What Others Are Saying About
Dr. Kenneth Polke and *Conquering Your Adversities*

"Kenneth Polke's life story stands as a true American success. A gritty tale that reflects on the true meaning of how one can overcome the most devastating adversity. Written with a challenge for all of us to look inside and face our own interpersonal reflections."

— Darin Watkins, author of *Chance for Glory: The Innovation and Triumph of the Washington State 1916 Rose Bowl Team*

"*Conquering Your Adversities* tells the dynamic story of one man who, through hard work and good decisions, avoided a life of crime to become a success. Dr. Kenneth Polke's story draws upon a nostalgic America of values, and it challenges us all to rise above our personal obstacles and strive for excellence."

— Deanna Becket, Author of *Cultivating Your Character*

"If you love tales of the Mafia, football, or stories of overcoming obstacles, then *Conquering Your Adversities* will knock your socks off, but best of all, it will inspire you to get out of your own way and go after your dreams. Ken Polke is the real deal when it comes to inspiration."

— Tyler R. Tichelaar, Ph.D. and award-winning author of *Iron Pioneers* and *The Best Place*

"If you want to achieve your dreams, just make a change, or in any way get more out of your life, then read this book. It'll help you become the champion of your life. It's a masterpiece!"

— Duane Martinz, Author of *Becoming Your Own Champion*

"Through personal stories and penetrating questions, Dr. Kenneth Polke provides the reader with a roadmap for finding your inner truth amid chaos. We can all rise above our problems, and *Conquering Your Adversities* shows us how."

— Nicole Gabriel, Author of *Finding Your Inner Truth*

"Ken Polke's story makes Rudy look like a fairy tale. *Conquering Your Adversities* tells it like it is—showing how a hardworking middle class American can succeed against all odds and do so honestly when he pursues his dreams. Ken, you are a true warrior. You are my kind of guy."

— Dr. Steven Rasner, DMD, MAGD, RealizingtheDream.com

"*Conquering Your Adversities* is a must-read book. It's a slice of Americana. It's a tale of an underdog achieving success. It's a story of following one's passion. It's a tale of dealing with disappointments. It's a great book for helping you make changes in your life and begin to create your own destiny!"

— Patrick Snow, Best-Selling Author of
Creating Your Own Destiny and *Boy Entrepreneur*

"As a fellow student, colleague, and friend of Ken Polke for over thirty-five years, I can emphatically say that when I find a roadblock, I ultimately head back to Dr. Polke's "blueprint" for ways to bounce and improve any situation. *Conquering Your Adversities* is a must read from the normal, work hard side of the tracks."

— Robert Adornetto, DDS

"In today's world full of glorified crime and declining values, Dr. Polke reminds us of an America that was better than that and can be again. He reveals his personal choices, including the occasional bad one, that led him to a lifetime of success, and now he's ready to give back by offering this book to others in need."

— Jimmy Hanlin, Host of *The Swing Clinic* and Co-Host of *18 Holes with Natalie Gulbis and Jimmy Hanlin*, Fox Sports

"*Conquering Your Adversities* is delightful. Ken Polke writes in the manner and style in which I have encountered him—engaging, smart, and reflective. Not only does he give readers insight into the Boomer generation, but his reflective questions at the end of each chapter give readers an opportunity to go deeper into their lives to make clearer choices for their futures. These questions come out of the author's faith background and are both self-help and spiritually-oriented. As a Catholic priest who lived through the years Ken writes about, I recommend this book for enjoyment and for the spiritual and historical journey you will encounter in its pages."

— Father Raymond Thomas, Pastor of Our Lady of Mount Carmel, Ashtabula, Ohio

"Dr. Kenneth Polke does not hold back in *Conquering your Adversities*. This inspirational, autobiographical tale tells the story of a true underdog rising up and claiming the American Dream despite formidable odds. Dr. Polke's writing style is fun and laid back and will make you laugh while imparting his heartfelt wisdom. If you've ever felt like the weight of the world was bearing down on you, then this book is for you. Thank you, Dr. Polke, for reminding me that the good guys can indeed win! Parents: Read this book now, and then pass it along to your children. You can thank me later."

— Julio A. Rodriguez, DDS, FICOI,
Dental Arts of Sunset, Miami, Florida

"Crime or sports? It's a hard choice many of our young people face today. Dr. Kenneth Polke shows how he made the better choice, and in the process, he encourages youths to do the same. *Conquering Your Adversities*, will inspire countless members of the younger generation."

— Lyssa Danehy deHart, MSW, LICSW, PCC
Transformational Coach and Author of *StoryJacking: Change Your Inner Dialogue, Transform Your Life*

"This powerful and dynamic book provides a 'how to' on converting the realities of adversity into a source of personal and professional leadership and success. It's an amazing 'must read' story of resilience and strength that helps you to understand what opportunities exist despite life's trials and tribulations."

— Susan Friedmann, CSP, International Best-Selling Author
of *Riches in Niches: How to Make it BIG in a small Market*

"*Conquering Your Adversities* is the spellbinding story of how Dr. Ken Polke, who grew up in the Mafia-controlled neighborhood of Cleveland, Ohio, succeeded in becoming an NFL quarterback and, ultimately, a doctor. If you love reading about the Mafia, and following the life of an accomplished athlete and doctor through his life, then this is the book for you. With Ken's 'how to' process, you will get guidance on how you too can succeed."

— Leo Higley, Founder & Past President of Higley & Company, Founder & Past Vice-President of Infoworld, Inc., aka Advizex Technologies

AN INSPIRATIONAL MEMOIR PROVING THAT YOU TOO CAN ACHIEVE SUCCESS

CONQUERING YOUR ADVERSITIES

FROM MAFIA-CONTROLLED STREETS TO THE NFL
AND ULTIMATELY BECOMING A SUCCESSFUL DOCTOR

DR. KENNETH POLKE

WITH STEVE EGGLESTON

AVIVA
PUBLISHING
New York

Conquering Your Adversities: From Mafia-Controlled Streets to the NFL and Ultimately Becoming a Successful Doctor

ISBN: 978-1-9443356-5-6
Library of Congress Control Number: 2017903651

Editor: Tyler Tichelaar, Superior Book Productions
Cover and Interior Design: Nicole Gabriel, AngelDog Productions

Published by:
Aviva Publishing
Lake Placid, NY
(518) 523-1320
www.avivapubs.com

Every attempt has been made to source properly all quotes.

Printed in the USA
First Edition

For additional copies visit: www.ConqueringYourAdversities.com

"Once a man has made a commitment to a way of life, he puts the greatest strength in the world behind him. It's something we call heart power. Once a man has made this commitment, nothing will stop him short of success."

— Vince Lombardi

DEDICATION

To my mom and dad, who through their love and countless sacrifices engineered a nurturing environment for me and my siblings to grow up in. Their strong core Christian values and principles created a foundation and safety net that I could always rely on for guidance. This well-lit runway always brought me home safely with a successful landing.

"I hated every minute of training, but I said, 'Don't quit. Suffer now and live the rest of your life as a champion'."

— Muhammad Ali

ACKNOWLEDGMENTS

I'd like to thank Cheryl "T" for her persistent persuasion (nagging) of me to write "my story." Her encouragement (kick in the butt) made me realize that this was a story to be told. Thanks also go out to Steve Eggleston, "the Eggman," for his organizational and writing skills; without him, I would still be "talking" about writing a book. His superb talents inspired me to achieve the proverbial "cream rising to the top" scenario. It would not be right for me to continue without a shout out to two special teammates Kevin Flynt (my high school full-back) and Steve Siewe (my college offensive center), both of whom contributed newspaper clippings and other memorabilia. Their anecdotal contributions, much like a good recipe, added spice and other seasonings to flavor this story. What started out as a story with a lot of meat became a "Big Fish Story" serving. Each of them is a great storyteller in his own right.

A final "Thank You" is air-mailed to Mario Houston, my Little Brother chosen for me by the "Big Brothers, Big Sisters" organization. My assignment was to aid this young black man who did not have an immediate adult male to offer him guidance. I would be lying in front of God and everyone else if I stated that Mario learned all he knows from me. Rather, if truth be told, the reverse is true. I learned more from Mario than he from me. This young black boy opened my eyes to a totally different world than I was exposed to. Growing up in a predominately white neighbourhood with just his mother must have seemed like a 24/7 horror flick. I tried to offer encouragement, a good example, and a set of values to carry him through the challenges I knew would come his way. Suffice to say, he exceeded my expectations. I wish I could take all the credit. I taught him the value of self-discipline, sacrifice, and hard work because these qualities aided me in life as I worked my tail off to become a doctor. Little did I know I could have just married a gorgeous good-looking doctor

(Candice) as Mario did. So, in retrospect, who is the smart one here and who is the dummy? Love you, Mario, like my own son.

CONTENTS

INTRODUCTION

Have you been surrounded by negativity your whole life, starting with childhood?

Were you told you were too slow, too short, or too small to play sports or do the things you wanted to do? Or, if you were good at sports, were you told you were a dumb jock—that you'd never be a doctor, lawyer, dentist, game designer, or engineer? Or, if sports were not even on your radar, that you were a geek—that you'd never get along with people, so you would never succeed.

Did that negativity follow you from childhood into early adulthood? Were people verbally abusive to you? Were you passed over and taken advantage of? Were you exposed to the lure of crime, getting high on drugs, skipping school, and goofing off? Were you so financially broke you couldn't find a dime in your car seat cushions?

Believe me, I've been there. I grew up in a poor family of six in a Mafia-ridden neighborhood. If someone dropped a penny in our house, it became copper wire before it hit the ground. I dreamed of playing football in middle school, but the moment I was old enough to qualify, the league was cancelled. I started only one football game in high school, yet needed a football scholarship to afford college. And for a broke kid like me with big dreams, temptation to pursue the romantic life of the Mafia was a jog down my street.

In this book, you will learn how to conquer your adversities, no matter who you are or what those adversities might be. In my case, I embraced the power of sports, faith, and determination to transform myself, though at the time I hardly knew it. You will see how being born poor can be overcome, despite the obstacles around you. You will follow the course of a family, perhaps like yours, that put everything on the line for the sake of its children, at enormous sacrifice. You will see how self-belief, hard work, determination, and values are much more than idle words.

The life-changing impact of good teachers, good schools, and good coaches will be demonstrated in these pages by the fate of my own life, perhaps resonating in part with yours, everyone's journey of course being different. Religion, faith, and values can raise up their lofty heads and reach out their caring hands, empowering you, your team, and your family to go that extra mile, just when you want to give up the fight and toss in the towel.

If you apply the insights offered in this book to your own life, you will have the tools to conquer your own adversities. You will see how your poverty can become your motivator, how your lack of physical size and strength in sports can be made irrelevant, how your family can become your engine, how your values will serve as your guide, and how your faith will inspire you through the darkest of times. You see, what the media elites, the Hollywood elites, and the political elites just don't understand is that, when wealth and privilege are not your roots, you must draw upon a Higher Power during those defining moments between failure and success.

Though I grew up poor, my parents did not see it that way. They worked full-time so all of us kids could escape the negative influences of our neighborhood and attend private Catholic school across the *crik*. Yes, that's what we called it—the *crik*. Though I didn't play in a single organized football game until high school, I made the team all four years as a second or third string quarterback. Though I only started one football game in all of high school, I received a full athletic scholarship to a major university, where I broke seven school records as the starting quarterback my last two years as a junior and senior.

In fact, in the four years of our high school play, we did not lose a single game (though we tied one as freshmen because I punted the ball backwards), and every single person on the team received a full-boat athletic scholarship to college. Did I learn something from this? You bet. Are there lessons in there for you? Absolutely.

Despite growing up on the streets of a Mafia town, often distracted by the lure of money, women, and hot cars provided by the mean streets, I did not succumb. And when no team in the NFL drafted me, I still got a personal call from Head Coach Don Shula, recruiting me to join his world champion Miami Dolphins, one of the greatest teams in pro football history. I kid you not—a story in itself.

Finally, when I left the game, that wasn't so bad, either: I attended dental school and became a dental surgeon...and now, ultimately, an author, speaker, athletic and life coach, and consultant. But man, oh man, it was not easy, and I fully understand how adversity can overcome you, rather than the other way around. I know first-hand that adversity—from poverty, to broken families, to physical inferiorities, to missed opportunities to plain ol' bad luck—can become overwhelming. These negative forces can threaten to take you down, to take you out, and to quash your dreams. But I also know that all of that is okay. You can get through it. You can win on every level, if you learn from the lessons taught in this book.

Because of all that I have received from so many people along the way, I want to give it back or, in today's vernacular, pay it forward. I want to be your mentor, your guide, your accountability partner, as well as the shoulder that you can lean on during tough times—just as I also want to be your friend, your coach, and your consultant, the person and resource that you can always reach out to as you work to conquer your adversities and achieve your dreams.

Are you ready to begin? Are you ready to step outside of your box? Are you ready to expand your comfort zone and step into the new person that you are becoming? Are you ready to achieve your goals and conquer your adversities? If so…good; let's get started and take this journey together, from the streets controlled by the Mafia to the NFL to the dental chair...or from wherever you come from, to wherever you want to go!

Now is your time. Ready, team? Let's Go!

PART I
THE GLORY DAYS

"The real glory is being knocked to your knees and then coming back. That's real glory. That's the essence of it."

— Vince Lombardi

Chapter 1

REFLECTING BACK

"Adversity introduces a man to himself."

— H.L. Mencken

It's early in the morning and I'm sitting on the back sundeck of my home outside Denver, having my morning coffee. The peaceful quiet and the crisp, Mile-High air provide a perfect backdrop for reflecting on my glory days. The McDonald's coffee, of course, plays an important role in the reminiscing, as the coffee-triggered defibrillator is what the doctor (that being me) prescribes to jumpstart my heart and brain. I wonder whether the Scarecrow and the Tin Man start their mornings with a hot cup of Joe. If it is, I'd be willing to pay for the Scarecrow's coffee if I could use his vast brain power to get the number 12 to stop flashing on my VCR.

Through the screen door, I can hear NBC-Denver's newscaster announcing the early morning headlines. Good news? Get outta here. It's all bad: Terrorists attack Paris in the deadliest assault since World War II; the U.S. opposes resettlement of Syrian refugees leaving thousands homeless; protests erupt in Minneapolis after another police shooting puts an African-American man onto life support; another politician is convicted of some kind of white collar crime or is caught sexting with a mistress. Seriously, if you were running for political office and your name was Anthony Weiner, would you not have thought seriously about changing it? Only in America!

This country's going to hell in a handbasket, I think. We have few moral leaders and little moral compass. Where are today's John Fitzgerald Kennedy (JFK) and Ronald Reagan—the two greatest U.S. Presidents of my lifetime—when we need them the most? Not to mention, no black leader has filled the shoes of Martin Luther King, Jr. Whatever happened to judging a person by the content of his character rather than the color of his skin? And if their spirits are watching us down on earth, I'm positive Ozzie and Harriet Nelson, along with Ward and June Cleaver, are rolling over in their graves. Seriously, is the public aware that some high schools are handing out condoms to their students as some sort of deterrent to having sex? Back in my day (the olden days) as a deterrent to having sex, the priests would hand out to us boys magazine covers of Barbra Streisand and Phyllis Diller. If that doesn't stop you dead in your tracks, nothing will. To modernize this tactic, all you have to do is add Whoopi Goldberg, Rachel Maddow, Joy Behar, Kathy Griffin, and Janeane Garofalo to the list. I mean, there is not enough alcohol in the world.

The clatter of dishes coming from the kitchen disrupts my reminiscing, reminding me that it's getting late. I'm boarding a plane to my hometown of Cleveland, Ohio, in several hours. It's just a visit this time, and I wonder whether I'll ever move back home as I've often wanted to do.

"Do you have everything packed, honey?" my wife Valerie yells to me. "Glasses, wallet, phone charger, tickets." At what point in a marriage, I think, do wives feel it is necessary to start nagging? Boy, I better not say that out loud, though my mother did the same to my father, driving me nuts as a kid. Or is it Val's sharp insight that I may be suffering from early-onset dementia? Speaking of which, did I leave the toilet seat up?

I chuckle to myself and, annoyed, reply, "Yes, dear," as I make my way to the bedroom, whereupon I gather my travel gear and belongings before sheepishly stating: "Honey, have you seen my passport?"

"I swear, Dr. Polke. If your head wasn't attached to your shoulders…."

After 23 glorious years of marriage, you can feel the love in the room. At least Marley Sue (our rescue Beagle) only looks at me with widened eyes. After locating my passport in my shoulder bag, I hear my brother's sarcastic faux Mexican humor in my ear: "Passports? What passports? We don't need no stinkin' passports."

"Are *you* ready, hon?" I yell. "We need to get moving."

"Ready!" she yells back. I hear the spraying water from the kitchen faucet go silent. "Meet you at the car," she adds to the quick click of her heels across the wooden floor, soon followed by the shutting of the door.

Valerie takes the wheel of our 2012 BMW, pulls out of our cul-de-sac, and speeds toward the Denver Airport.

"We're not that late," I say as she hugs the bumper of the car in front of us. She smiles, acknowledging our running narrative over her tailgating. I unsnap my black satchel, remove a small stack of typing paper, then arrange the stack neatly on my lap.

"Are you working on your induction speech for the Hall of Champions, Dr. Polke?"

"Yes, well, no," I answer. "This isn't the speech for Cleveland. I doubt I'll be speaking there, what with all the other famous athletes in attendance."

"Oh?" she says.

"No, I'm reworking the speech I gave to that high school football team in California last month. Next time, I want it to go faster...and smoother. In light of everything that's going on in the world, I need to emphasize better *the fundamental importance of values* to coaches and to our younger generation."

I pull the visor down to block the glare of the rising sun, thinking to myself. In my humble opinion—actually meaning: *in my strong opinion*—athletic coaches do not fully appreciate the remarkable influence they have on the value systems of their players and, thus, of millions of young men and women.

"You know, in today's secular, broken culture," I say, "coaches more than ever need to fill in the moral gaps. They need to instill in young minds the values that are missing. Teaching basic techniques and fundamentals in sports is one thing, and it is important, but it is not enough. Coaches also need to supply the emotional and spiritual support once provided by parents, teachers, and clergy."

Valerie nods her head in agreement. "Sounding very erudite, Dr. Polke, and opinionated."

"You know something?" I continue on a roll. "The baby-boomers—our generation—are much to blame for this vacuum in values. If our parents' generation was 'the Greatest Generation,' as they say, it goes without saying that we baby-boomers are 'the Selfish Generation.' We were given everything and haven't improved societal values one iota."

"I couldn't agree more," Val says as she turns on the radio. At once, a bass-pounding hip-hop song about some girl's big booty thumps from the speakers. We both look at each other, bust out laughing, and then shake our heads in affirmation of my point. "Your receptionist's son," she says to explain the music. "I gave him a ride the other day.

He's in high school." She quickly punches a button that automatically finds our favorite station, 710 News/Talk KNUS Denver, one of the homes of the nationally-syndicated *Hugh Hewitt Show*.

We love Hugh Hewitt. He's a Cleveland boy like me—from Warren, Ohio, to be exact—and a huge fan of all things Cleveland: the Ohio State Buckeyes, the Cleveland Browns, the Cleveland Indians, and the Cleveland Cavaliers. He is enormously accomplished—a law professor of Constitutional Law, a popular author, a guest TV analyst, a moderator for several of the 2016 Presidential debates, and a regular commentator on NBC's *Meet the Press* and CNN.

Though Hugh normally broadcasts out of Sacramento, California, several years ago he did come to Denver. For that show, he was gracious enough to invite me on as a guest to discuss football and our mutual home state of Ohio.

We had a heck of a time, a lot of laughs, and I remember him presenting me with a tricky trivia question. Here's how it went: "Name four universities that have produced both a U.S. President and a winning Super Bowl quarterback," he said.

I thought about it for a moment, then quickly replied: "For Navy, Jimmy Carter and Roger Staubach, and for Michigan University, Gerald Ford and Tom Brady."

"Not bad," Hugh said, "but what about the other two?"

"Okay, how about Jim Plunkett...and John Elway, both from Stanford?"

"Right! And the President?"

"Got me there," I said with a big smile.

He laughs a big laugh. "Herbert Hoover. And number four, Miami of

Ohio. Benjamin Harrison, President. Ben Roesthlesberger, quarterback."

"Ohhh, no," I replied. "I missed the guys from our home state. I will burn in hell for all eternity for missing that one."

Like myself, Hugh embraces the principles of our founding fathers, and of faith, and he tells it like it is…no holds barred. When it comes to *the importance of values*, we clearly share a common thread. We also share a huge disdain for Steeler fans. I informed Hugh's radio audience that Steeler fans are the result of the fetus not getting enough oxygen. Also, in the Pittsburgh public school system, it is taught that chewing tobacco is one of the major food groups.

Thanks, Hugh, for having me on, and thanks for being a spokesman for my dental practice and a friend to the game of football.

Twenty-five minutes later, we're slowing to the curb-side baggage check, where I get out.

"Have a great trip, honey," Valerie says demurely, her tone revealing that she's happy for me but sad I'm leaving.

"I will," I reply and then lean over and kiss her goodbye. "I love you."

"I love you, too, Dr. Polke."

~ ~ ~

Standing curbside, I wave as Valerie drives away, a slight anxiety building in my chest. The upcoming event in Cleveland (to be fully videotaped by NFL films) will be a proud moment and rare opportunity in my life to reunite with my old teammates, which may explain the anxiety…or could it be that the morning coffee is finally giving me the jolt I need?

Inching along the security line allows me time to reflect further on the "glory days of high school." Amazingly, our entire 1969-70 St. Joseph Vikings football team will be inducted tonight into the Hall of Champions, together with a handful of younger NFL and NBA superstars who graduated after we did.

But the "glory days" in reality were not so glorious, at least not for me. The truth is that the glory days came with great adversity, a lot of struggle, and tremendous pain.

It is hard to imagine so many great players (25 NFL stars in all) all graduating from one high school, and all invited to be here tonight. I mean, we have London Fletcher, who finished his pro football career having played in 256 consecutive games and started in 215 games, an NFL all-time record for consecutive starts at the linebacker position.

Then there's Mike Golic, who everyone knows as the co-host of ESPN's popular *Mike & Mike* show, as well as host of the longest-running syndicated sports highlights, bloopers, and gag fest called *The Lighter Side of Sports*. Not to mention, he's an eight-year NFL defensive tackle whose brother, Bob Golic, same high school, enjoyed a fourteen-year NFL career as defensive tackle…and who also was an All-American at the University of Notre Dame, as well as an actor appearing in several sitcoms.

And who could forget Elvis Grbac, who holds six all-time records with the NFL Kansas City Chiefs, including most touchdown passes in consecutive games (15), lowest percentage passes intercepted (3.04), and most yards gained in a single game...or the legendary Desmond Howard, who currently serves as an ESPN college football analyst and regular on ESPN's *College Gameday*, and who in his day was a Heisman Trophy winner at the University of Michigan, MVP of Super Bowl XXXI, and the ninth greatest kick return specialist in NFL history?

CONQUERING YOUR ADVERSITIES

We are not talking minor guys here, and football isn't the only sport with honorees tonight. Clark Kellogg will be inducted for his basketball prowess, a veteran NBA player who now serves as Vice President of Player Relations for the Indiana Pacers, lead basketball analyst for CBS Sports' coverage of the NBA, and a regular commentator for college basketball's March Madness.

"Wow! What company I'll be in," I think, as I rush to the nearest men's room. I pull up to the urinal and utter under my breath as I begin to relieve myself, "Man, that's almost as good as sex." The guy next to me tries to hold back, but he can't. He starts laughing as he tries not to spray his foot and mine.

I board the plane and take my usual aisle seat near the front, pull out my speech papers, and quickly doze off. Before I know it, I hear the pilot say, "Folks, we have begun our descent into Cleveland Hopkins International Airport, where the current weather is sixty-five degrees, with slight winds off Lake Erie. We will be at the gate in about twenty-five minutes."

"Holy Cow, Batman!" I think. Miracles do happen: sixty-five degrees in November in Cleveland? Someone needs to call Mother Theresa pronto. If she were here, this would count as her third miracle and sainthood would be only days away. (Actually, she would receive sainthood shortly after. I must have had ESPN—oops, I mean, ESP.)

Now, folks, don't get me wrong. I love Cleveland dearly, but the winters can be downright brutal. That's why Val and I moved from Cleveland to Colorado in the first place. But it's not the only reason. There were other adversities in Cleveland that I needed to leave behind— negative, life-crushing adversities. Sometimes leaving *is* conquering.

I collect my papers and push up the tray table, thinking about the importance of that speech. Do kids growing up today have the same guidance I did? Is there something about my own life story that, if told the right way, might provide you, the reader, the tools to overcome adversity in today's secular and cynical world?

I glance down at the stack of papers now on my lap, replete with scribbled, handwritten revisions, and start reading the revised version to myself as the plane descends.

~ ~ ~

"If I assembled a highlight reel of my life in sports," my speech begins, "I would start with high school. Between 1966 and 1970, I attended St. Joseph's Catholic High School (called Villa Angela—St. Joseph today) in Cleveland, Ohio, an all-boys school of 2000 students. Our football team was the St. Joseph's Vikings."

I pause, thinking about a statistic I had heard recently: "Today, more people watch American football on Sunday than go to church." *Football functions culturally as the new religion.*

I continue reading my speech to myself.

"I played quarterback for the St. Joseph Vikings for all four years of high school, freshman to senior, and our football team went undefeated all four years...."

I lean back my head, shutting my eyes. I visualize myself in scrimmages on our high school football field. My hands are tucked tightly under the center's crotch, yelling, "Blue 29 K, Blue 29 K, Red, Red, Hut, Hut, Hut," and the ball is snapped into my hands."

"The thunder rising from thousands of pounds of angry muscles slamming into one kid wearing twenty pounds of protective gear momentarily deafens me. The first string varsity defensive linemen crush my scrimmage squad offensive line, literally running over them in mad pursuit of me, the scrimmage quarterback."

"Before I can hand off or pass, a forearm across my jaw from John Shinsky pops off my chin guard. My helmet flies one way and my teeth the other…. By high school, John was a legend, a tough and mean upperclassman from Mayfield Road rumored to be an orphan who once killed another boy in self-defense. If he was angry about that, he certainly brought it all to the field. When John Delamileur, the All-Pro and Hall of Fame offensive guard who played for the Buffalo Bills and Cleveland Browns, was asked who was the toughest defensive lineman he ever played against, without hesitation, he said, "John Shinsky." And they had only played against each other in college, not the pros.

"Sir, sir," the attendant says, "please bring your seat up. Did you hear me, sir?"

"Oh, sorry," I say, opening my eyes and jerking my head forward. "I was just, ah, daydreaming, thinking back…."

She smiles, nods, and walks away as I move my seatback up and return to reading my pages.

"Under Coach Bill Gutbrod, we *never* lost a game, chalking up 33 victories in four years against some of the best high school football teams in northeast Ohio and surrounding states. Our reputation as a powerhouse even forced us to go out-of-state to find teams willing to play us. Many sports writers consider our team to be one of the best in Ohio high school football history.

"Coach Gutbrod was a hardworking career high school football coach who turned down offers to coach college and maybe even the pros. Our graduating class serves as proof of what a dedicated career high school coach can achieve. Not only did we go undefeated in four years, but every single uninjured player on our 1969-1970 senior (graduating) roster received a full-boat, four-year scholarship to some university or college in America. That's why the entire team is being inducted into the school's Hall of Champions tonight—an honor never before conferred on an entire class.

"Myself, I was recruited by the Naval Academy and a host of other universities, including several Ivy League schools, but for reasons I'll explain later, I took the four-year ride offered to me by the University of Dayton Flyers. In my junior year at the University of Dayton, I started as quarterback. That year, I was fortunate to lead the nation in passing yardage and completions by mid-year. And by the time I had completed my senior year, I had broken seven UOD offensive records.

"The same year that I was a junior at UOD, 1972, the Miami Dolphins were in the process of achieving the best win-loss record in NFL history. Under Head Coach Don Shula, also a Cleveland boy, that year the Dolphins won every game—they went 14-0 in the regular season, won every playoff game, and won Super Bowl VII, beating the Washington Redskins. Many sports gurus consider Shula's 1972 Dolphins to be the best NFL team of all time.

"Needless to say, as a college quarterback setting some records of my own, I had my eye on the NFL. I wanted to go pro. It had been a dream of mine for some time. Just as I had prayed for a scholarship to college, I prayed for an offer from the NFL. And then, as if from above, the phone call came and my dad answered. 'Son,' he said, 'it's Coach Don Shula of the Miami Dolphins.' 'Don't pull my leg, Dad,' I replied.

"Within weeks of graduating from college, I was on a plane to Miami, Florida, *en route* to playing for one of the greatest NFL football teams of all time."

I shuffle the papers in my hands as the wheels of the big plane hit the tarmac. I smile. *You've come a long way, Poke Salad*—a name they used to call me as a kid, some with teasing affection, some to get my goat.

"Now, gentlemen," my speech concludes, "if you just consider my highlight reel, you might think my life walked right off the pages of a dream-come-true storybook—that everything was handed to me on a silver platter, that I got every break a guy could get, that I was blessed in all things. Well, that was hardly the case, I assure you."

So please buckle your seatbelts while I tell you, to quote the late Paul Harvey, "the rest of the story...."

EXERCISE:

Despite all my past success, before I wrote this book, I was downright unhappy with my station in life as a highly successful dental surgeon. Pardon my puns, but I'd had my "fill" of dentistry and going into my beautiful office in Westminster Colorado was becoming a real "grind." How I got there and where I would go next are the subjects of this book—*Conquering Your Adversities*. So before we get started, ask yourself these fundamental questions and write out your answers.... Then go back to these answers when you finish the book.

What adversities did you conquer to achieve your current state of success?

_____

_____

_____

_____

_____

_____

Have you ever shared your secrets of success in conquering your adversities with others?

_____

_____

_____

_____

Despite your current successes, do you feel that you've reached a dead end in your life and/or career?

_____

_____

_____

_____

Are you afraid to make a life and career change and embark on a new journey to do something for the rest of your life that you really love? If so, why?

_____

_____

_____

_____

Despite any fear you may feel, are you ready to make a huge leap in your life and career that will transform you forever? Say, "Yes!" Then write out how you plan to do it. Let's take the leap together!

_____

_____

_____

_____

PART II

THE REST
OF THE STORY...

"The answer is always in the entire story, not a piece of it."

— Jim Harrison

Chapter 2

TAP DANCING AT EUCLID BEACH PARK

"I don't make love by kissing, I make love by dancing."

— Fred Astaire

Inspired by New York's Coney Island, Euclid Beach Park embodies the mixed spirit of 1950s Cleveland. It laid the foundation for current modern-day amusement parks such as Cedar Point in Sandusky, Ohio, and King's Island further South in Cincinnati, Ohio. Today, both parks compete for bragging rights as to which has the World's Tallest Roller Coaster rides.

Euclid Beach Park in the 1950s is the focal point for summer fun. On the one hand, it exists for families. No alcohol is allowed, and it's a wonderland of sights, sounds, and smells, all designed to climax the five senses. Colorful lights that make it feel like Christmas morning outline the carousels. Screams from the thrilling roller-coaster rides and the taste and smells of the original popcorn ball and Candy Kisses (taffy squares), which are to die for, permeate the park. Betcha can't eat just one!

On the other hand, for young couples in love, there is no better place to go than a day and night at the popular Beach Park. With its Flying Turns, the Dodge 'em electric bumper cars, and the Swinging Rotating Cages that couples try in earnest to flip in a complete circle, daytime thrills turn into a night-time romance. When the sun begins to set, it's time to sashay to the Ballroom, where the world's biggest stars perform within arm's reach of the wooden dance floor. Performers like Frank Sinatra, Tony Bennett, and eventually, Elvis, all took that stage.

The cool breeze coming off the shores of Lake Erie and through the super-large ballroom doors sets the stage for a wanderlust of unforgettable and sometimes downright sizzling romantic interludes. The giant mirrored ball rotating from the ceiling transports young lovers to a solitary tropical paradise, only for them to be rudely awakened when the music stops.

On this particular night, the stage is dark. Thursdays are devoted to dancing, with Dizzy Gillespie's "A Night in Tunisia" energizing the room in harmony with the spinning disco ball. Spotlights sweep the floor as a young couple emerges from the perimeter shadows. He's tall, athletic, and handsome; she's eye-catching with her slim waist and fiery-red hair. They twirl on light feet as he spins her around. Then he releases her, breaking into a dazzling display of tapping, a budding white Bojangles.

Suddenly, the young man stops and drops to his knee, her hand cupped in his. The music ceases. "Lois," he says softly, all eyes on them, "will you marry me?"

Her hand jerks to her gaping mouth; she has been caught totally by surprise. For a long moment, she's speechless. Then, as tears stream down her cheeks, she says, "Yes, yes, yes, Gene Polke. I will marry you, and it's about time you asked."

Allow me to introduce to you my future parents.

~ ~ ~

Several years later, I'm still only a twinkle in my dad's eye when, at 4:00 a.m. on June 25, 1950, seven divisions of helmeted North Korean troops invade South Korea by crossing the 38th Parallel. The aggression hits America like an unforeseen tsunami, washing away our idyllic, feel-good, post-World War II peace and prosperity.

"This is the first coast-to-coast television broadcast in history," the staid man in the gray suit and gray tie—Walter Cronkite—narrates from within the square screen of our brand new black-and-white television on September 4, 1951.

"Honey, come quick," Dad says, standing back and admiring his work in setting up the new TV set, their first purchase as newlyweds.

"You got it working," Mom says, her stomach large with me and eyes growing in wonderment at the new contraption.

Dad beams a big smile as he adjusts the rabbit ears to sharpen the picture while Cronkite continues with the live broadcast: "This first transcontinental television broadcast originating from the Opera House in San Francisco will bring you the President of the United States, Harry S. Truman, addressing the welcoming ceremony of the Japanese peace conference...."

"What is this about, Genie?" Mom asks with confusion. "The Korean—"

"No, it's historical. It's about when we signed the peace treaty to end World War II. It's never been televised before. The public has never seen it before."

"Wasn't that, how long ago—when was that?"

"Shhhh, Lo," Dad says, bordering on rude, a quality very out of character for him; he is typically a gentleman with whom every woman falls in love due to his politeness and romantic gestures. But in his defense, he sensed the importance of history in the making.

To a thundering applause, the President with the homespun voice takes the televised podium and says: "I'm glad *ta* welcome you to this conference for the signing of the Treaty of Peace with Japan. The people of the United States are honored to serve as hosts to this meeting. Six years ago, the nation's representatives at this conference were engaged in a bitter and costly war. Nevertheless, these nations and others came together here in this very hall to set up the United Nations as the first essential step toward a firm and lasting peace. Today they meet here again...."

There, in the living rooms of millions of Americans, including my parents and me *in vitro*, we see for the first time what our President had said *six years earlier* (not six minutes earlier or live like today). And in his speech, Truman quotes deceased President Franklin Delano Roosevelt from comments he made on the 1941 attack on Pearl Harbor: "'When we resort to force as now we must'," said Roosevelt, "'we are determined that this force be directed toward ultimate good, as well as against immediate evil...for a world...safe for our children. That's our purpose here today.... We are trying to build a world in which the children of all nations can live together in peace.... Unfortunately today, the world is faced with new threats of aggression.... There are thugs among nations, just as among individuals....'"

~ ~ ~

Ironically, outside technology, even after 70 years, the world has not changed so much (with the likes of North Korea, China, Iran, Syria, Russia, and ISIS all ongoing threats), though in late 1951 and early 1952, of course, I'm oblivious to it all, kicking in my mom's womb as

America gets drawn deeper and deeper into the aggression known as the Korean "Conflict," initiated by thugs known as the Korean People's Army.

"Thank God we are winning the war," Mom says one day.

Dad looks up from one of the many borrowed library books he's reading in the living room and puts his hand to his chin the way he does before he's about to disagree with her, as if tactically planning his approach. "Lois, I don't think we're winning. They caught us with our pants down."

"Don't say that, Genie Boy."

"No one knows why we are there," Dad says. "Supposedly it is to stop the spread of Communism."

"But Truman says we're winning. I read it in a magazine."

"Truman won't even call it a war. He calls it a police action."

"What the heck is that?" Mom says.

"Who knows, but did you know that Truman's military guys are thinking about dropping an atomic bomb on China because of this 'police action'?"

Mom stops cooking for a moment and looks at Dad, speechless. He has forgotten that she has new life inside her—me. She rubs her protruding stomach.

"Can we please talk about something else?" she asks, then mumbles to herself, "May the Good Lord keep us safe."

~ ~ ~

On that same television, Dad watches the first NFL football broadcast of a Cleveland Browns game. He's excited and looks forward to seeing more games since he can't afford tickets to attend a game at the stadium. Then everything comes to a halt. The "police action" requires everyone to drop what they are doing and prepare for another war.

At the time, Don Shula, the man who would later be Head Coach of the Miami Dolphins, works as a second-string running back for the Cleveland Browns. But in January 1952, he's deployed to the Ohio National Guard. His military service will keep him away from football until his unit is deactivated later that year.

After leaving the Guard, Shula signs a $5,500-a-year player contract with the Browns. Yes, that's right. The Browns will pay him a mere $458.33 per month, and he will play in five games to end the 1952 season, starting first-string only because of injuries occasioned to other players. That year, the Browns again advance to the championship game, but lose to the Detroit Lions for the second year in a row.

I don't know it at the time, but football coaches like Don Shula will ultimately have a profound influence in the shaping of my life, character, and career. Coaches like Vincent Lombardi, Paul Brown, Ron Marciniak, John McVay, and Bill Gutrod will join the ranks of Coach Shula—each contributing in his own unique way to my struggle, survival, and success.

Likewise, the Green Bay Packers, the Cleveland Browns, the University of Dayton Flyers, the St. Joseph High School Vikings, and the Miami Dolphins—the teams associated with these coaches—will influence me for better or worse in my trek to conquering the adversities of my youth and becoming a man.

EXERCISE:

Do you find yourself depressed due to the negativity in the world, with terrorism, war, and hostilities seemingly all around you? If so, how?

_____

_____

_____

_____

_____

Are you excited yet overwhelmed by the vast volume of current information from around the world that enters your life on a daily basis, much of it negative? Write out some examples.

_____

_____

_____

_____

_____

If you are constantly struggling to understand what it all means and how you will carry on against the negativity and adversity around you, propose some solutions.

_____

_____

_____

_____

_____

Chapter 3

LOVE, BIRTH & FIRE

"The family, founded upon marriage freely contracted, one and indissoluble, must be regarded as the natural, primary cell of human society. The interests of the family, therefore, must be taken very specially into consideration in social and economic affairs, as well as in the spheres of faith and morals. For all of these have to do with strengthening the family and assisting it in the fulfilment of its mission."

— Pope John XXIII, *Pacem in Terris*, 1963

No wonder I'm born in 1952. My dad loves crooner Vic Damone, and he's churning out love songs like nobody's business. "So in Love," "Almost Like Being in Love," "Love Letters," "A Time for Love," "Once I Loved," and "Our Love Is Here to Stay" -- all blare from the table top radio in our inner city Ansel Road apartment during my venture in the womb. With a little bit of Frank "Chairman of the Board" Sinatra and Dean Martin thrown in for good measure, it's a perfect fit for the nascent baby-boom.

Dad is Eugene Polke, aka "Genie Boy." His cousins are "Buddy Boy" and "Pettie Boy" (pronounced Pete-e). All are Slovenian, meaning they hail from one of the five tribes of Yugoslavia. The Slovenians love their nicknames, so by the time I'm a teenager, people call me "Poke Salad." Mom doesn't have a nickname to anyone but Dad, who sometimes call her Lo, but if she did, it might be "Fireball," on account of her vibrant red hair and fiery personality. Before she married Dad, she was Lois Price, of strong, German stock. Both Mom and Dad were born in the U.S.A., as were their parents before them.

Arriving April 14, 1952, and weighing in at nine pounds, eleven ounces, I enter the world a sickly baby due to a chronic brush with asthma caused by severe allergies. Before I'm two, I turn blue and almost die three times, or so I'm told by my mother. Maybe that makes me tough later, having overcome these adversities early, just to stay alive, except it leaves a psychological scar, an Achilles heel if you will. Whenever I'm claustrophobic and can't get enough air, to this day, I go into panic mode.

Fortunately for me, my parents find Dr. Harold Friedman. Doc Friedman is one of the few doctors of this era who knows how to treat asthma as it should be treated. Cleveland had—and still has—some of the best physicians in the world as part of the downtown medical complex, and fortunately for me, Dr. Friedman is one of them.

In 1916, Mt. Sinai Hospital relocated from its original location on East 32nd Street to the larger facility at East 105th Street, which is where I am born. After I enter the world, Mom tells everyone, "You could hear Ken screaming from the top of the actual Mt. Sinai!"

Thankfully, despite its origination as a Jewish hospital, by the time of my debut, Mt. Sinai Hospital has become the number one healthcare provider to Cleveland's urban poor, irrespective of race or religion. That includes me and my brother and sister soon to come since our parents are not financially well off despite their strong Christian work ethic, and despite the fact they would *never* in a million years describe themselves as poor.

From the windows of the Mt. Sinai maternity ward, one can see Case Western Reserve University, including the Dental School where I will alight 25 years from now as a freshman dental student. That's the same year—1977—that a so-called "Trojan Horse" car bomb (a bomb planted in an adjacent car) horrifically explodes, taking the life of Cleveland's notorious Irish mobster, Danny Greene, described by the police as the "King of Racketeering." Danny reigned as king in my childhood neighborhood of Collinwood. His life and times will one day be made infamous on the big screen in the Hollywood movie *Kill the Irishman*.

Quite ironically, Danny will die in the parking lot of his dentist, with whom he had made an emergency appointment to fix a loose filling. The dentist will be Dr. Alfonso Rossi, a professor in the dental program where I will enroll several years after departing the NFL. A reason to brush your teeth if there ever was one. But I get ahead of myself....

EXERCISE:

Do you love dance, music, or the arts to the extent that they might become a source of empowerment for you to conquer your adversities? If so, how might they help?

_____
_____
_____
_____
_____
_____
_____
_____

Were you or your parents born into controversial times yet able to overcome the negativity? If so, list some ways you did.

_____
_____
_____
_____
_____
_____

Do you have family stories that you might call upon to provide strength in difficult times?

_____
_____
_____
_____
_____
_____

Chapter 4

THE BROWNS & THE MAFIA

"I don't teach kids to be No. 1. Organizations and people that tell you you have to be No. 1; that's not it. You don't have to be No. 1. What I teach is to be as good as you can be. Use what you have and be as good as you can be. That's all you can do, anyway."

— Jim Brown, Legendary Running Back, Cleveland Browns

Though I will never devour books with the hunger of my dad and my brother, I will find time to read whenever my busy life permits it. One of my favorite subjects will be the history of the Cleveland Browns football franchise (as well as the history of the greater Cleveland area and politics). How a new professional sports team comes into being, rising from a mere idea in someone's mind and inspiration in his heart, and grows into a championship franchise that influences generations of players and fans to come, has always fascinated me.

From 1944 to 1953, Arthur "Mickey" McBride owned the Cleveland Browns—first in the All-American Football Conference (AAFC), which originated in Canton, Ohio, and then in the nascent National Football League. I'm one year old going on two in the 1953 season, but the groundwork for what comes later—for what will directly impact me in my life—is being laid. That is why I cover it here.

During McBride's tenure, the Browns will win five league championships and reach the championship game twice. An early legacy responsible for attracting many die-hard Browns fans. Absolute shame that when success comes too soon, it remains difficult to live up to future expectations. McBride's tenure will, thus, comprise the most successful era ever for a Cleveland sports franchise.

In the beginning, long before he acquired the Browns, McBride was only a boxing and baseball fan, openly conceding he knew little about professional football. However, after attending a "Fighting Irish" game at Notre Dame in 1940, where his son Mickey attended college, McBride's interest in owning a football team apparently changed. Like football fans before him, he was riveted by the energy and excitement of the new game. And given his golden touch with capital, he left the Notre Dame game believing a professional team might be within his reach, as well as loads of fun and possible profit.

At the time, McBride was already a prosperous real estate developer with projects in Cleveland, Chicago, and Florida. He also owned taxicab companies in Cleveland and a horse racing news wire that sold information to bookmakers, thus exposing him to the gambling world. It was said the wire service created ties to organized crime figures, but to be absolutely clear, to my knowledge, he was never charged with, arrested for, or convicted of any crime. In fact, he consistently and adamantly denied ever engaging in any criminal activity despite the public speculation. McBride's storyline runs parallel to that of the DeBartolo family, the same DeBartolo family of San Francisco 49ers' fame. The DeBartolos reigned from the Youngstown, Ohio, area just southeast of Cleveland where they developed the concept of big shopping malls. It has long been rumoured that the DeBartolos financed all their big mall projects with mob (Mafia) money, though again, to my knowledge, they have never been charged with, arrested for, or convicted of any crime. Eddie DeBartolo later became owner of the San Francisco 49ers during the legendary Joe Walsh and Joe Montana Super Bowl era.

On a side note, George Steinbrenner of New York Yankee fame, also much like the DeBartolos, made his vast wealth in the shipbuilding business in Cleveland. Had these two families kept their fortunes in Cleveland and invested in the Cleveland sports scene, Cleveland may have dominated the sports world for many years. Another sports powerhouse, International Management Group (IMG), headquartered in Cleveland, is a major player in the golf world because it has represented the likes of Arnold Palmer, Jack Nicklaus, and Tiger Woods.

In 1942, McBride approached Cleveland supermarket heir Dan Reeves to buy his Cleveland Rams, a team from a different football league, but Reeves turned down his offer. In 1944, *Chicago Tribune* sports editor Arch Ward proposed a new professional football league called the AAFC. McBride, who had met Ward during his newspaper days, promptly came on board as the owner of the brand new Cleveland franchise in the eight-team AAFC.

New to the game, McBride took the advice of *Plain Dealer* sportswriter John Dietrich to contact Paul Brown, former coach of the Ohio State Buckeyes. At OHB, Brown had just won his first national collegiate championship. McBride offered Brown $17,500 a year to take the reins as head coach (about $255,000 in current dollars), the largest salary ever offered to any football coach at any level, plus an equity stake in the team. Brown took the position, telling anyone who asked, he couldn't "turn down this deal in fairness to my family."

Once Coach Brown was on board, McBride put his money where his mouth was, as the saying goes, sparing no expense in promoting his new team and giving his new coach wide discretion over talent and personnel. This permitted Coach Brown to use his own judgment in signing future stars such as tackle and placekicker Lou Groza, wide receiver Dante Lavelli, and quarterback Otto Graham, reportedly paid $7,500 a year and $250 monthly for living expenses to sustain him through the end of World War II.

Separate and apart from needing a roster of good players, the new team also needed a resonate name. To excite the public, McBride held a contest in May 1945 to come up with a fitting moniker. When the votes were counted, the name "Cleveland Panthers" prevailed over the other entrees. Apparently a tad superstitious, Brown rejected this name because it was the same name as an earlier failed football team. "That old Panthers team failed," Brown was quoted as saying. "I want no part of that name." Then in August, McBride caved to popular demand, adopting the name "the Cleveland Browns" over Coach Paul Brown's objections.

To this day, I am amazed that a major franchise city can have both the best logo symbol (Chief Wahoo for the Indians) and the worst logo symbol (the plain colors of orange and brown for the Browns). If you ask me, this defies all tenets in the marketing world related to "branding."

The Browns were an immediate success, both financially and on the field. A capacity crowd of nearly 36,000 fans attended the Browns' first preseason game, and between the years of 1946-1949, the team led the league in attendance. But that attendance did not come in a vacuum. During the same time, the Browns won every AAFC championship, which explains the mushrooming legion of dedicated Browns fans, my dad among them. Then, after the 1949 season, the AAFC dissolved and three of its teams, including the Browns, merged into the better-established NFL.

But that did not slow the Browns, who won the NFL conference championship that year and reached the title game in both 1951 and 1952, the year I am born. However, all is not roses for Mc-Bride. In January 1951, with Mafia pollen floating in the air of greater Cleveland, he was subpoenaed to testify at the nationally televised Kefauver Committee hearings, where Congress sought to establish the existence of organized crime in America. Millions of Americans watched the broadcasted hearings as McBride was grilled about his Continental Press wire service and alleged ties to organized crime and illegal gambling. He denied any Mafia connections, repeatedly claiming under oath that he had never broken any law of any kind.

But the hearings must have impacted McBride. During the summer before the 1953 football season, he exited the game, stage left, so to speak, selling the Browns franchise for $600,000 (about $5,300,000 today), thereby departing the business of professional football. Apparently, that sum proved more than double the amount ever previously paid for a professional football franchise. (In 2012, Randy Lerner sold the Cleveland Browns franchise to truck-stop magnate Jimmy Haslam reportedly for in excess of $1 billion.)

While McBride never said so, many people opined that the Kefauver hearings and the growing public perception that he was associated with the Mafia caused him to leave, though McBride explained it differently. He said he simply had "had his fling" with professional football and wanted to focus on other businesses and business interests.

"Well, I came out clean after all," he also said. "Considering what happened to some of the other fellows who started the old All-America Conference with me, this isn't so bad. I never made anything, but I didn't lose anything either, except maybe a few thousand dollars." Not too bad given the speculative risk involved.

Though I'm an adolescent in these early post-McBride years, the reputation of the team as composed of hard-working champions permeated the culture of Cleveland, reaching especially the youth.

CONQUERING YOUR ADVERSITIES

There is nothing like a popular professional franchise—for example, to-day's Golden State Warriors and Stephen Curry—to motivate the spirits of impressionable young men and women. While Dad never became an avid Cleveland Browns fan (as a baseball fanatic, his first love always lay with the Cleveland Indians), I become a diehard fan as soon as I am old enough to comprehend football. Later, when my brother Dennis and I play football in high school, Dad will religiously join us in the living room to watch every Cleveland Browns game that's broadcast on television—if only to support his sons.

~ ~ ~

The Korean War over by a few years, 1957 shines the first bright light of history on the NFL. That year's rookies will help alter the game forever. Syracuse's Jim Brown signs to the Browns, where he will become the most feared and talented backfield runner of all time. Notre Dame offers up Paul Hornung, who presents not a double but a triple threat: runner, receiver, and blocker extraordinaire.

Playing for the Green Bay Packers from 1957 to 1966, Hornung will ultimately become a revered Hall of Famer, win four NFL titles, and take home a Super Bowl ring. Quarterbacks Sonny Jurgensen from Duke, John Brodie from Stanford, and Len Dawson from Purdue will all enter the NFL and change the game with their precision passing techniques. As such, all will serve as inspirations to yours truly.

For those of us growing up in Cleveland, Jim Brown will become a legend unto himself. He will play his entire career with the Cleveland Browns, from 1957 to 1965, sharing the same name with the team and the coach, as if all three were delivered there by destiny. In 1957, Jim Brown ends his rookie year by leading the Cleveland Browns to a championship win over the New York Giants, where Vince Lombardi first landed after leaving the Army. Within months, Jim Brown is known to every football fan in Cleveland.

When he leaves the NFL eight years later in 1965, Jim Brown will hold countless records, including single-season rushing yardage (1,863 in 1963) and career rushing yardage (12,312 yards), as well as all-time leader in rushing touchdowns (106), total touchdowns (126), and all-purpose yards (15,549). He will also be the first player to score 100 rushing touchdowns. To eliminate any doubt, in 2002, Sporting News will crown him the greatest professional football player—and one of the greatest athletes—of all time…noting that he also was an all-American lacrosse player at Syracuse University.

When I join the Browns in 1974, nearly two decades later, I will be overwhelmed with pride, notwithstanding the team's total fall from grace in the early '70s. That pride will have its roots in guys like Jim Brown and the early Browns teams. There is something about a legendary status that cannot be erased. I think it is the underlying values that support such an achievement. Building a team, believing in yourself against all odds, being the very best that you can be, and the pride of winning—these values survive long after the glow of championship glory grows dim.

When these values permeate a culture or community, somehow they take on a life of their own, infusing themselves into the minds, bodies, and souls of everyone who grows up with them. The game of football will eventually endear itself in the hearts of many millions of Americans. Ultimately, football will metamorphosize into a bigger-than-life continuation of that winning "we-can-do-anything" spirit that mushroomed over America after the Second World War.

Americans embrace winners, heroes, and winning. When a newcomer on the block like America can take on and defeat the likes of well-established world powers such as those of Germany, Italy, and Japan, the floodgates of achievement open up. What was once action taken just for survival now carries over into peacetime activities. Cheering and rooting for the "underdog" becomes a national pastime alongside hotdogs, baseball, and apple pie.

Values like these, I will later learn, are the bedrock of conquering your adversities.

EXERCISE:

Growing up, did you and your parents have any heroes—in sports, science, adventure, or otherwise—that provided the rallying point for positive achievements in your home? If so, who were they and what was their impact on you then and now?

_____
_____
_____
_____

Identify the early childhood values that were most important to you and your family and had the biggest impact on you both while growing up and now.

_____
_____
_____
_____

To what degree does America's historic values—things like success against all odds, the pride of winning, and having a winning spirit—permeate your life?

_____
_____
_____
_____

Chapter 5

APALACHIN & THE MOB

"J. Edgar Hoover knew perfectly well that organized crime existed before 1957. In the 1940's he had been known to sit at the same table in upscale clubs with known underworld figures like Meyer Lansky.... He preferred to not acknowledge the Mafia's existence so he would not be obligated to assign FBI agents to build cases against them. He chose to assign his agents to cases like unorganized interstate crime ('Pretty Boy' Floyd, John Dillinger, 'Baby Face' Nelson), infiltrating the Communist party, and spying on and harassing civil rights leaders. It was only the blatant publicity of the Apalachin Meeting, after it was raided by state and local police, that forced the FBI director to admit that the Mafia was an actual organization."

— Curt Gentry, *J. Edgar Hoover: The Man and the Secrets*

On April 16, 1957, five years after the Kefauver hearings, I turn five years old. We had recently moved from our downtown apartment to a 1,400 square foot, three-bedroom prefab in Collinwood, a rough and tumble neighborhood on the outskirts of Cleveland that would become known in the '70s as "Bomb City USA."

Years earlier, our prefab had been inserted onto the lot by the protruding blades of a large tractor, then connected to the community via public utility pipes and electrical wires. Looking at it from the street, few people could tell that it was a prefab since we donned a green grass front yard and pitched roof just like our neighbors.

At age five, I, of course, do not know the difference between a prefab and a regular house, and I do not care. My world revolves around the only home I know, and Nottingham Grade School, where I am now attending kindergarten. In fact, my world starts the same way each day, with Mom yelling.

"Kenneth Jeffrey, you and your brother need to get up, and I mean NOW!" Whenever the middle name was used with the full first name, you knew immediately it was not a good thing!

I look at my brother. He's snoring, mouth wide open, at the other end of the bed. We share a twin, my head at the top, his at the bottom. I kick his shoulder. When that doesn't work, I tickle one of his feet.

"Denny, wake up."

He grunts and frowns, but doesn't move, mumbling, "Leave me 'lone."

Rolling out of bed, I crash into the wall a foot from the edge of the bed, then leverage myself against it to stand up. Our room is tiny, just like the house. Tiny has its advantages and disadvantages.

"Denny, let's go. Come on; get up. Mom's getting mad," I say with a final, futile urging.

"How many pieces of toast?" Mom yells. I squeeze between the bed and the wall, open the door, then walk into the kitchen, which is about four feet down a short hall.

"One piece, please, with lots of jelly. Do we have grape, Mom?"

"Yes, but only one spoonful, so your teeth don't rot out."

The smell of fried ham and eggs wafts into my nose, making my stomach growl. The chair leg scratches on the new floor tile, recently laid down by Dad from a pile of extra tiles occupying our closet, as I settle into my seat at the Formica and chrome drop-leaf table, adjusting my rump on the sticky plastic seat.

Dennis walks out, rubbing his eyes with one hand and dragging his favorite blanket with the other. He sits opposite me, a frown on his face. Already he is as tall as me, despite being one year younger. His rapid growth as he grows older, in fact, will scare Mom, so much so that (in my opinion) she will not push him as hard because she feels his growing body needs more rest.

"Hi, honey," says Mom, referring to Dennis. "Did you get a good night's sleep?"

Dennis only frowns deeper.

"He hates getting up early," I say.

"The early bird gets the worm, boys. Remember that."

Dennis and I look at each other and I mouth, "*Yuck*," thinking to myself, *Here we go again with another momism*. (She had a million of them, and as we grew older, we swore we would never in a million years repeat any of them. But never say never, as life has a way of rearing its ugly head only to bite you in the behind (and that's behind, with a double *S*). There was a lot of home-spun wisdom in those momisms.)

Mom looks at the grease-covered wall clock. "It's almost eight. Genie Boy, you'll be late!" she yells.

Mom dabs the ham (canned Spam) with a Scott paper towel, then scoops easy-over eggs onto our plates and drops two slices of ham onto each.

"Ouch," she says as she pulls the hot toast from the toaster, elbow jerking, then flips the squares onto our plates.

Gripping two plates in one hand, she opens the fridge with the other, snags the jelly, then drops all three onto the table like she's working the local diner. "Only one spoonful of jelly," she affirms to me with an evil eye.

When she turns her back, I quickly scoop two large spoonfuls onto my toast. She doesn't catch me, having already moved on to worrying about Dad.

"Genie Boy," she yells toward the back again. "It's getting la—"

"I'm over here, honey," Dad says from the living room.

"Oh, I didn't see you go by."

"You won't believe this," he replies.

I turn my head toward his voice. He's staring at a gray-green TV screen with some words on it. Our living room is so tiny the television console barely fits into the room when combined with Dad's overstuffed Chaise recliner and our three-cushion sofa.

Mom wipes her hands on her apron and hustles toward the living room. I look at Dennis and we both jump from our chairs and follow her as she scoops Cheryl from the floor and onto her hip. By this time, Cheryl is about two-and-a-half, literally our baby sister.

Updated from the earlier model, our latest TV screen still offers programs only in black and white, but it is a larger console model, with a bigger screen and better speaker. The screen flashes fuzzy, prompting Dad to bang the side before adjusting the wobbly rabbit ear antennas to obtain a clearer picture. On one occasion, the TV repairman had to come service the TV because Dad did not know exactly where to bang on it. I was amazed by the huge TV tubes inside the TV. After he replaced a couple of old tubes with new ones, I thought for sure that after a few more TV repair visits we would be able to collect all the old tubes together and bring Frankenstein back to life.

"What's it about?" Mom asks as she adjusts her footing so as not to trip over our long legs since Dennis and I have already taken positions on the couch. Even before we grow into large athletes, the whole family barely fits into the room. (Picture the visual, and if later after we grow up you don't have a big smile on your face, write me and I'll send you a signed George Washington $1 bill.)

"Shhhh," Dad says sharply. "It's a CBS news bulletin." He points to the words on the screen. "He's about to—"

Mom walks over and twists the volume nob just as a deep, grumbling voice begins to speak. I recognize the grumble, but don't know the name that goes with it. I do know that whenever the voice comes on, Mom and Dad stop talking, just like they do when the priest starts talking at church. Today, that rarely happens—part of the same moral crisis, I say, because national news programs today are more focused on scandal, popular spin, infotainment, and the short-term bottom line. Not to mention, there's breaking news every minute of the day, it seems.

"Good morning," the voice grumbles, then follows with words to this effect: "This is Walter Cronkite, CBS News. We interrupt our regularly scheduled program for this special report. In Apalachin, New York, the Federal Bureau of Investigation has broken up a meeting of suspected criminal figures gathered there from all over the world. Fifty-five men, all with alleged ties to organized crime, have been arrested. The Director of the FBI, J. Edgar Hoover, claims this is the first ever definitive proof that nationwide organized crime exists in America."

"Oh," Mom screams, "the grease!" At once I smell smoke and turn toward the kitchen. A small fire has erupted from the skillet. Mom rushes over and tries to grab the handle, but she quickly flings her hand up from the scorching heat, causing the pan to clang to the floor. "Honey, help!" she yells.

As Dad leaps over the couch, he grabs a blanket strewn across its back, and in the blink of an eye, he throws it over the flaming pan. "Stand back!" he screams to Mom as he grips the pan's handle through the blanket, wraps the whole shebang around his hand, then races out the side door. We all converge on the doorjamb to watch, but the excitement is over as quickly as it started. Dad sprays the mess down with the garden hose, then turns off the spigot and walks back inside as if nothing happened.

"We need to get one of those new smoke alarms, Lois," Dad says as he reaches for the black Bell rotary phone sitting on the counter, puts the cradle to his ear, then spins the dial with his index finger.

"What's a smoke alarm?" Mom asks.

"I read about it in *Popular Science Magazine*. They're working on a smoke detector that you can put in your house. Runs off batteries, like those new wall clocks. It goes off and makes a loud sound whenever it detects smoke. They say it will save thousands of lives."

"No kidding," she says.

"Eddie," he says while still looking at her but directing himself to the person on the other end of the line. "Thank God. I just wanted to make sure that you—. Did you hear the special news report about the maf-, organized cri-, in Apalachin? You did. Okay, I just, well, wanted to make sure you were all right. Okay, great; I'll tell Lois. Goodbye."

He turns to Mom. "Uncle Eddie says hello."

She stares at Dad for a moment, then says: "Good, I'm glad he wasn't there."

Our eyes grow big with curiosity, but we have no idea what they are talking about. Years later, I will learn that Great-Uncles Eddie and Frank Simms (brothers to our paternal grandmother, Alice Simms), were both very colorful characters, to say the least. Rumor had it that both worked in some vague way in connection with the Las Vegas mob.

Later that year, our favorite uncle visits us for the holidays. "Hi, Uncle Eddie," Dennis and I yell as we race to the open front door, having waited for him with great anticipation for hours.

"Hi, boys," Uncle Eddie says, sweeping both of us up into his massive arms at the same time and twirling us around. Our smiles engulf our faces with joy because we know our uncle will soon be giving us boxing lessons.

"Hi, Eddie," Dad says as he reaches out his hand.

Mom smiles and takes her hug, then offers Uncle Eddie something to drink. "Whatever you have, Lois." (He would ask for a beer, but he knows we don't keep any in the house on account of Dad not drinking.)

"Come on in and rest your feet," Dad says as he walks back to the living room. Then over the next hour, we listen as Uncle Eddie tells one colorful story after another about how he escorts celebrities and casinos owners around Las Vegas, watches people gamble thousands of dollars, and acts as a bodyguard to movers and shakers. Dennis and I don't know the names or understand the nuances, of course, but we are in awe of his exploits.

To be honest, however, as kids we don't really care about any of this, and Uncle Eddie eventually can see it in our faces. "You ready?" he says to us. We jump to our feet and take the boxer pose—legs bowed, dukes up, fists curled. He extends his flat, meaty palm towards us, and we take turns punching it with our fists.

Now Uncle Eddie is on his knees. "Great, hit harder," he says. "Right in the middle of my hand." I swing so hard I miss and fall to the ground. Dennis and Eddie laugh. I get back up and blast a pointed knuckle into Dennis' bicep.

"Ouch!" Dennis yells.

"Ken," Uncle Eddie says, "let me talk to you about that. We only hit someone in self-defense. Your fists are weapons, and we have to handle them in that way."

Dennis and I look at each other. "Sorry," I say.

Uncle Eddie had a unique (very gruff) speaking tone and slow speech pattern that I am sure many actors in Hollywood copied when imitating boxers or mobsters. So after Uncle Eddie's professional boxing career was over, he was a "natural" as they say in show business to portray a "punch-drunk" boxer or hitman mobster. This is probably why he appeared in almost twenty-five "B" movies—because he really wasn't acting. So when he talked, like everyone else, we listened.

Uncle Eddie climbs to his feet and gets into his patented boxing stance, the former professional boxer that he is. "This is how you do it. Right hand in front, left hand back. Jab with your right, cross with your left." He demonstrates a blazing flurry of punches. We're both frozen in wonderment and admiration. Then we try to copy him—two little guys madly jabbing the air like future pugilists.

And though head-butting isn't legal in the ring, Eddie prided himself in teaching us how to do it without getting caught. "Once a pugilist, always a pugilist," Uncle Eddie would say. And speaking of pugilist, the word fit Uncle Eddie like a glove, known far and wide for his large forehead and flattened nose.

After Uncle Eddie leaves, I remember Dad telling Dennis and I all about Uncle Eddie and his brother, Frank, being professional boxers. "Guys," he would say with excitement when boxing matches were playing on the TV, "do you know what a professional boxer does?"

"Yeah, Dad," I would say. "You told us about it last week. They hit each other until someone gets knocked out."

"Well," he says, ignoring me, "your uncle Eddie, he was big time in his day. He was a heavyweight and he fought over 200 fights. At one time, he had eighteen straight knockouts."

"Wow," Dennis and I say at the same time as we giggle at Dad telling us the same story again (like older people do) with the same relish.

"Eddie's biggest moment came when he fought the great Joe Louis, right here in Cleveland at the Cleveland Public Arena. It was a charity match sponsored by the *Cleveland News*. Do you know what charity is?"

Dennis and I look at each other and shrug.

"A charity is when you volunteer. You do it for free because it's a good cause. It helps other people who are less fortunate."

"Oh," I say.

"Like when I help shovel the driveway?" Dennis asks.

"Yes—" Dad starts to say.

"You don't, either," I assert. "You just stand there while I do all the work."

"Okay, that's enough," Dad says. "I was just a kid myself back then. It was December 14, 1936. Unfortunately, Eddie was not a match for the great Joe Louis, who was considered the best fighter in the world. He knocked Eddie cold in the first round, with his first punch, in only thirty-six seconds."

"Thirty-six seconds," I say, dropping my jaw.

In all fairness, as Dad went on to explain, Uncle Eddie was no match for the much younger and faster Joe Louis. Joe was entering the prime of his boxing career and Eddie was on the tail-end of his. The newspapers also reported that Eddie had nothing left in his legs in the Louis fight, having just returned from a long road trip out to the West Coast by train, sometimes fighting every other week.

As I grew up, I would learn that the mob had extended its long fingers into the boxing game. Had Uncle Eddie not been hit so hard, and had it not been for a worthy charity, his fight with Louis might have garnered cries of "fix," but apparently it never did. No one dared take on or embarrass the mob, despite Hoover not knowing it existed.

On top of that, Dad tells us, "Your Uncle Eddie enjoyed an impressive film career. He appeared in movies with some pretty big stars, people like Humphrey Bogart, Lauren Bacall, Dean Martin, Ricardo Montalban, Fred Astaire, Jerry Lewis, and James Dean." None of those names mean anything to us at the time. If he had made an appearance on *Captain Kangaroo*, that might have been different.

"But there is more," Dad says, adding yet another layer about our illustrious uncles. "Both Eddie and Frank were world-class Cleveland-Style Polka squeezeboxers." Dad sees the blank look on our faces and points to a squeezebox laying in the corner of the living room. "There, that's a squeezebox, remember."

"Oh, yeah," I say. "I know what that is. Uncle Eddie played it last year on Christmas." Dennis shakes his head in agreement, though I wonder whether he really remembers. He was only three at the time.

"I know this is a lot to remember," Dad says, "but Eddie and Frank, they joined their step-brother, my Great Uncle Matt Hoyer, in the Matt Hoyer Trio. A trio is three. The Trio recorded the first Slovenian polka and waltz records ever released in America. In fact, in his heyday in the so-called roaring '20s, Eddie played accordion and banjo on ninety-seven songs recorded for Columbia and RCA Victor Records in New York City. They ultimately made him an honorary inductee of the National Cleveland-Style Polka Hall of Fame."

At the sound of the number ninety-seven, our eyes grow wide. At our age, ninety-seven is a number we rarely hear, but we both know it is a lot. Plus, Dad used it with the word "ultimately," so it must be big.

According to Dad, since Eddie himself never told us, one of Uncle Eddie's favorite stories and proudest moments was when he got to hang out with Dean Martin. Apparently he was filming a movie with Dean Martin and Jerry Lewis when the director called for a break. Dean came over and started singing as Eddie sang along and played. Eddie knew all the words to the song and joined in on vocals. The stagehands gave them a standing ovation after they howled through several songs together.

But as my brother and I grew older, we both secretly felt that Uncle Eddie must have had ties to some big-time gangsters, such as New York gangster Bugsy Siegel. That's who he followed to Hollywood and then to Vegas. Nothing to prove this, just suspicions based on things we would overhear him saying to Dad and Mom. Sorry, Eddie, if that wasn't the case. But young guys are impressionable, a lesson to remember.

"Ken, school time," Mom says suddenly, looking over and giving me a sharp jerk of her head.

"Ahh, Mom, do I have to?" I moan.

After a pause, Dennis says, "I have a stomach ache."

"You do not," I say, then realize I'm working against my own interests. "Me, too, Mom. I ate too much jelly."

By now, Mom's hands are on her hips, not believing a word, at least not from me.

"Maybe Ken should stay home today, Lois," Dad interjects. "In light of—" He nods toward the TV in the living room.

"Can I, Mom; can I?" I beseech her.

Mom considers it a moment, then shakes her head from side to side. "You can be anything you want, but you won't be anything if you don't go to school."

"Mooommm," I whine.

"Brush your teeth," she says.

"But Dennis doesn't, isn't—"

"Listen to your mother," Dad says.

I drag myself into the bathroom and brush my teeth. As you can see, in matters like this, Mom rules with an iron fist. After combing my hair, I return to the kitchen.

"Genie," Mom says as she lights a cigarette from the blue and orange flame of the stove. "Tell me the FBI is not just now realizing there's organized crime in America."

"That is a ridiculous notion," Dad replies. "The Mafia families go back to the 1920s in New York and Chicago. They ran liquor during Prohibition. Mom and Dad were bootleggers, as you know, Lo, so I'm afraid I know more about it than I care to. When I was a kid, I often couldn't take a bath because they were distilling gin in the bathtub, for Christ's sakes. If truth be told, we've had organized crime here in Cleveland for at least thirty years, ever since the bootleggers."

"In Cleveland? How about Collinwood?" Mom adds with her signature sarcasm, as she pulls another strong drag from her cigarette and blows a smoke circle high into the air. (Back then, smokers did not go outside to smoke.)

I jump into my Machine Gun Kelly stance and start firing away with my imaginary machine gun. "Bbbddddddddddddd."

Dennis grabs his heart with both hands and crumples to the floor, pretending to be shot dead.

And so it is when we are growing up. The mob is a natural part of our lives, beginning with the almighty television, from the time we can walk.

EXERCISE

When young, were you exposed to any negative or criminal element that you romanticized? If so, explain how you overcame that influence?

_____

_____

_____

Growing up, did the media have an influence on your dreams and your ability to achieve them? If so, explain the impact.

_____

_____

_____

List other negative influences that might steer young minds in the wrong direction, and suggest ways to conquer them.

_____

_____

_____

Chapter 6

THE CLEVELAND MOB

"It is not possible to go forward while looking back."

— Ludwig Mies van der Rohe

Despite J. Edgar Hoover's public statement that the Apalachin arrests provided the first *definitive* proof of nationally organized crime in America, my mom and dad were totally correct in knowing better. Indeed, my dad's parents—raging alcoholics, speakeasy operators, and brawlers who, according to Mom, abused Dad as a child—were bootleggers in Cleveland in the 1920s, and the bootleggers obtained the corn sugar needed to make liquor from the Cleveland mob, which controlled all corn sugar coming into the city.

As for the Cleveland mob, Dad told us—in bits and snippets over the years—that it actually originated in Cleveland in the early 1900s. Apparently that's when Joe, Frank, John, and Dominic Lonardo, and the seven Porrello brothers, all migrated to America from Sicily, home to La Cosa Nostra. As the story goes, the brothers Lonardo and Porrello first started with legit businesses, then moved to presumably more profitable criminal enterprises like robbery and extortion.

As a voracious reader, Dad was like a walking history book. On many nights over the years after we came home from playing baseball or football, he would be reading in the living room. He loved books about World War II, but he also read many books about Cleveland, the Mafia, and America in general. You never knew when he would start talking about his latest book interest.

"When Prohibition began," Dad starts one day after Uncle Eddie had called, "Joseph 'Big Joe' Lonardo was said to be the boss of Cleveland's organized crime families. He was the second oldest of the four Lonardo brothers, who supplied bootleggers like my parents with corn sugar. His top lieutenant was Joseph 'Big Joe' Porrello."

"Two 'Big Joes'," I say, laughing.

"Yeah, "Big Joe'," Dennis says, also laughing and pumping his right hand high in the air.

"By the mid-1920s," Dad explains, "the Porrellos had branched out on their own, establishing their home base near Five Points." Dad points west. "You know, the place where all the streets come together."

Dennis and I shake our heads in the affirmative since we've driven by there often.

"As time passed, the Lonardo and Porrello brothers started fighting between themselves. They battled over corn sugar and controlling bootleg liquor."

"What is liqa, Dad?" Dennis asks.

"And corn sugar?" I add, hoping we don't get in trouble for asking, knowing already that the subject of liquor is *verboten* in the Polke household.

"It's something adults drink, and it makes them do silly and sometimes

mobs of Five Points. A guy named Alfred 'Allie' Con Calabrese was the leader, a true gentleman gangster from the old school, I've read. His turf ran from the 152nd Street Bridge, up to Five Points and Ivanhoe Road, down Mandalay and across London Road to Wayside and then over to Saranac, which bordered the Collinwood train yards where you guys ride your bikes." (My brother and I both played Little League ball and were coached by many in the Iacobacci family, who reported to Allie Con Cabrese.)

"But the biggest guy of them all," Dad says, "was John Scalish. He ruled the Cleveland mob beginning in 1944 for eight years, Kenny, before you were born." Neither Dad nor I knew it at the time, but, in fact, Scalish's reign would last until he died in 1976, the year after I left the NFL and only months before I started dental school at Case Western Reserve.

Scalish would mix with some of the most colorful characters in mob history, guys like Lucky Luciano, Myer Lansky, Alex "Shondor" Birns, Moe Dalitz, and Tony Accardo...the guys mentioned in mob movies. He even became allied with the so-called Chicago Outfit and the Genovese crime family. The Cleveland mob thus expanded its influence to the Midwest, California, Florida, and Las Vegas, where my great-uncles, the Simms brothers, spent many years. Did the Simms mix with these guys? I couldn't say for sure, but if I had to guess, I'd say they did.

During my childhood in the 1950s, the Cleveland mob reached its peak with about sixty *made* members, and several times as many associates, I read. Growing up, my brother and I knew kids in the neighborhood who chose the route of organized crime, some of whom no doubt became these one of these made members. Especially in high school, I would notice young Italian guys all of a sudden driving by in fancy cars, wearing fancy cloths and watches, and getting all the babes. Like a scene from the feature film *Scarface*, which would not

81

hit theaters until 1983.

The intoxicating lure of crime calls out to every kid growing up in a mob town like Collinwood, just like it called out to Henry Hill (played by Ray Liotta) in the 1986 Martin Scorsese masterpiece, *Goodfellas*. As a kid growing up in the shadow of the mob, Henry Hill said: "For us to live any other way was nuts. Uh, to us, those goody-good people who worked shitty jobs for bum pay checks and took the subway to work every day, and worried about their bills, were dead. I mean they were suckers. They had no balls. If we wanted something, we just took it. If anyone complained twice, they got hit so bad, believe me, they never complained again...."

In 1976—only ten years before *Goodfellas* hit the big screen, and four years after *The Godfather* swept the Oscars by romancing the mob—John Scalish would die. After word of his death swept the underworld, Scalish would be accorded a funeral befitting a king. Not one but three priests would come together to deliver his solemn Requiem Mass. Roads were barricaded to accommodate the streams of cars and mourners attending the funeral. But no sooner was he buried than the Cleveland underworld began to implode, erupting in a battle for who would succeed him, since he had failed to name a successor.

The battle for control of gambling, loan sharking, unions, and even legitimate businesses, so carefully manicured by Scalish during his tenure as don, would make Collinwood the bombing capital of America, earning it the infamous title, "Bomb City USA." Many lives would be lost, but more importantly, the battle between the mob and the FBI would turn Collinwood into a war zone.

Why? Because the FBI's sacrosanct data on confidential informants would be disclosed by someone at the Bureau to the very mob figures it was hunting. The leak would have disastrous repercussions, necessitating a complete revamping of the FBI's methodology for managing informants. In some ways, it was just as much a shocker as the Snowden incident that rocked America's intelligence community in 2013.

At the center of this incredible situation—The Mob War and The Leak—was the bombing murder of Danny Greene, the Robin Hood of Collinwood whose life became the subject of a book by Rick Porrello and the motion picture *Kill the Irishman*. Greene was bigger than life, with goals of running the Teamsters and the Longshoremen. Both an FBI informant and a mobster, the guy who would give away dozens of free turkeys over the holidays to people in need...would die a tragic death.

Like so many things in Collinwood, Greene defied all the rules of the game and lived on myth and borrowed time, considering himself a tough Irish kid unwilling to cave in to the iron will and blind allegiance required by the Italian mob who, for that very reason, was hell-bent on putting him six feet under.

Accordingly, no story about a kid growing up in South Collinwood would be complete without outing the Elephant in the Room. The Mafia or La Cosa Nostra was part of our lives, whether we were Italian, Irish, Polish, or Slovenian. Everywhere we turned, it was lingering 'round the corner, up the alley, down by the crik, rearing its ugly head—from the neighborhood church and little league, to the local merchants and garden centers.

Though I will later escape through football, prayer, and determination, organized crime will live on in my neighborhood for years, intertwined with the greed, self-destruction, killing, crime, pride, lust, money, power and legacy on which it thrives. That I was able to escape with my life and my integrity is nothing short of a miracle—and thus a prime mover for this book.

EXERCISE:

Did you or your family grow up under the shadow—the adversity—of the mob, criminal gangs, or any kind of criminal element? If so, explain what it was?

_____

_____

_____

What did you, your family, and your friends do to escape the clutches and attractions of crime?

_____

_____

_____

Does the criminal element that you grew up with or to which you were exposed still haunt you? If so, how?

_____

_____

_____

What advice would you give to young people growing up under the influence of negative influences, and how might this advice enable you today to overcome your own adversities?

_____

_____

_____

Chapter 7

NUTS, BOLTS & HEART

"My mother was the most beautiful woman I ever saw. All I am I owe to my mother. I attribute all my success in life to the moral, intellectual and physical education I received from her."

— George Washington

"A child miseducated, is a child lost."

— John Kennedy

Between 1952 and 1954—in April 1952, September 1953, and December 1954, to be exact—Mom gives birth to me, my brother Dennis, and my sister Cheryl. We aren't Irish, but if we were, we might have been dubbed Irish triplets, traveling through school and life a mere one year and several months apart.

I'll be more like Mom, and Dennis and Cheryl, they'll be more like Dad. That means I'm going to be more assertive, aggressive, and outspoken, while Dennis and Cheryl are going to be more quiet and laid back, though as he grows older, Dennis will never stand down to anyone—nor will he have to, ultimately growing to 6' 7½". LeBron

James is only 6' 9"!

Within months of me starting kindergarten at Nottingham Grade School, a public school close to our prefab, Mom and Dad reach a profound decision: They agree Mom will take a job, a rare choice for any working family in the 1950s. In this era, men work and women mind the home. In later years, they will explain to us in more detail why they chose the road less travelled, but it's actually quite simple.

"We want you and your sister to have a better life," Mom explains to Dennis and me one Saturday afternoon in the living room, justifying the announcement that we will be leaving Nottingham public grade school and attending St. Paul's Parish grade school beginning next fall.

Even in the 1950s and 1960s, the public schools suffered from a poor reputation. Everyone agreed that the Catholic school system was far superior. The nuns walked softly, but they carried a harsh, disciplinary stick. Their educational philosophy demanded they set the highest possible standards in behavior, education, and faith, pushing every student to the limit.

One may not agree with their methods, but it is hard to argue with the results. In my opinion, the reverse philosophy of setting a bar so low that everyone can pass fails miserably in preparing students for the harsh realities of a competitive world. On this I'm sure I'm not alone.

It will be years later, of course, before I appreciate the gravity of that simple decision that my parents made. By sending us off to private school every day, they also removed us from the harsh, rough and tumble streets of South Collinwood—even though it's a decision that would wrap them in a financial straightjacket for their entire lives.

Of necessity, Mom's job decision required a careful calculation and balance of many factors.

"How will you do it, Lo?" I hear Dad ask her after she has informed the family that she plans to start working in a few weeks, a decision she has reached largely on her own.

"Well," she replies, her hands carefully rubbing a kitchen towel as she thinks. In her mind, she must be juggling how she will raise three young children while being absent from home eight hours a day in a family with one car. Since Dad works in downtown Cleveland, that means, among other things, she will have to walk to work since he must drive to work and owning two cars is out of the question.

"I've got to get something close by, Gene. If I get the kids off to school before seven, that will give me time to get to work. Then I need to be off work by three so I can rush over to pick up Cheryl at day care and get home about the same time the boys do. It takes the boys about thirty minutes to walk home, so I'm good if I'm home by 3:30 p.m. I can hide a key under the mat, so if I'm running late the boys can let themselves in."

As it turns out, Jergens' manufacturing plant is located a block up the street, since in these times residential neighborhoods like ours are mixed use. Homes, family shops, corner drugstores, and factories all occupy the same block. It's not like today, where different uses are sectioned off into different parts of town per force of the local zoning laws. Back then, people understood the importance of close proximity if they wanted to survive with limited resources.

Years later, after decades of growth and success, Jergens would become a multinational company and move out of Collinwood. When Mom takes her job there, it's still a small nuts and bolts factory, squeezing its employees for every ounce of work it can get out of them for the least possible wage. At least that's how Mom sees it, and it doesn't take long for her to react to the perceived minimal wages and severity of her new workplace.

While the rest of the workers suffer in silence, the fiery redhead raising three young children openly protests the working conditions and wages offered by the growing company whose owners wear fine suits and drive expensive cars. Of course, it's the mid-1950s, the peak of union growth in America, so she has a national liberal wind under her wings, as the battle rages over who will rule the workplace: management or organized labor.

"Genie Boy," she says with great defiance one evening after work. "Look at these hands." She withdraws them from under the running water of the kitchen faucet and holds them up for us to see, palms facing out.

Dad stands up from his seat at the kitchen table and extends his neck toward her to see them better. "Oh, honey," he says sympathetically.

Dennis and I, doing our homework, become curious because of the concern in Dad's voice. We both stand and look over as well.

When what we see registers in our minds, we all look at each other aghast. The skin on Mom's palms is shredded and scarred. Blood is running through sharp grooves that slice across her palms, akin to a scene from a bloody horror movie. "Those nuts and bolts," she says, "they are mixed with sharp metal shavings that cut right through the thin gloves they give us, when they give them to us. This isn't right."

Many times at night, I will hear Mom crying from the pain of her hands. The solvents used by the nuts and bolts shop cause her to suffer a life of rashes and hives. Being a doctor today, I now understand the epidemiology of her suffering, which gives me an even greater admiration for all she did as our mom.

"Why don't you tell them how much your hands hurt?" Dad asks.

"I'm going to do more than that. I'm going to unionize that shop."

"Are you sure you want to do that?" Dad says meekly.

"Darn right. Stand up for what's right, even if you stand alone. That's what I say."

"My guess is you won't be alone. I just don't want you to get fired."

"They can't do that, Genie."

"I know, the National Labor Relations law protects you. But that's just the law. Reality is another thing, dear."

"Well, we'll see about that."

Unlike today's Marxist-elitist, Communist-leaning Democrats, Dad and Mom will become so-called "Kennedy Democrats." They are proud of America, proud to be Americans, and believe in God and Christian values. They haven't the slightest reservation in thinking America is the land of the free, the home of the brave, and the greatest place on earth to live and raise a family. Burned in my mind are JFK's famous inaugural words, "And so, my fellow Americans, ask not what your country can do for you; ask what you can do for your country." How did this country ever get so far off track?

Mom would reject out-of-hand today's weak, apologetic attitude. She and Dad were as far from being socialists as one could be, but they believed in fairness and compassion. Funny how times have changed. My parents—staunch, died-in-the-wool Democrats—would sooner have died from starvation than endure the embarrassment of accepting welfare. They were far too proud to accept handouts from the government, money taken off the backs of other hardworking Americans.

Something makes Mom driven. As silly as it seems, we jokingly attribute it to her being a redhead. She wears her values on her sleeve, and she makes her opinions clear by her words, which she backs up by her actions and fiery temper. If virtue means acting to secure proper values, Mom qualifies as a saint.

For a few days, Mom mulls over what she plans to tell the other workers to rouse them into signing her union petition. Dad supports her since he works for the Railroad Engineer's Union himself and is a true believer. A quiet bookkeeper, perhaps because of his abusive upbringing, he keeps the books for the union pensioners, making sure each and every retiree receives his pension check on time and for the correct amount. As Mom told it, the quiet demeanor of my dad usually resulted in "one less beating" when he was a kid.

These union railroad men, Dad often brags, "Do not get rich on stock like the owners and top management. They do not get bonuses or company cars or fancy lunches paid for by the company. What they do is hook and unhook box cars. Many lose their fingers or worse. And when they become conductors, they drive the trains that connect America and make her great."

From many locations in Collinwood, my brother and I can see the Cleveland Railroad Yards. Dad says there are nearly "fifty acres of crisscrossing rails. We are a major hub, the headquarters for all the railroad unions in America. Just because we are not rich, does not mean we are not proud. Don't ever let anyone tell you differently."

When Dad inquires at night of Mom's latest unionizing efforts, she tells him everything is "fine." Despite her assurances, however, he repeats his concern that she might get fired for shaking things up. Time and again he cautions her: "Please, be careful."

When he does that, Mom raises her voice in objection. "Genie, stop that," she yells. "We've got to get the boys into private school, and unless I work, we don't have the money. But if I work and make nothing, and destroy my hands in the process, that won't work, either."

Finally Dad succumbs, if for no other reason than to avoid the losing battle of arguing with Mom. Between the two, ironically, she wears the pants.

Ultimately, Mom fails. The other workers are afraid of retaliation by management and most decline to sign the union petition. They just want to keep their jobs. But Mom does not get fired. In fact, before she is done, she gets a small raise because she is a good and reliable worker. For this, we are thankful to Jergens, and nothing I've said is meant to disparage the company. It provided Mom and thousands more with jobs, and for this we are forever in its debt. Unionism was simply a cross-current of the times.

Knowing of Dad's relative passivity, you might naturally assume he shirks sports, except perhaps as a fan or so-called Monday morning quarterback. You would be wrong. Something in the Polke genes aspires to athleticism. His Slovenian ancestry seems to have a penchant for big and gifted athletes, as evidenced by many such athletes playing in the NBA today. Put a baseball in one hand and a glove in the other, and Dad is like a kid again. He's the first out the door to play a game of softball with the local league, or simply to play catch with me and my brother.

Mom always says Dad could have been a professional baseball player, and would have fought in the Second World War, except for one thing: during the Great Depression, he contracted rheumatic fever, which left him with a weakened heart valve. The random occurrence of him contracting the fever thus profoundly changed his life and ours.

But like so many other people of that generation, his heart never became a source of excuses or justification for government entitlements. He never collected disability or welfare. Instead, his heart defined his character. If nothing else, Genie Boy's weak heart fostered a strong individual will, a trait he passed on to all of us.

EXERCISE:

What traits—and values—do you admire in your mother and father?

_____
_____
_____
_____
_____

Have those values enabled you to conquer your adversities and hardships? If so, how?

_____
_____
_____
_____
_____

What values do you wish to pass on to your children, students, or team?

_____
_____
_____
_____
_____

Chapter 8

ST. PAUL'S, CATHOLICISM & THE PADDLE

"Catholic schools, which always strive to join their work of
education with the explicit proclamation of the Gospel, are a
most valuable resource for the evangelization of culture, even in
those countries and cities where hostile situations challenge us
to greater creativity in our search for suitable methods."

— Pope Francis

In 1959, nearly a quarter of my life later, I'm seven going on eight.
By this time, Dennis and I are veterans of St. Paul's, which will take
us through eighth grade. Just as Mom and Dad planned, going there
gets us out of the neighborhood each school day and into the adjoining city of Euclid. Euclid is across the crik "where the rich kids
live." Rich, of course, is relative. To us, it means not poor like us. To
a political scientist, it would mean middle class.

St. Paul's introduces me to a brand new universe: Catholicism.
Though we had always attended Catholic church on Sundays, this
universe involves the whole new experience of sisters, pastors, paddles, flash cards and, of course, daily religion. To this day when

meeting new folks, I'm often asked if I'm Christian, and I emphatically say, "No, I'm Catholic." For those who don't take themselves too seriously, I often get a big laugh, especially from Catholics who realize how absurd my reply truly is...

Why do I say universe? Because the word "Catholic" derives from the Greek word "katholikos," which, originally, meant "universal." In the early days of the Catholic Church, many Roman citizens described the new, upstart religion that heeded the "ways" of a fellow called Jesus of Nazareth as being "Katholik." What made these followers "Katholik" is they could be found universally throughout the Roman Empire.

As time passed, the word caught on, becoming part of the Roman—and eventually world—vernacular, denoting a religious faith open to any people anywhere. Race, ancestry, wealth, or social status did not matter; the arms of the Catholic Church open wide for all who wish to worship the Christian God who was first described in the Old Testament. Indeed, even to this day, when asked if I am Christian, I give the same answer: "No, I'm a Catholic."

On a typical day, on his way to work, Dad gives us a ride several blocks down the street, then drops us off to walk to school from there. Our route takes us past the postage stamp homes of South Collinwood, the neighborhood factories and corner stores, and then over the footbridge that stretches over Euclid Creek from South Collinwood and Euclid, where the homes are mostly colonial, with porch columns and pitched roofs, and where the cars in the driveways are newer and fancier.

St. Paul's School resides off of Chardon Road and East 200th. The main building is an imposing two-story brick edifice that faces the road in the manner of a large rectangle. Next to it on one side is the church, complete with pitched cathedral. Surrounding the adjoining buildings are parking spots for the parishioners attending Sunday Mass. Monday through Friday, the parking lot serves as our recess area.

On a typical day, we arrive a few minutes early, goof off outside on the playground with our friends, then hustle inside to homeroom the moment the morning bell sounds. Like most Catholic grade schools at the time, the nuns teach most of the classes with some lay teachers intermingled, and run the day-to-day operations of the school. At our school, the nuns report to Father Herman (the parish pastor), who officially oversees the operation of the school as well as the adjoining St. Paul's Church of Euclid. Discipline, protocol, and the Gospel are the tripartite pillars of our education, which means when Sister Mary Margaret arrives at homeroom each morning, we come to order and sit to attention.

After Dad gets home from work or on holidays and weekends, our favorite father-son pastime is playing catch.

"Son," Dad could say on any given weekend, "grab the gloves and ball and let's go out front."

"Out front" means the sidewalk that runs between the front yard and the street. Dad takes one side, where he squats and holds up the catcher's mitt. I take the other, where I work on my windup and rip a fast ball down the length of the sidewalk as fast as I can throw it.

"Whoa," Dad says as the ball sails wildly over his head. He races back to snag it before it rolls into the voracious jaws of the street sewer. Turning, he yells, "Son, coming at you!" He whips a long throw and, after backing up a few steps, I snap it with my glove.

He hustles back to his spot and squats. "Okay, right here," he says as he pops his stuffy mitt with his fist. "Fast as you can."

I wind up, kick my leg high, and release a rocket right down the shoot. Smack! "Ouch!" Dad yells.

Dad thoroughly enjoys our games of catch, as if it were food for his soul. Never once does it seem a fatherly burden to him, and as the strength in my arm grows, he beams with pride when he shows Mom the stinging red skin on his palm, evidence of where the ball hit the mitt, his counter to her slices from the nuts and bolts.

I have vivid memories of him in his squatting, catcher's stance simulating signals to me just like the major leaguers did. The sound of his voice yelling, "Harder! Throw it harder!" still to this day sends chills down my spine. And this is how we do it, leaving many fond memories stored in my brain forever, treasure troves for inspiration when times get tough.

On one particular morning, I'm sitting at home on the living room couch before school studying the leather straps of my old, worn-out baseball glove. I smack the ball into the pocket several times and the webbing literally disintegrates, falling off the fingers to which it was attached. "Mom," I ask, "can I get a new glove?"

Mom stops drying dishes and frowns at me. "Honey, I'm sorry, but we don't have the money right now. Maybe Santa will get you one for Christmas."

"Christmas? That's a year away," I bemoan, then stand up, pouting, and amble to the kitchen table to grab my books.

"No, it's not. It is only a few months away," she says as she hands me my lunch bag. "You better get on to school or you will be late."

Because Dad left early to work, and Dennis has a cold, that means I'm walking to school by myself, which means I can go an extra block to drop by Nottingham Hardware Store without Dennis tattling.

An uneventful, square brick building, the hardware store is located at the corner of Nottingham Road and Saint Clair Avenue, serving in these times as a sort of general store offering everything from garden tools, hammers and screwdrivers, to cookware, clothes irons, seasonal things like Christmas bulbs, and even fringe items like footballs, baseballs, bats, and gloves.

Adjacent to the hardware store, but right across the street, is Red's Drug Store. For years, I will work there as a soda jerk behind Red's old-fashioned soda fountain—serving sodas, shakes, and sundaes. Red was the first Jewish man I ever met, and like other religious practitioners, seemed to fit nicely into the multicultural mix of the neighborhood. (It is here that I will get my first exposure to girlie magazines such as *Playboy*. I will sneak daily peeks at them as puberty set in.)

When I get to the hardware store, I walk directly to the large toy rack to the left of the front counter, and there, on the middle shelf, a line of Spaulding glove boxes beckons me. I grab the box labelled "medium" and insert my fingers through its open face to see whether the glove fits. It does.

From behind me, a voice in an Irish brogue says, "Eh, young man. What's that sad look on your face?" The voice startles me. I turn and see the figure I recognize from Dad's newspapers as Danny Greene, the Irishman who will one day be called Robin Hood by some and a notorious gangster by others.

"Hi," I say. "My glove's, ah...." I pull the leather strings on the boxed glove. "It's falling apart, but Mom can't afford to buy me a new one."

"May I see it?" Mr. Greene asks.

I hand the box to him and he turns to the clerk at the counter.

"How much?"

"It's on the box," the clerk says imperiously.

Danny gives him a look that could kill. This man has no tolerance for disrespect, no matter how slight. Later, I will learn that Danny demanded deference from the merchants in the neighborhood in return for his unsolicited protection…and usually got it without the necessity of putting an edge on his expectation.

Danny pushes the box toward the clerk and repeats himself. "How much?"

The clerk, taken aback by his tone, suddenly recognizes who he is and turns the box sideways, panicking to find the price sticker. "Sorry, Mr. Greene. Sorry, sorry. It's right there." Danny removes his wallet, hands him a few bills, throws him a menacing don't-let-it-happen-again look, then hands the box over to me with a smile.

"It's yours, mate."

My jaw drops.

He crouches down so his eyes meet mine at my level. "From Danny Greene. If you ever need anything, you let me know, okay?" He reaches out and musses my hair with his large hand.

"Sure, Mr. Greene," I say. "Thank you!"

"Go on, then," he adds. "Better scoot to yer school."

"Thanks!" I yell as I race out the store, make a beeline to the crik, then start over the foot and car bridge. That's when a troublesome gaggle of boys enter from the other side and stop, shoulder-to-shoulder, blocking my path.

"What do we have here?" the large, freckle-faced boy with bad teeth says.

"I'm just going to school," I say after some hesitation. "And I'm late. I need to get by."

Bad Teeth steps forward. I brace my feet and stand firm, gritting my teeth.

"A wiseass, I sees," he proclaims, grabbing my books from my arms and flipping them over the railing before I can react.

"Hey!" I yell to the sound of the books splashing into the crik water below.

That's when Bad Teeth rams a fist square into my mouth, which spurts blood like a geyser. With me stunned by the sucker-punch and blood gushing over my face, he easily rips the glove box out of my clutched hand and pushes me sideways. I bounce off the bridge railing, then fall to the ground and land hard on the bone of my rump.

Towering over me, he growls: "I'm a fuck wit you ever' day of your life if you tells anyone, asshole."

I stand up and brush myself off. He and his friends (four in all) push me aside and saunter over to the Collinwood side, hooting and hollering as they go, truant bullies with nothing better to do than pick on a kid half their size. They then drop down to the crik bed and start making their way upstream.

I run all the way to school, heart beating a hundred thumps per minute, arriving late. My face and shirt are a bloody mess, the former smeared from wipes by the latter. My right knee stings and my pants are torn. Though my mind is still frozen from shock, I know conscious enough to know that I'm in big trouble.

I throw open the front door to the school and head to homeroom, doing my best to sneak in quietly and take my seat without being noticed. I don't get ten feet before Sister Mary stops writing on the blackboard, turns, and looks directly at me. "Children," she says to the class, "please give me a moment with Mr. Polk-e."

She takes me into the hall and asks, firmly, "What in God's name happened to you, Mr. Polk-e?" That's when I realize the blood from my broken lip is still running down my numb chin and dripping onto my shirt. "I was, well, well, well—" I stutter, before she cuts me off.

"Have you been fighting again?" she asks calmly.

"No."

"Where's your books?"

"I—"

"Here, let's go to the nurse's office." She sticks her head into the classroom and tells them to read from their books, then gently takes my elbow and leads me to the office. She's compassionate, but also thinks I'm a hooligan. That I come from the other side of the crik no doubt influences her thinking and her resolve. Confirming my suspicion, as we're walking down the hallway she says, "You're from Collinwood, aren't you?"

I say, "Yes, ma'am," with both pride and worry. Back then, you were proud of your neighborhood, even if you wanted out. And everyone knew what neighborhood you were from *and* what it meant to be from that neighborhood.

When we get to the nurse's office, she tells the nurse, "It looks like Mr. Polke has been in another fight. He—"

"No, I have not," I interrupt.

"Then what happened?" the nurse asks.

"Some boys, ah, ah…. I tripped and fell on the bridge."

"So, you weren't in a fight?" she asks.

"Yes, I was." I think about my lie for a minute. "I, okay, no, I didn't trip and fall on the bridge."

That afternoon, I'm required by Sister Mary to stay after school. I do. That's when I receive my first paddling, for being late and lying, twin felonies in the disciplinary universe of Catholic school. Little could I anticipate the number of additional paddlings that would come my way, some deserved, some not, before I would be done.

I would later learn that this same gang had been dropping down to the crik from the path next to the bridge and burglarizing auto body shops upstream. Their *modus operandi* was to break into the shops through the back door where no one would expect them. Coming up from the crik allowed them to steal thousands of dollars of valuable car parts from the collision-damaged cars awaiting their turn to be repaired, without being detected. The owners of the shops had assumed, of course, that the steep terrain rising up from the crik would act as a natural barrier to intruders, and video security cameras were a long way away.

Once again, however, the lure of crime was all around me.

CONQUERING YOUR ADVERSITIES

EXERCISE:

As a child, did you ever have to deal with bullies or highly negative people? If so, how did you conquer this adversity?

_____
_____
_____
_____

As an adult, have you ever had to deal with bullies or pushy or highly negative people? If so, how did you conquer this adversity?

_____
_____
_____
_____

Did religion play a role in your upbringing? Does it do so now? If so, how?

_____
_____
_____
_____

Did you have any heroes growing up who turned out to be bad people? If so, how did you address this change in perception?

_____
_____
_____
_____

Chapter 9

COMMUNION & A PADDLE WITH MY NAME ON IT

"I always have a funny story at communion time that underscores that no one is perfect, and that communion is not for perfect people but for hungry people."

— Greg Boyle

My first paddling at school does not deter me one bit. Several weeks later, I'm sitting in my seat in homeroom looking ahead like everyone else, except the tip of my right foot is toying with the books of my friend, Genie Fiorelli, who is also from Collinwood and sitting directly in front of me.

Ironically, Genie's first name is the same as my dad's nickname, but not so ironically, he's a good Italian boy like so many of the kids from our predominately Italian neighborhood. Like me, he's being sent across the Euclid Creek boundary for a better education.

I'm up to no good, trying to spill his books, which are stacked precariously on the rack below his seat. Anything to get a few laughs.

Standing erect at the front of the class in her black and white cassock and habit, Sister Mary Edwards says, "Children, please give me your undivided attention." When we all look forward, she nods her head toward a kind-faced man, similarly dressed, who has just stepped into the room. Quickly, we all stiffen further to attention, for Father Hancock (coincidentally, my mother's favorite priest) is blessing us with his presence this day, a rare occasion.

"Good morning, Father Hancock," Sister Mary says.

"Good morning, Sister," he replies. "Rather than make an announcement on the loud speaker, I wanted to come by each class personally...." Now he turns his head from her to us. "Class, I wanted to remind you that we have a very special Easter Sunday Mass this week, and we are looking forward to seeing you and your families in attendance...."

When he speaks, his words roll softly off his tongue, lapping our ears like warm water, his hands pressed together like pancakes before him, with occasional dipping gestures of his chin. Something about him bespeaks serenity and respect. It's as if God were speaking to us through the presence of the body of Father Hancock.

We all shake our heads and say in unison, "Yes, Father."

"Thank you, Sister Mary," he says, and he leaves as quietly as he arrived.

"Kenneth Polk-e, please see me after class," Sister Mary Margaret says after Genie's books slide to the floor from the last dig of my shoe. *Oh, Christ*, I think as I tuck my feet beneath me, straighten my slouch, then jerk my head to attention.

"Yes, ma'am. I mean, yes, Sister Mary. Ah, it's Polke."

"I'll try to remember that, Mr. *Polke*."

Seeing Sister Mary after class means only one thing: another paddling. Looking back, I'm chagrined to say that I had a special relationship with that paddle. Unlike today, the paddle in those days asserted itself as the primary mode of punishment when the transgression required something more than staying after school and writing "I won't talk in class" a hundred times on the chalkboard.

Truth be told, the nuns actually have two paddles. One is solid wood and the second has a grid of little holes in it resembling Swiss cheese. My fellow students and I surmise that Sister Mary Edwards, a tiny little woman with little muscular strength, uses the one with the holes in it because she needs a running start and, therefore, needs as little wind resistance as possible in order to deliver a good whack. Whereas, by contrast, Sister Mary Margaret (aka "the Moose") has plenty of muscle and uses the solid one. Either way, I will autograph both paddles with my you-know-what more times than I care to admit.

In regard to the paddle, the hottest water I would ever get myself into at school was in sixth grade, when I was twelve. The regretful incident stemmed from me being an altar boy. For those who did not grow up Catholic, being an altar boy is a dead serious matter held in the highest regard by the church and its congregation.

First and foremost, altar boys help the church preserve the sacred tradition of Mater Dei by sacrificing their time and effort. In earlier times, we had to learn Latin prayers and songs, behave in an exemplary manner, and strictly abide by all the rules at all times, many of us preparing for priesthood later in life.

By the 1950s and 1960s, the altar boy-to-priesthood tradition had certainly tapered off. However, being an altar boy still remained a coveted honor and still allowed us to participate at the Lord's Altar for any Mass. Our Sunday duties at St. Paul's are to help the priest do whatever he needs to do at the altar during the Sacrifice of the

Mass and other liturgical events. And since our visibility is so high, the church expects us to be little saints, always being on our best behavior, setting an example for the whole congregation.

Many parts of the rituals associated with Sunday Mass intrigued me as a young altar boy, but the act of giving Communion was my favorite. The bread and wine represent the body and blood of Christ at the Lord's Supper. So this is, to say the least, a vital and sacrosanct ritual that requires a large storage of wine to be kept in stock. Being altar boys also means we know the ins and outs of the church, including the location of the Communion wine.

One day, Genie, Joey, Bobby, and I are assigned by Father Herman to do some chores needed in the church. While being sent to the church to work during normal school hours (I wonder whether we were violating any child labor laws back then), we decide to visit the secret wine closet, sneaking quietly through the church hallways until we find the hidden, recessed door.

"Get in here," I whisper.

The guys all huddle inside the doorjamb.

"Joey," I say, "is anyone coming?"

Joey cranes his head out the recess and looks up and down the hall. "No, coast clear."

I giggle as I turn the doorknob, but it's locked, putting a frown to my face. "Turn it harder," Genie says. He's the shortest among us, thin and frail from always being sickly.

I follow his direction, and this time the knob turns. We all lean against the heavy door in unison until it pushes open; then we close it behind us. At first, it's pitch dark. When someone flips the light switch, we find ourselves staring at a half-dozen crates of bottled wine.

"Everyone grab a box," I say. We each pull down a box and tug at the flaps. "Mine's open," Joey says. We crowd around his box. Not knowing how to uncork a wine bottle, we scan the bottles until we find one with a cork sticking up from the opening.

Joey grasps the bottle with his left hand and tries to pull the cork out with the fingers of his right hand. No luck. "Give me that," I say. I jam the cork into my mouth, clench it tightly with my teeth, then pull. After an initial resistance, the cork pops out, causing my head to jerk back. Wine spills all over me. I laugh. "Got it."

"Take a gulp," Joey says. I slug back a large gulp, cringe from the bitterness, then pass it to Genie. Genie takes a chug, cringes, and passes it to Joey. Joey barely takes a sip before he gags. Bobby tries it and swears he's swallowed a mouthful, but I have my doubts. In short order, despite the bitter taste, Genie and I finish the bottle off. Gulping down and finishing off a bottle, of course, is quite different from sipping from a tiny paper cup at Communion.

Not surprisingly, all of us are tipsy by the time we get to class, Genie and I far more gone than Bobby and Joey. We must be walking funny and giggling because Sister Mary Margaret instantly senses something is off. Before we know it, she has us marching to the pastor's office, our hearts thumping hard against our chests. It never occurred to us that she might have such a sensitive nose as a nun that she can smell liquor from a dozen paces.

"Please sit down," the pastor says softly, pointing to four chairs opposite his desk.

We all stare at the floor, hands clasped in front of us as if we're praying.

"Who wants to talk first?" he asks.

We glance up at each other, intuitively knowing we should keep our lips zipped. Neither Genie nor Bobby say a word, which gains my utmost respect. However, before we know it, Joey is spilling the beans. Damn rich kids can't keep their mouths shut. So Joey tells the pastor exactly what we did and how we did it.

After receiving a stern lecture, we receive an even sterner paddling. The pastor, though not angry as such, is not messing around. He means business. To teach us a lesson and deter anyone else who might want to follow in our shoes, he turns on the public address and announces what we've done. He then paddles us one at a time with the flat paddle, each of our names announced first, so all the students in the school know who's getting paddled and doing all the crying. For five minutes, you can hear four kids yelling and sobbing with every stinging smack.

No way I'm telling Mom, and since she was not there, I figure she will not find out. Wrong. The moment I open the door, she's standing in the kitchen staring directly at me like I just broke all Ten Commandments. From the rigid look on her face, I know I'm in deep trouble. As she looks at me, her face turns as red as her hair, one big red ball about to explode.

"Kenneth Jeffrey," she says. *Uh oh*, I think, *there's that middle name following my full first name. That can only mean one thing. I'm in deep trouble.* "What's this I hear about you drinking the Communion wine?"

How did she know? Sheesh! "I, ah, I, we—"

She wipes her hands on a kitchen towel and marches over to where I'm standing. With her left hand, she grabs my shoulder and turns me sideways and down at the same time, causing my rear-end to stick way out. Then she whacks it with the stiff palm of her hand until

I start yelling out in pain. Point made, she stops and says, "Now go to your room."

So far I've held them back, but now the tears start flowing, a virtual waterfall, which prompts Dennis to smile.

"Wipe that smile off your face, Dennis," she says, "or you'll be next." He frowns immediately. "You are lucky you don't get a spanking, too," she adds.

"Me?" he says incredulously.

"Yes, you," she replies. "You said you were sick today and didn't go to school, but it certainly didn't stop you from watching television non-stop, did it?"

"But, but…." He decides to stop while he's ahead.

I shut the bedroom door behind me and fall face first on the bed. My butt stings like the dickens, a spanking on top of a paddling being a double-whammy. Not to mention, my pride has taken quite a walloping as well. The whole school heard me bawling. I will never be able to show my face there again.

The door to the bedroom suddenly swings open. Mom's standing there with one hand on her hip and the other on the door frame.

"I'll let you know when you can come out," she says. "I just want you to understand the importance of behaving at that school. They could have expelled you, you know."

I wipe my tears, give her a pouty look, then say, "Sorry, Mom."

"Apology accepted," she says. "Now sit there for a bit and think about what happened. When you're ready to tell me why you did this, you can come out."

"Are you going to tell Dad?"

"We'll see."

A half hour later, I come clean. "We just wanted to have some fun," I say. I consider blaming Joey, but she will know better, so I avoid compounding the error with another lie. I also come clean about the day that Danny Greene gave me the new glove and I lost my books, figuring I better lay it all on the table along with any other incidents I could throw in.

"Drinking is the devil's tonic," she says. "Do you understand?"

"Yes, ma'am," I say, though I'm not sure what she means by tonic. Whatever it is, it must be bad. That much is clear.

"Okay, why don't you and your brother go play some catch in the front yard. I'll have dinner early for you today. You're probably starving."

I smile. "Sure am. So I can come out?"

"Yes."

After that, I try hard not to get another paddling. However, I am mad, really mad, at those clowns who jumped me on the bridge, tossed my books into the crik, and stole my new glove. I tell Dennis I swear I will get my revenge.

EXERCISE:

Think back to times when you got in trouble as a child. What did you learn from it, and how can you use that knowledge to overcome obstacles you face today?

_____

_____

_____

_____

_____

Do you find yourself mindlessly using techniques to which you were subject as a child—yelling, anger, aggression, paddling, and the like—or being subject to such techniques by others today, despite feeling they are inappropriate? Explain how you might alter these techniques by turning a negative into a positive today.

_____

_____

_____

_____

_____

Chapter 10

RAILROADS, NO CRIME OR POLICE

"You can get much further with a kind word and a gun
than you can with a kind word alone."

— Al Capone

The older I get, the more our neighborhood comes into focus, like the adjusting lenses of an optometrist's phoropter. Collinwood is a family-oriented, lower middle class town—many families being second or third generation—culturally rich with all slices of life. We have pride of ownership, our lawns are green and well-groomed with lots of trees and flowers, and many backyards from the older sections include family graveyards with headstones honoring several generations of decedents. These graves tend to be covered by small vineyards, kept for the sole purpose of making homemade wine.

Blanketing everything are the ubiquitous sounds, smells, and sights of the railroad, with multiple tracks crossing at virtually every street corner. Collinwood's staggering 50 acres (or 2.178 million square feet) of railroad tracks service hundreds of ingoing and outgoing trains daily, all of which spike the air with shrill, tooting train whistles around the clock.

CONQUERING YOUR ADVERSITIES

On every horizon, smoke stacks from industrial manufacturing plants belch black and gray plumes into the air all hours of the day and night, while church bells gong on the hour, 24 hours a day, 365 days of the year. Church bells were, in a way of speaking, the first 24/7 service. Add to all that the aroma of simmering tomato sauce, sizzling sausages, and cooking vegetables wafting into the nostrils of anyone walking a dog, riding a bike, playing in the streets, or rocking on a porch.

In good weather, families sitting on their porches was routine, a way of life with grandparents rocking while young children played games in the yards and streets. All of them—the Italians, Slovenians, and Polish—represent a melting pot of European immigrant families who have migrated to America in search of a better life, and who have found a way to get along. The two central binding forces are the Catholic Church and, believe it or not, *sports*. I truly believe that religion, Motown records, and sports have done more to improve racial relations than any positive law ever passed by Congress.

Ironically, despite our rough and tumble streets and modest income families, Collinwood reports little to no "ordinary" crime. The police rarely enter the neighborhood, having no reason to do so. Dad attributes this to "the presence of the Italian Mafia and the Irish gangster, Danny Greene." In her usual sarcastic tone, Mom says, "There's nothing to steal, anyway." But being a kid raised on the streets, I know there is swift and severe retribution for any outsider foolish enough to rape, murder, rob, or kidnap anyone from our neighborhood. Odd as it sounds, the mob embraces a twisted code of ethics, committing horrific crimes when it serves its purposes, while having zero tolerance for any crimes committed by anyone else.

To give you an example of the irony, suppose one of the parish priests in Collinwood had molested one of the neighborhood boys, as chronicled by *The Boston Globe* following its investigation of child sexual abuse at the hands of Catholic priests in the Boston area, and then turned into the movie, *Spotlight.* The *Globe*'s articles led to the resignation of the once-powerful Cardinal Bernard Law, former archbishop of Boston. Though the newspaper won a Pulitzer Prize in 2003 for its coverage, a decade earlier, when the same paper reported on abuse allegations against the Rev. James R. Porter—accused of molesting up to 100 children in the 1960s—Cardinal Law famously (or now, infamously), condemned the paper. "We call down God's power on our business leaders, and political leaders and community leaders," Law said. "By all means we call down God's power on the media, particularly *The Globe.*"

If that had happened in Collinwood, I guarantee you this: any priest violating a child in any way would, as the neighborhood saying goes, "Be food for the fishes." He'd be at the bottom of Lake Erie where sheephead and carp (both bottom-feeders) are nibbling away at his flesh and bones for eternity. If you think I am kidding, well, I am not. It was not uncommon for bodies to wash up on the Lake Erie shores, and I assure you none of those bodies were the result of boating or water-skiing accidents. So common was this occurrence that, when one such body washed up onto shore behind our high school during football practice, Coach Gutbrod simply ignored it and went on with practice as if nothing unusual had happened.

Another popular story illustrating my point is the lore that circulated the neighborhood for years and found its way into both the book and the film, *Kill the Irishman.* The book's author, Rick Porrello, openly a descendant of the infamous Porrello brothers crime family in Cleveland, is now a policeman with several publications under his belt. This story starts with Danny Greene confronting the Hell's Angels who, as Dad tells it, "thundered into Collinwood like they owned the place. Most of the homes were occupied by families, so they found an old shanty house. Bikes were parked all over the street, with loud, obnoxious bikers coming and going and music blasting all hours of the day and night."

"Before long," Dad says, "local residents were up in arms. They were scared and upset and their concerns reached the ears of Danny Greene. Without hesitation, Mr. Greene marched right up to the front door of the bikers' shanty, holding three sticks of dynamite. He knocked. When a biker opened the door, belligerent with a 'What-do-you-want, asshole' attitude, Greene ripped the wick off one of the dynamite sticks and lit it. As it sizzled in his hand, he said: 'Next time, the wick stays in the stick.' The next morning, the bikers were gone."

The irony should not be lost. The mob, an organization built on systemic violence, had secured a monopoly on the use of force within the neighborhood, resulting in no crime being committed except by its own members according to their own code. Put another way, while the Italian Mafia and Irish mobster commit countless acts of atrocity in the name of their families and to secure their turf, they don't allow strangers to enter the neighborhood to do so. Any crime committed on our community is a crime committed on them.

It's a zero tolerance game. You pay us and we will protect you. That's the business plan. Though I am not Italian, the temptation to hang out and be a part of that culture is quite tempting to me as a young man whose other options include physical labor and poverty at the top of the list. Making big money, buying nice things, being popular—all will have their allure for me as time passes. "It is a serious option to consider," I think more than once when times get tough. The road to crime is always there, always calling like the mythical Sirens, always alluring. Not to mention, it would allow me to settle some scores.

Figuring out why the criminal beast did not devour me is another driving force behind me writing this book. And by me figuring it out, which in my humble opinion I have, I know I can offer hope to you, your family, and young men and women everywhere.

EXERCISE:

Were you ever drawn to a life of crime? If so, how did you overcome that urge?

_____

_____

_____

_____

_____

Were you ever faced with options, one of which was the wrong but alluring path, even a moral dilemma? If so, how did you choose the right path?

_____

_____

_____

_____

_____

If you chose, or are thinking about choosing, the wrong path, how did or might you correct your path and set your moral compass straight?

_____

_____

_____

_____

_____

Chapter 11

RITE OF PASSAGE

"Years ago a boy applying for a newspaper route would come in and ask, 'Can I get a job peddling papers?'.... Today on most newspapers the carrier is known as a carrier-salesman.... He is taught the fundamentals of salesmanship and learns that there are definite steps he must take to accomplish desired ends...."

— Rex Fisher, *East St. Lois Journal*, 1935

The turbulent '60s have begun, and I'm ten years old, entering fourth grade. My brother is right behind me, entering third, and my sister right behind him, entering second. Do you suppose we pass our books, jackets, and toys down from year to year? You bet your life we do. And this applies equally to school books, which we cover with cut-off brown shopping bags, folded and taped over the cover.

When I pass my third grade books to Dennis, he tears off the graffitied brown bag covers and puts on his own. Not fighting there. I do it my way, he does it his way. But Dennis and I always fight over the same pants. Because we are the same size until he passes me in height in high school, Dennis can fit into my pants just as easily as I can.

When I'm turning ten, Danny Green is turning 29, scoring points as Collinwood's Robin Hood while flexing muscle as President of International Longshoremen's Association Local 1317. If he can scratch his way to the top of the Longshoremen, the kid who dropped out of high school and is notorious for his brutal alley-fighting, knows he can get an iron grip over a bunch of criminal enterprises if he puts his mind to it, and he proceeds to do so. A stick of dynamite and a fuse will get you a long way if used strategically.

Two years later, on November 13, 1964, Robin Hood Greene will be indicted by a Cleveland federal grand jury and convicted of embezzling $11,542.38 in union funds and falsifying records. Though his conviction will be reversed on appeal for procedural error, he will be forever banned from participating in union activity. But that ban does not stop him; it doesn't even slow him down. Instead, it speeds him up. The pull of the streets—and the pull of crime—is like heroin to the heroin addict, or fuel to a dragster.

Apparently, Danny's initial strategy had two parts: first control the Longshoremen, the dockworker's union, and then take over the Teamsters, the truck driver's union, which included long haulers. Think of the simple brilliance of this strategy: together, these two national unions control all commercial transportation in America, on land and water. Had he gained control of both unions, nothing—literally nothing—could be shipped and moved anywhere in America without his approval. He would possibly have wielded more influence and power than the President of the United States. As a young man with ambition, I have access to, and could easily be a part of, that burgeoning power structure. It's intoxicating, at the least. But you still gotta wake up in the morning and look in the mirror and, unfortunately, keep looking over your shoulder.

By this time, the Polke family has long settled into its prefab and has found its stride. On April 14, 1963, for my eleventh birthday, I wake up to a new Spaulding glove and baseball and a Micky Mantle bat laying at the foot of my bed. For dessert after dinner, Mom makes me her famous homemade chocolate cake. To this day, I remember these as the best birthday gifts I have ever received. And here's where Danny Greene and I part philosophies. Though we grow up in the same neighborhood, my addiction is sports, while his addiction is crime.

Comfortable in its skin, the Polke family has also established a routine. Monday night is spaghetti night; Tuesday night is liver; Wednesday and Thursday nights Mom mixes it up; and Friday is always fish. Either Mom bakes the fish at home, or we go to the church for fish buffet (and, as Dennis and I get older, practically break the church's bank we eat so much). Saturday nights can be anything, and Sunday nights are usually a formal sit down with roast beef preceded by a morning of church and afternoon of playing ball at the park or catch out in front of the house.

"Boys!" Mom yells at the sound of the Sunday church bells chiming five p.m. "Dinner!"

I whip a final pitch toward Dad and it pops into his glove. Dad tosses one to Dennis, who flips it to me. I whip another one.

"Boys," Mom says as she walks out to the front yard. "Dinner is up."

"Aw, Mom," I say.

Dennis races toward the side door, yelling: "Dibs on the chair."

"Oh, no, you don't," Dad says, then hustles after him.

I follow everyone in and happily take my place on the living room floor, which allows me to sit closer to the TV.

To this day, I have warm memories of all of us jamming into our tiny living room on those Sunday nights. Unlike other nights when we are allowed to stay out until dark, on Sundays Mom insists that we be inside the house by 5 p.m. sharp. And if we are not all home together on Sundays dining in the living room, which is especially the case during the winter months, then we are piling into Dad's dark blue Chevy Biscayne to go visit cousins and grandparents.

On Sundays, it is rare not smelling spaghetti sauce permeating the whole Collinwood neighborhood, and in particular, coming from Grandma Bossi's house across the street. In our home, not being Italian and Dad being a meat and potatoes kinda guy, our mainstay is Mom's famous roast beef. I remember Dad driving to the University of Dayton to watch me play while in college and surprising me with Mom's roast beef and her tremendous potica, a moist, buttery Slovenian nut raisin bread roll. What I wouldn't give to have some of that right now. Cousins, aunts, and uncles would drive for miles to claim their loaf. It took a whole week to fill the requests just from family members alone.

When we stay at home, everyone takes his or her place. Dennis has Dad's chair and Mom and Dad sit next to each other on the couch. Their plates are overflowing on those chrome-legged foldout TV trays with metal legs. Cheryl and I are on the floor with plastic trays, and though my plate is also overflowing, it does not stay that way for long.

Walt Disney's *Wonderful World of Color*, *Bonanza*, and *The Ed Sullivan Show* are the Sunday night staples, all playing on the tube, which is what we called the television in those days because the picture was produced by those tubes that created Frankenstein. After dinner, Mom serves up her homemade apple pie. We clear the trays and shovel the pie into large bowls with as much vanilla ice cream as the bowls will hold.

"Mom, you make the best apple pie in the world," I say.

"Yeah, Mom," Dennis says in agreement, his mouth re-stuffed as quickly as he can swallow his last bite.

Needless to say, the Polkes love their food. In fact, eating is so integral to our lives that it is rare for any of us to sit down to a meal without two forks—one for eating, and the other for stabbing any intruder daring and foolish enough to attempt to snatch some food from someone else's plate.

Cheryl, now seven, says: "I helped."

Dad just smiles. If Ozzie and Harriet were here, they'd be proud to call us relatives.

One TV show that worked its way into the Polke way of life—though it did not show on Sunday—bears special mention. Following on the heels of his popular Sunday night radio show, to which my parents did not listen, Bishop Fulton Sheen (later Archbishop), started airing an unpaid, unscripted Catholic TV show every Tuesday liver night at 8 p.m.

Initially being broadcast by only three television stations nationwide, Sheen's show quickly goes national. The compelling man with the hypnotic gaze, disarming smile, and dramatic delivery gains huge traction by delivering religion directly to millions of Americans like us. Religion joins war and football as a force that enters the privacy of our homes and thus impacts the days of our lives.

Evidence of his mushrooming influence, *Life* and *Time* magazines run a feature story on Bishop Sheen. Mom gets copies of both, and for months, they seem to have legs, making their way from the kitchen table and counter to the living room floor and her nightstand.

Having insinuated himself into people's everyday lives, the bishop starts receiving 34,000 fan letters per month, Mom's among them.

Demand for tickets to attend his live show skyrockets, often to four times his live audience capacity, or so the magazines report. As a result, he becomes the first ever Catholic bishop—and very first religious figure of any kind—to broadcast a live religious service into American living rooms, thereby reaching millions. His success reflects the new and growing power of television, so radically different from when I was born.

The show itself—first known as *Life Is Worth Living*—is so popular that it battles neck-to-neck in the ratings with "Mr. Television," known to most Americans as "Uncle Milty," the celebrity host of *The Milton Berle Show*. As early as 1952, Bishop Sheen wins an Emmy Award for "Most Outstanding Television Personality." Weekly viewership eventually rises to 30 million, a number unheard of at the time and that today would still be highly respectable.

Bishop Sheen will later credit the Gospel writers—Matthew, Mark, Luke, and John—for their invaluable contributions to his success, and will often go on the attack, making controversial statements against Communism and Socialism. In a 1953 episode, he recreates a reading of the funeral scene from *Julius Caesar*, substituting the names of Soviet Premier Josef Stalin and his political minions, Beria, Malenkov, and Vyshinsky, for Julius Caesar and his minions, Cassius, Marc Antony, and Brutus. In one prophetic scene, he dramatically proclaims: "Stalin must one day meet his judgment." The next week, the Russian dictator dies of a stroke. Sheen's popularity does somersaults.

Bishop Sheen's powerful messages notwithstanding, as a young kid from a family where money is always tight, I'm of the age where I want some spending money—you know, some money to buy the things that the richer kids at school have. Nothing big, mind you, but enough change in my pocket to enjoy an occasional soda pop or milkshake, get some cool bubble gum baseball cards, play some pinball, drop a quarter in a jukebox, go to the movies and order some popcorn and candy, ride a new bike perhaps, maybe even own a new basketball and football, God forbid—all the things that are cool at the time.

To earn some legitimate "bread" (the new term for money), I undertake the boyhood tradition of applying to become a paperboy. In a manner of speaking, for guys from families of modest means, having a newspaper route is a rite of passage. It's an opportunity to make some money, of course, to buy these things I want, but it comes at a big price: I have to wake up at the crack of dawn every single day, come rain, snow, or shine. For a pre-teen, this is pushing the impossible, but I do it. In our modern, no-paper, digital age, the obsolescence of the paperboy constitutes, in my opinion, a huge loss on the road to building character in millions of young boys. Has any character builder of equal effectiveness replaced the paperboy? Sadly, I think not, and without getting ahead of myself, that is one of the challenges for parents and coaches in today's world.

One particular Sunday morning offers another kind of lesson—the kind of lesson you learn growing up in a neighborhood like Collinwood. Dark clouds blanket the sky, and it is, as the saying goes, raining cats and dogs. I'm donning my yellow raincoat and hat and tossing bundles of *Cleveland Plain Dealer* newspapers into the open trunk of Dad's car. Dad is holding a large umbrella, bracing it against the gale winds, and fighting a losing battle to keep the papers dry.

Nearby, a light flickers on inside Red's Drug Store, officially called the Nottingham Drug Store. The day of the large franchise drug chain has not yet caught on. Red has just arrived and is going about his daily pre-opening duties. But the store lights also reveal the dark image of another person, that of Mr. Cavotta, the local owner of Cavotta's Garden Center. Oddly, he's knocking on the drugstore door with no apparent reason for being there at 5:00 a.m.

"Hi, Mr. Cavotta," I yell, in hopes of selling him one of the extra newspapers that don't have a subscriber attached to it.

Dad quickly says, "Kenny, mind your own business."

Mr. Cavotta turns toward us, waves, and hustles in our direction. I think I hear Dad curse under his breath before beaming a big smile.

"Hi, Kenny, Mr. Polke," Mr. Cavotta says as he ducks under Dad's umbrella and reaches his arm around Dad's shoulder.

I dig a dry paper out of the trunk and extend it to him. "Do you want a plastic bag?" I ask.

"No, thanks," he says as he puts two quarters in my hand (the paper costs twenty-five cents on Sundays, ten cents during the week) and winks. Red has since opened the door and is waving at us. Dad and I both wave back.

I push the quarters deep into my front pocket. Mr. Cavotta glances up at the sky, then dashes back to the awning that covers the entrance to the hardware store. When he reaches Red, Mr. Cavotta flips the newspaper over and stabs it with his finger at a certain spot. Red shakes his head, throws up his hands, then pulls out his wallet and gives Mr. Cavotta what appears to be a stack of bills. Mr. Cavotta looks around, stuffs the bills inside his jacket pocket, then turns and walks to the next shop on the street, Ed's Barber Shop, where Ed—I forget his last name—is also just arriving for work. They repeat the same exchange.

Years later, Dennis and I will talk about Mr. Cavotta and his garden center from time to time. The way we see it, he was always loitering more than working. And his brother, Francis, never seemed to be working either, despite having lots of valuable cars and machinery on their lawns (they all lived near or adjacent to each other) and both had families to feed. We wonder how they did it, running a garden center and landscaping service but never doing any gardening or landscaping that we could see. The only conclusion we could reach is that they are Italian and must be running the numbers or doing something for the mob, though we have no way of proving it. But that's what was going through our minds, and I'm sure we were not alone.

In researching our neighborhood, I do learn that, as early as 1931, police estimated that the daily take of Cleveland's Mafia in the numbers racket alone (sometimes referred to as the poor man's lottery) was somewhere between $6,000 and $10,000. If true, that's between $2.19 million and $3.65 million per year in 1931 dollars, or between $31.9 million and $53.1 million in today's dollars. Man, oh man, what I would have given for a piece of that.

When finished loading the papers in the trunk, Dad and I jump into the car and head out. Dad honks and waves politely to Mr. Cavotta and the barber, then drives to the beginning of the paper route. We park under a large tree that somewhat blocks the rain, then proceed to put plastic bags around the papers. We deliver most of the blocks together, him driving and me tossing the papers, but toward the end we split up, Dad taking one direction and me the other.

As I'm heading in my direction, the rain starts to let up and I pass a man who's taken the opportunity to walk his dog. I offer him a paper since I don't recognize him from my route. He takes me up on it, and I stuff his quarter into my pocket, in which I've now accumulated about $1.50 in change. On a typical day, I sell about a dollar's worth out of the bag, but the rain has caused more people to buy from me today rather than get wet walking to the corner store.

After I flip my last paper onto a porch, I head back the way I came and start looking for Dad's car. Sometimes he finishes first and then drives to find me, but today, I see the car still parked where we left it. I'm jingling the change in my pocket, enjoying the warmth from the sun as it peeks through the clouds, when suddenly a tall, skinny teen with slicked back hair steps out from behind the bushes. In the cocky voice of a budding young thug, he states, "Your money, punk."

I stop in my tracks, then instantly recognize who he is. He's Tony Milano (name changed to protect the guilty). His family is from the Saint Clair area near Five Points. I often see him when we ride our bikes to Collinwood High School. Years later, it will be rumored that he has become an associate (wise guy) in the Danny Greene mob.

"Screw off, Milano," I say with foolish bravado.

Milano shoves me hard to the ground, whereupon he produces a switchblade from the inside pocket of his black leather jacket and ejects the blade, jerking it upward toward the sky. He looks like one of those menacing greasers from a Brooklyn street gang movie.

"Yell for your old man, asshole, and I'll slit your throat."

"What do you want?" I ask.

"What do you think? Your money, clown."

Already several dimes have spilled from my pocket due to me landing hard on my rump on the sidewalk. I collect the spilled few, then reach up and put them in his cupped hand.

"All of 'em," he huffs as he jams them into his pocket.

We stare at each other for a moment, a sort of visual standoff, until I rise to my feet, brush myself off, then dig the remaining change from my pocket and hand it over to him. About that time, the man with the dog happens back along the sidewalk. Seizing the moment, I say as loud as I can, "Hey, pooch."

Milano jerks his head toward the man and dog, then quickly pops in his blade and tucks his knife sheaf under his coat sleeve. The man stops and starts to engage in small talk, having no idea what is transpiring. Impatient, and not wanting to get caught, Milano turns and walks away, saying, "I'll get the rest later, asshole."

About this time, I see my dad returning to his car. I thank the man—who does not know for what—and race off in Dad's direction, arriving out of breath.

"Was that Mr. Milano's son I saw?" Dad asks.

"Yeah," I say.

The look on my face tells him I'm mad as hell.

"Everything all right, son?"

"The…the…. Dad, he robbed me. He pulled a knife on me and took my paper money. I'm gonna kill that guy."

I remember Dad gritting his teeth and shaking his head. "No, you're not. That's not the way to do things."

"But shouldn't we at least call the cops?" I stammer.

"No, there's nothing we can do, son. Sorry."

"Why not? Why can't we call the cops on 'im," I beseech.

"That's not the way it works. I'll tell you when you get older," Dad says, though later in life he will not need to.

So, while the newspaper boy's rite of passage serves an important purpose in my early life, it also teaches me a valuable lesson about thugs and getting robbed. Indeed, by the time I become a teenager in Collinwood, I will already learned a thing or two about alley fights and surviving on the street.

"Let's get home and get ready for church," Dad says. "And if the weather clears"—he looks up to the clouds—"we'll play some catch later, as long as you don't burn my hand again."

We laugh and I say, "I can't make any promises," since my fast ball is already something to contend with.

EXERCISE:

List some things that you, your friends, and the neighborhood kids did when you were young and broke to earn money.

_____

_____

_____

_____

If you need more money today, for a vacation or car or even a house, how might the lessons of your childhood jobs pay off for you now?

_____

_____

_____

_____

What rituals might you adopt for yourself today that would assist you in achieving your financial and non-financial goals, drawing from your childhood experiences and anything else that comes to mind?

_____

_____

_____

_____

Chapter 12

BASEBALL, BABY

"'Somebody once asked me if I ever went up to the plate trying to hit a home run. I said, 'Sure, every time.'"

— Mickey Mantle

Papers delivered, it's later in the same day—or any given Sunday, really—and we're back at the house getting ready for church.

"Mom, you sure are pretty," I say. Mom adjusts her hat and smiles.

"You have your line memorized," Dennis says.

Tall and model thin, in her red hair and green dress, Mom looks more like a glamorous movie star than a mother of three headed out to church in gritty Collinwood. Dad walks up behind her, puts his hands on her waist, and gives her a peck on the cheek. He's dressed in his Sunday navy blue suit, handmade by the local tailor, accented by a red, white, and blue Cleveland Indians tie that's smartly accented by the Indians insignia.

Though a bookkeeper by trade, Dad is powerfully built like his uncles, looking more like a boxer than a pencil pusher. The consequent impact on his Sunday suit is that, no matter how nicely it's tailored, when he flexes his muscles, it goes taut at the seams.

Cheryl, Dennis, and I are also attired in our Sunday best, Cheryl's hair in curls, military crew cuts for me and Dennis. We're looking handsome in our matching blue suits, white shirts, and red ties, and Cheryl looks pretty in her blue dress with red and white polka dot belt and bow. Note the emphasis on Cleveland Indians colors, which is by no means an accident.

Our parents typically drive to church, while we typically walk. Heading down the street, looking our family finest, I always feel *proud* to be a Polke. I don't put that word on it when I'm ten, because it's glaringly apparent to me that we are lower middle class, but looking back, that's what it was. Put differently, our parents are proud of what they have accomplished with their hard work, and that feeling of pride rubs off on all of us.

When walking to church, our inclination is to wave only to those neighbors who wave to us first, but otherwise to avoid interacting with adults like kids tend to do. Invariably impatient, we hurry to get to church, to get where we're going, which is ironic since once we arrive we are equally in a hurry to leave and get home. Of course, when I'm working as an altar boy, everything is different, as I must arrive early and stay late.

On one particular Sunday, Dad drives up beside us in the car and engages us in small talk as we're walking down the street. If memory serves me correctly, I think he's mentioning something about the Cleveland Indians winning or losing the latest game, or their chances of taking the pennant. As we approach the nursery, we see "old man Cavotta"—what Dennis and I call him— and pause our talk and wave. He's standing on the sidewalk admiring the colorful displays of flowers that the garden center always puts out on Sundays. When we turn back and look ahead, a long, low Lincoln hardtop rounds the corner in the distance. Dad suddenly stops the car and points. The driver is smiling and waving to everybody out the driver's window, as if he were someone running for office.

Mom says, directing herself to Dad, "That's the guy who bought your oldest son a baseball glove a few weeks ago."

"What?" Dad says, his tone elevated to one of strong disapproval.

Mom looks piercingly at the moving car, then quickly glances away when it appears that the driver might make eye contact with her. She lifts her chin in defiance.

"He bought your son a new baseball glove the day you went into work early. His glove was falling apart."

"Son," Dad blurts out, but then he lowers his tone to maintain his cool. "Never take gifts from a stranger."

"Mom already told us that," Dennis replies.

I nod my head in agreement.

"Who is he, Dad?" Dennis asks.

"He's Danny Greene," I answer.

"He may look like a good man, but he is not," Dad says. "Please do not have any contact with him except to say hello if he first says something to you. Do you understand me, both of you?"

"Yes, Dad," my brother and I reply together, though we are quite intrigued.

"Yeah, he's the local Robin Hood," Mom says sarcastically. "Kills the rich and gives to the poor."

"Don't say that, Lois," Dad says in a rare moment of open defiance. "You know you can't say things like that." Dad looks over at me and says, "You kids get in the car. You'll ride with us today." And we do.

When we arrive at the newly renovated church, first built in 1926, the old church bell is clanging resonantly, motivating those of us arriving late to hustle up the front steps and take our seats in the crowded pews.

Inside, the slick, burnished seats offer some entertainment since we can slide on our rumps. But countering that is the thick fragrance of men's hair tonic and women's perfume. Dennis and I look at each other and plug our noses, then giggle until Mom shushes us.

The church, although remodeled, still has a European feel, from the architecture to many immigrant parishioners. Italian Byzantine Stations of the Cross (commemorative moments of the crucifixion of Jesus Christ) hang from the walls, and the atmosphere feels rich in a sense of tradition and respect. Donation baskets are circulated, and I am always shocked by how much money Dad gives, considering our financial situation at home.

Years later, I will learn that Mom and Dad actually tithe in addition to donating to the basket each week. I will learn that "tithe" means giving a tenth of what you make. So the more you make, the more you give. For Catholics, the payment of tithes was adopted from the Old Testament Law, and early writers spoke of it as a divine ordinance and obligation of conscience. Though I support the church and tithing, I do wonder how much has been racked in over the years. Must be in the trillions.

Each week, the priest tells a moral lesson, often one based on a biblical story from the New Testament, and as always, the sermon seems to take an eternity to finish. The only saving grace today is that the priest talks about the Sermon on the Mount, one of my favorites.

"One day Jesus taught His disciples the gospel on a mountainside by the Sea of Galilee. He told them how to live so they could be happy and live with the Heavenly Father again. The things He taught them can make us happy too. Jesus said we should be gentle, patient, and willing to obey our Heavenly Father. We should try as hard as we can to be righteous. We should forgive people who hurt us or make us feel bad. If we forgive them, our Heavenly Father will forgive us...."

What I like is the idea of a mountainside near a sea, reminding me of Lake Erie, which is the closest I've come to a real sea. I've never seen a real mountain or a real sea before, and it sounds fun. His last injunction—forgive people who hurt us or make us feel bad—does not sit well with me, however, which is another reason I'm intrigued by it. I'm pissed at those guys who took my glove and Tony Milano, who stole my money, so revenge, not forgiveness, is pointedly on my mind. I look around the church to the solemn worshippers, everyone quietly taking it in. Sometimes the world doesn't make sense to a young man, especially when the pastor contradicts my natural feelings.

When Mass concludes, everyone gathers outside the church, shakes hands, and says hello. Mom and Dad chat with old friends and, as usual, introduce us to a few people we seem to have met a dozen times before. You know, "Boys, do you remember the Smiths?" Whoever they are. Then we have a few words with the pastor, who always comes out on the steps and chats with as many families as he can.

In truth, of course, given our age, all Dennis and I do is go through the motions. What we want to do is get to the park and play ball as quickly as possible; that's probably why we were in such a hurry to get here: so we could leave! As soon as we get home, we males grab our gloves and bat and ball and head to Nottingham Park, tossing the ball between us as we walk. If asked, truth be told, Dennis and I would both no doubt confess that baseball is *our* religion and playing catch is *our* Mass.

Nottingham Park is the crucible of the neighborhood, drawing everyone together. Filled with elm, birch, and hemlock trees, it is the place families go whenever they want to get away from the confines of home. Every kind of game is played there, from football and baseball to kickball, tag, and building snowmen. Except in the winter, football and baseball predominate.

Throughout the tree-covered grounds, families also enjoy picnics, BBQs, kite flying and, of course, the new phenomenon known as throwing Frisbee. Of course, no Sunday would be complete without me burning Dad's hand with my fast ball. "Throw it again," he says, "but harder. This kid's got speed." Dad always says this out loud, more as an announcement of pride in his son than a salutation to me. "I have to get a thicker glove," he says, laughing. "Harder, Kenny. Harder!" Smack. "Ouch!"

~ ~ ~

Baseball holds a unique spot in our culture. It is so deeply, so pervasively, so perfectly American that the game is imbued with a glowing sense of patriotism—the sense that this is what young American boys in the name of democracy must do. The phrase "As American as hot dogs, baseball, and apple pie" includes baseball as part of the patriotic trilogy. In the movie *Field of Dreams*, famed author Terence Mann, played by James Earl Jones, says this about the cultural power of the game:

The one constant through all the years, Ray, has been baseball. America has rolled by like an army of steamrollers. It's been erased like a blackboard, rebuilt, and erased again. But baseball has marked the time. This field, this game, is a part of our past, Ray. It reminds us of all that once was good, and it could be again. Ohhhhhhhh, people will come, Ray. People will most definitely come.

The very essence of Mann's speech pierces the heart and soul of my dad at an early age. Like many Americans, including the early immigrants, baseball brings refuge from the harsh realities of day-to-day living. The joy and excitement of the game, albeit temporary, transports him to another dimension, ushering him into his own version of Rod Serling's *The Twilight Zone*. Through it, he can escape the residual memories and scars of his abusive upbringing and experience some happiness. So as soon as we can walk, Dad infuses us with his passion. Today, looking back, I sense that America has been steamrolled again and is longing for "all that was once good" to return to our lives. Just put forth the right leadership with the right ideas and "Ohhhhhh, people will come, Ray. People will most definitely come."

~ ~ ~

Like millions of young boys growing up in America, my brother and I start playing little league baseball the very day we turn old enough to be eligible. For us, that's age nine and it carries on to age 13. In Collinwood, there are two divisions, north and south. The north teams play at Humphries Field, while we in the south play at Lindsay Wire Field. Lindsay Wire Weaving Company built our baseball diamond on its property to support the kids and give back to the community (though the company will be sold to an East Coast company in the 1970s when cloth wire, which is what it made, becomes obsolete).

The league has lots of great players, and I am fortunate to be one of them. Right-handed, I toss my wicked fastball and a drop-off-the-table curve ball, catch behind the plate when I'm not pitching (pitcher and catcher being a rare combination in one player), and bat clean-up because I can clobber the ball. Dennis pitches and, because of his height, plays first base. The teams are selected by lottery, so as the chips fall, Dennis and I always play on different teams. Dad coaches a number of teams over the years, which sometimes puts him in a quandary because we have to play his teams and each other. Somehow, he always seems to support both of us, focusing more on our play than the final score.

Over the years, we make a lot of friends playing little league. One of them is a guy named Glenn Pauley. We both know him, and although he is Dennis' age, he hangs more with my childhood friend Joe Saviano and myself. Much like my brother and me, Glenn and Joe are gifted athletes and usually got voted, like us, onto the Collinwood All-Star team. This entitles all of us to travel and compete against other teams in what is still known as the Little League World Series. Indeed, for a small neighborhood team, we are highly competitive and always make Collinwood proud. We also make our Aunt Jean (Uncle Eddie and Uncle Frank's youngest sister) proud. I mention Aunt Jean because she was inducted into the Baseball Hall of Fame. As depicted by the movie *A League of Their Own*, Aunt Jean played in the All American Women's Professional Baseball League during World War II.

Several years ago, over 45 years later, Dennis calls me in Colorado from his home in the Cleveland area. Unlike me, he never left our hometown, instead becoming a lawyer and keeping his practice there. We talk about the things that brothers talk of at our age—family, the holidays, sports, local happenings, this book, and so forth. But before we are done, he says, "Hey, you remember Glenn Pauley? He played baseball with us."

"Sure, of course," I say. "Didn't he get in trouble a while back, go to jail?"

"That's right. Can you believe it? He has just been released from prison after spending several decades behind bars."

A year is a long time, I think. *Several decades is a lifetime.*

I mention Glenn because his life trajectory, as juxtaposed to mine, goes to the very essence of this book. Here is a guy who, in the famous words of Marlon Brando in the motion picture, *On the Waterfront,* "coulda been a contendah." But like dockworker Terry Malloy, he succumbed to the dark side early on, but unlike Malloy, when the judgment day arrived, he chose not to redeem himself by testifying against the criminals who directed his crimes. Apparently, he chose the honor of *omerta,* the Mafia code of silence, over his own freedom, and for that choice, spent a lifetime behind bars. Wow! What a price to pay for honor.

As a kid, Glenn is a phenomenal baseball player. He's so good that both Dennis and I see him rising to the pros one day. But obviously, when he faces the crossroads in life that so many young men face, he takes the road of crime. My research shows that his name is tied to a number of criminal transgressions—from minor crimes like carrying a concealed weapon to major ones like racketeering and murder.

Indeed, articles in the *Plain Dealer* tie him closely to legendary Cleveland mobster Sam Lucarelli. At one time, the FBI considered Lucarelli one of the most powerful figures in the Cleveland mob. In his early days, Lucarelli ran the Hotel Sterling operation, meaning he controlled traditional mob rackets like gambling, loansharking, and prostitution. Years later in 1989, after decades of mob affiliation, he was convicted of racketeering along with William Denova, Michael Panzerella, Dennis Francis, Benny Bonnano and, sadly, our old little league pal, Glenn Pauley.

I imagine that is the prison sentence he had just finished serving when my brother and I spoke. Sadly, other newspaper articles further describe Glenn as an "underling" of mobster Jack White, working together with or having some connection to White's criminal associates, guys like Butchy Cisternino, Joe Iacobacci, Allie Calabrese, and Joseph Bonariggo. As underlings of White, these guys were accused of attempting to assassinate mobster John Nardi following his return from Florida, where he was tried and acquitted for some alleged mob-related crimes there. Nardi was another mobster vying for control of the Cleveland Mafia. For years, he was secretary-treasurer of Teamsters Local 410 (the union for vending machine service employees), where he lived in the shadow of John Scalish, the last great don of the Cleveland Mafia that I mentioned earlier.

The upshot of the Pauley story is that, in Collinwood, organized crime permeates the whole neighborhood, from little league to numbers to jukeboxes and vending machines and garden centers. Its octopus-like clutches reach out invisibly into every home and family in Collinwood and other towns like it across America, preying on the next outgoing, energetic kid who "coulda been a contendah."

In Martin Scorsese's Mafia movie *Goodfellas*, that I also mentioned earlier, actor Paul Sorvino plays crew boss Paul "Big Pauley" Cicero, who runs a cab stand across the street from Henry Hill, the guy played by Ray Liotta. Cicero is based on the real life of Paul "Big Pauley" Vito, who worked for the infamous Lucchese crime family. In the film, Cicero is involved in violent crimes like extortion, hijacking, bootlegging, and the numbers racket. He and his brother also run some legitimate businesses, including a cab stand, a restaurant, and *a florist*. Imagine that.

In *Goodfellas*, it's the poverty, idle time, and neighborhood proximity of the mob that sucks in Henry Hill. These are the hobgoblins that expose susceptible young kids to the sticky lure of crime. The "Hey, kid, can you run an errand for me" coming from Big Pauly, and the "Wanna make a few dollars?" coming from a guy like Danny Greene, soon lead to the, "Can you deliver this message for me" and ultimately to the "Hey, I got $2,500 for you to pop a guy. Should be easy. Here's the gun. Just toss it in Lake Erie when you're done."

It saddens me deeply when I think of Glenn and guys like him. *Yet if I'm being honest, but for the grace of God, that coulda been me.*

EXERCISE:

Give some thought to how sports—football, baseball, soccer, basketball, any of the other dozens of Olympic sports—influenced you in a positive way growing up. List those ways.

_____
_____
_____
_____
_____

How can you take the power of sports and athletics and use that power today to achieve your goals and dreams, both at home and at work?

_____
_____
_____
_____
_____

Some kids you grew up with made the wrong choices in life. Do or did you know any such kids, and how can you, your family, and your friends not make the same mistakes today?

_____
_____
_____
_____
_____

Chapter 13

RACISM & KNEE FOOTBALL

"I have a dream that one day little black boys and girls will
be holding hands with little white boys and girls."

— Martin Luther King, Jr., "I Have a Dream" Speech

"Smack!" A white, bare-knuckled fist collides with the jaw of a black teenager on the muddy banks of Euclid Creek. Shattered teeth fly as some Italian goons beat the small black boy into a pulp, eventually kicking him into the creek. These guys look like the same punks who sucker-punched me, bloodied my nose, and took my new baseball glove; but I'm not certain, because they are not from Collinwood and when I shared what had happened with some of my friends, none had any idea who these guys were.

The black boy's motionless body floats away with the current, bumping and twirling from collisions with the large boulders that spot the shallow crik bed. The oldest one, who looks like he should be in high school, or just graduated, assuming he didn't drop out, wipes his face with the back of his bloodied sleeve. Self-satisfaction appears to be the emotion of this budding sociopath.

I watch the brutality, hidden behind scraggly bushes growing from the crik's banks. Nauseated by the shock of seeing someone killed right before my eyes, I get sick to my stomach and tilt forward, bracing the ground with my outstretched fingers to avoid falling into the water. Hearing a branch crack, one of the punks yells, "Who's that?" Like a scared jackrabbit, I take off running for my life, weaving in and out of trees and shrubs before scaling the tall creek bank leading up to the backyards of my neighborhood.

As I'm running, I think I recognize the black man. If I'm not mistaken, he's one of the young welders who works at the auto body shop up the crik where Dad sometimes takes his car. And Dad recently talked about some hoods who were breaking into the shops, sneaking up from the crik where they couldn't be detected, telling Dennis and I to be careful going to school. This must be the same guys.

But I'm scared shitless, to be honest, and getting away is all that's on my mind. Like I'm racing for the Olympic gold, I leap familiar fences, weave in and out of clotheslines, and dodge behind trees and bushes. There's no way in the world these guys, strangers to the neighborhood, could follow me, and they certainly don't want to walk into the muzzle of a shotgun in some stranger's backyard. Better luck next time, *suckers*.

As it turns out, my worry quickly shifts. Though I've shaken the punks, in one yard it's not clothes that are pinned to the line. An angry watch dog with bared, growling teeth stares me down when I leap into his territory. Tethered to the clothesline with a long leash, which allows him to run freely up and down the yard, he rips into me like a hungry wolf, tearing my pants leg, shaking his head with ferocity, his sharp fangs digging deeper into the meat, and drawing blood—lots of blood. To this day, I still have a scar on my inner left thigh where that dog clamped down on me like I was a Porterhouse steak. Thank God for the short length of the leash or I might have been Grade A hamburger.

Having escaped Fido's jaws and leaped the fences to a half-dozen fences in a single stride, I crash through the side door into the safe and warm confines of our house, totally out of breath. Already home from Jergens, Mom is standing in the kitchen and puffing on a cigarette. She looks over at me and gasps, "What on God's earth?"

"Tree tag, Mom," I say, hands on my knees and gasping.

"Kenny?"

"Honest, Mom, I caught myself on a branch."

"Let me look at that." She pulls down my torn pants and her chin drops. On my left leg near my groin are a row of wicked slashes across my flesh, thick red blood oozing all over the place. She screams to Dad, who races in, carries me to the car, then rushes me over to Euclid General Hospital, where they know Mom and me on a first name basis, as this was not my first visit by any stretch. The previous year, I had broken my arm while fighting in the schoolyard, and after the Sisters had sent me home, Dad had left work early to come home and take me to the same hospital.

The nurses practically snort in contempt as I retell my tall tale of tree tag. One nurse smiles and looks at my dad. "Mr. Polke, not to contradict your son, but I'd bet my two front teeth that this is a dog bite."

"Son?" Dad says sternly.

I duck my head sheepishly, wait a few seconds, then tell the whole story between sobs and snorts.

"I'm afraid he's going to have to get a rabies shot," the nurse says to both of us. The shots that follow are something I would not wish on anyone, except maybe the guys who chased me or took my glove. The shots hurt more than the dog bite, times ten.

~ ~ ~

Funny how Mom often asks us, when we walk into the house after school or after playing at the park, "You boys hungry?"

"Duh. We are *always* hungry," Dennis says.

"How's grilled cheese and chips?" she says one day, her hand already on the refrigerator door, a bloody cloth wrapped around her palm, the result of another hard day of working in the metal shavings at Jergens.

We both smile and bob our heads up and down. Then I remember to say, "No pickle, please."

"Me neither," Dennis enjoins.

After consuming two sandwiches and a large bag of potato chips, we start contemplating what we want to do next. Mom senses this and intervenes.

"If you two derelicts don't start opening up some books, you're going to be cutting your hands to pieces all your life, or worse, just like me." She unwraps the bloody cloth from her hand and raises up her palm. "Do you see this? You need a good education to make something of yourselves." We later discover that, in addition to the sharp metal shavings that are tearing up my mother's hands, she is also allergic to the metal solvents used in this process—a case of double jeopardy for my poor mom.

Dennis and I mope around for a few minutes, go to the bathroom, start to wrestle between the walls, and procrastinate as long as we can until we finally grab our books and plop down at the kitchen table. But don't get me wrong. It's not that we are bad students; we aren't. We both get good grades and we like to learn. But we are kids, so we'd prefer to do anything *but* homework.

"I hate homework," I say, speaking my mind as I always do.

"I love to read, Mom," Dennis counters, trying to get one up on me with Mom. "If I were a betting man, I'd say I could read better than Kenny," he adds, deliberately trying to bait me, "even though he's one year ahead of me."

I give him an evil look as he flips open his history book. He's only nine years old and already he loves boring subjects like history and taunting me.

"Me, too. I *love* reading," I say, not to be outdone in Mom's eyes.

"Liar, liar, pants on fire," Dennis mutters under his breath.

"Shut up," I say.

"Boys," Mom intervenes. "That's enough."

We both hunker down for a half hour until, as if choreographed, we both simultaneously shut our books and say, simultaneously, "Done, Mom! Can we go now?"

"Okay," she says, the word following a long, doubtful stare. "Find something constructive to do."

I stand up to head to our bedroom when Dennis lurches forward, driving his head deep into my back. I reach out to the wall to prevent a collision, then drop to my knees and twirl. Dennis drops to his knees, facing me. The game is on: knee football. *How's this for constructive?* We take knee football just as seriously as league ball, except we do it in the hallway of our tiny house.

I reach over to grab a bundled pair of socks, which I tuck under my armpit like a football. Bobbing left, then right, I shoot between Dennis' shoulder and the wall. He leans his bulky frame hard left, squashing me against the wall.

"Shit, Denny," I say. "That hurt."

"Kenneth Polke," Mom says sternly, intolerant to any cussing. "You watch your mouth or I'll wash it out with soap." (In fact, on one occasion, Mom did wash my mouth out with soup when I called a neighbor lady who lived down the street a "fat witch.") Mom looks down at us, putting her knuckled hands to her hips.

"Sorry," I say, hoping she doesn't carry out her threat if I slip again. Meanwhile, Dennis has been cleverly calculating his next move. After feigning left, he snags the socks from my hand and leaps high over my head, his gangly length practically crushing me.

"Touchdown!" he yells. "Six-zero!"

I snatch the misshapen bundle from his hand, toss it over his head, then leap into the air like a wide receiver stretching for a touchdown. Before he can adjust, I've caught my own pass and tumble past him.

"Touchdown right back at you," I say, breathing hard.

"That's unfair," he huffs. His huffing gives me a small opening to swipe the ball from his hand again and pull it in tight to my chest. "Fumble!" I yell. "Poke Salad has it on the five-yard line, first and goal."

Dennis frowns and charges into me with all his might. He knocks me backwards and the socks fly from my hand. We both scrabble for them, but this time I overpower him, plow him into the wall, jabbing my knee into his chest, then shuffle on my knees for another touchdown.

"Twelve six!" I yell. "Foul!" he replies. "Cry baby," I say as I start to laugh.

"Mom," he yells. "Ken—"

"Sissy," I whisper.

"Moomm," he whines louder.

"Big baby," I say. "I'm never playing with you again."

I leap forward and grab his head tight in a headlock with my muscled right arm. He starts to yell because I've gotten his head clamped in the wedge of my armpit, which is like a vise grip. Mom reaches down and pinches my ear until I let go.

"Ooouch," I scream.

As I release him, I foot-sweep the socks past Dennis like a hockey puck. "Field goal, three points. Fifteen to six. Slaughter." Then I laugh again.

"Mom, Ken cheated *again*," Dennis says.

"Both of you, one hour detention. Different rooms."

Thirty minutes later, Mom lets us off the hook. She's a softy when it comes to carrying out the full sentence, but we still exit the bedrooms (me from our bedroom, Dennis from Cheryl's) with our chins hanging low.

"Would you boys like ham for dinner?" Mom asks, ignoring our sullen looks. "I've been saving it for a special occasion."

"What's an occasion?" Dennis asks in a sulking voice.

"It's when something good happens, dummy," I reply.

"Mom, tell him to leave me alone."

"He's right," she says. "I got a raise, on account of a little union work I did and a raise that resulted." She smiles, knowing we have no real notion of what "union work" means. "I'm making $5.75 per hour now."

"Wow," I say.

Dennis grabs a pencil and scribbles on a piece of paper. "That's not even $250 a week, Mom," he says.

"230 is what I get now, and 230 dollars is not bad in this day and age for a week's work. Not bad at all."

"Really?" I say.

"Yes, really," she replies.

Dennis' history book now lays open from his removal of the pencil to add up Mom's weekly wage. It reveals a folded section of Sunday's newspaper with the Cleveland Indians' box score wedged in the crack. The only homework he had done was study the box scores.

EXERCISE:

Prejudice can present one of life's biggest obstacles to overcome. List out instances of prejudice against you or others.

_____
_____
_____
_____
_____

How did you or others overcome that prejudice?

_____
_____
_____
_____
_____

Take the lessons of overcoming prejudice and apply them to other adversities you are seeking to overcome.

_____
_____
_____
_____
_____

Chapter 14

HEROES, BASEBALL & MISSILES

"The way a team plays as a whole determines its success. You may have the greatest bunch of individual stars in the world, but if they don't play together, the club won't be worth a dime.

— Babe Ruth

From his living room chair, Dad looks up from his latest book and says to me and Dennis (we are lounging on the couch), with his tell-tale instructor's voice, "Who said this: 'You just can't beat the person who never gives up'?"

We look at each other and snicker. "Santa Claus," says Dennis.

"Very funny. Denny," he replies.

"Babe Ruth," I say.

"Correct."

I lick my finger and mark one in the air.

"Who said: 'Never let the fear of striking out get in your way'?"

"Ken Polke," Dennis says, another wisecrack that he just can't resist. He starts giggling at his own humor.

"Very funny, jerk," I say.

"The Babe," Dad says. "And finally, who said: 'Every strike brings me closer to the next home run'?"

"Genie Boy!" we both yell.

Every generation has its heroes. For Dad, that hero was Babe Ruth. "The Babe," as he is affectionately called by his fans, including, no doubt, millions of dads like ours, died on 16 August 1948, about four years before I was born. But that doesn't matter. Whether he intended to or not, he cast his bigger-than-life shadow on generations of young boys. In the minds and hearts of his adoring fans, he stood— and to many still stands—for everything that makes America great.

The day after his death, *The New York Times* ran a piece written by Murrah Schumach. In his obituary for the Babe, Murrah wrote with great elegance:

Probably nowhere in all the imaginative field of fiction could one find a career more dramatic and bizarre than that portrayed in real life by George Herman Ruth. Known the world over, even in foreign lands where baseball is never played, as the Babe, he was the boy who rose from the obscurity of a charitable institution in Baltimore to a position as the leading figure in professional baseball. He was also its greatest drawing-card, its highest salaried performer—at least of his day—and the idol of millions of youngsters throughout the land.

But the Babe does not stand alone, despite his larger-than-life image. He is a member of a team, America's team, the New York Yankees. In 1961, the previous year when I turned nine, the New York Yankees won the American League pennant again and took the World

Series. But while the Babe remains my dad's hero, the '61 team fields three of mine: Mickey Mantle, Roger Maris, and Whitey Ford. That year, Maris is named the American League MVP and the AP Athlete of the Year. Ford takes the Cy Young and Babe Ruth Awards. Mantle is arguably the greatest offensive threat in baseball history at center fielder, and arguably the best switch hitter ever. All three make the American League All-Star Team, and many sports writers agree it may be the greatest professional baseball team of all time.

Inspired by my heroes, I want to be good at everything there is to do in baseball: hitting, pitching, and catching. In 1962, our local practice diamond—Aspenwall Field—is where I, as an aspiring ten-year old, try to make it happen. Aspenwall, however, is not your ordinary baseball diamond. It looks like something out of *The Outer Limits* TV show, as if located on Mars and played on by Martians. For starters, there is no grass. Then, between the backstop and the dilapidated home run fence, there lies hard dirt and broken cinder, the former giving way to the latter as the infield becomes the outfield. Everyone's uniform is shredded from sliding on the abrasive hard pan. But to a kid, none of that matters, because we're doing what we love—playing baseball.

Beyond the home run fence are a tangled crisscross of steel railings known as the Collinwood railroad yards. I point my bat toward the tracks as I step up to the plate, *a la* Babe Ruth, and glance over at Dad. He smiles. By habit, I paw my cleats at the edge of the small depression that's developed next to the rubber home plate, planning to smash one into an empty boxcar.

"Hey, batta. Hey, battta. Hey, batta," chime the players on the field, like crickets at sundown. A loud train horn blasts the sky, as I hunker down in concentration of the first pitch.

Several throws later, it's two balls, one strike. *Perfect position,* I think. I'm waiting for a fastball, high and outside, and if this clown on the mound throws one, well, goodbye Mary Ann. I glance down at the catcher, who chirps, "Strikeout king at the plate. Strikeout king at the plate."

Bullshit, I think, and I crouch down even deeper as the ball rockets toward me. I grit my teeth and swing so hard I lose my helmet. The ball smacks the catcher's glove with a loud "Pop!" I jam my bat into the ground to stop from falling.

"Sttttrrrike!" the ump yells.

I look over to my dad, who's the team coach this season. "Settle down, son," he yells, hands cupped to his mouth. "Make him throw you one."

I take two quick warm-up swings, then step back up to the plate, bouncing like a crab on two legs, left elbow flapping. The pitcher lets loose with another rocket, except this time it doesn't drop low. It starts to lift high. I curl up my left foot, flap my left elbow, then let loose with all my might. "Crack!" The ball whistles over the pitcher's head and climbs into the sky like it's a rocket ship headed to Mars. The center-fielder takes off running, glove-arm stretched to full extension. He's running, running, running, then slams into the fence as the ball disappears into the oblivion of the train yard. Another train whistle toots loudly as if saluting my homer. I jab my cleated foot on first base and trot toward second. *I love this*, I think. *I really love this.*

Our crowd, about half those in the bleachers, are on their feet screaming and yelling. My homer is the winning run in the bottom of the sixth, breaking the tie and putting us into the playoffs. I slowly round the bases, taking it all in. It's also my twenty-fourth home run of the season, a little league record for Collinwood. I wish Mom were here, but she never attends any of our games. She's afraid we'll get hurt. If she had her way, we'd be at home reading. Sports just isn't her bag.

There's good reason for her concern, of course. Games don't always go like this. In a previous game, I was a runner on first base. My teammate hit the ball hard to the right field corner, causing me to turn my head while running toward second base to see whether I should hold up at second or stretch it to third. Knowing it would be close, I turned on the jets and tore for third. In the process, I ran smack dab into the back of the second baseman's head. My two front teeth got knocked out so hard they stuck into the roof of my mouth. Blood was squirting from my mouth like a fountain. The exsanguination (how's that for a fancy medical term) was so profuse I literally gagged on the blood that was pooling in my mouth.

My dad almost fainted from all the blood. Thank God one of the opposing coaches was less squeamish. He had the presence of mind and ability to quickly stuff a towel into my mouth to stop the flooding, then race me off to the emergency room because Dad was too light-headed to drive. Thank God for the second time when the Emergency Room doctor on duty had enough sense to put the two teeth right back in their sockets. Though my teeth were saved, the ensuing dental bills set my parents back a tidy sum.

Mom "just knew it." Her worries were affirmed completely. For the next year, more than ever, she would wring her hands in worry every time we left the house to play ball.

Game over after my game-winning home run, we burst through the side door and into the house with Dairy Queen ice cream cones dripping onto our hands and shirts.

"Mom, we won!" I yell. She's in the kitchen cooking burgers and homemade fried potatoes, my favorite dish. She turns from the oven and smiles. "Ah, Ken, that's wonderful. Are you okay?"

"He hit a homer to win the game," Dennis says excitedly.

"I'm so proud of you son, really," she says. "Now wash up for dinner, and when you're done, how about cutting the grass for dessert?"

My smile turns south, wind sucked from my sails. "Sure, Mom, whatever you say."

~~~

A few months later, the Cuban Missile Crisis hits the front page and puts the nation on high alert. One day, Dad walks in from the side porch after grabbing the morning paper in the driveway and exclaims, "This could be the end of everything!"

It doesn't mean that much to me, but I know it must be something big because Dad is rarely prone to pessimism or exaggeration.

"What is it?" Mom says from the kitchen.

"The Russians, they want to rule the world," he says.

"What else is new?" she replies. "Look what they did to us in Eastern Europe."

Several days later, on November 22, 1962, Dennis and I are sitting in the living room watching cartoons. A special news bulletin disrupts the regular show. "Dad," I yell, "the President is going to say something on the television." He and Mom stop whatever they are doing and rush over.

Mom turns up the volume as President John F. Kennedy's voice blares loudly in his nasally, Irish brogue. "Good evening, my fellow citizens," he says, standing at a podium like the pastor at church. "This Government, as promised, has maintained the closest surveillance of the Soviet military build-up on the island of Cuba. Within the past week, unmistakable evidence has established the fact that a series of offensive missile sites is now in preparation on that imprisoned island. The purpose of these bases can be none other than to provide a nuclear strike capability against the Western Hemisphere...."

The speech goes on and on. I try to follow it, but every time I start to ask a question, Dad shushes me so he doesn't miss a word of it.

"Our policy has been one of patience and restraint," the President continues, "as befits a peaceful and powerful nation which leads a worldwide alliance. We have been determined not to be diverted from our central concerns by mere irritants and fanatics. But now further action is required, and it is under way; and these actions may only be the beginning. We will not prematurely or unnecessarily risk the costs of worldwide nuclear war in which even the fruits of victory would be ashes in our mouth; but neither will we shrink from that risk at any time it must be faced...."

For a young guy, it's all too much. I zone out and lay my head on Mom's knee. Finally, it sounds like the Irishman is about to finish... but he is not done yet.

"The path we have chosen for the present is full of hazards, as all paths are; but it is the one most consistent with our character and courage as a nation and our commitments around the world. The cost of freedom is always high, but Americans have always paid it. And one path we shall never choose, and that is the path of surrender or submission...."

"Our goal is not the victory of might, but the vindication of right; not peace at the expense of freedom, but both peace and freedom, here in this hemisphere, and, we hope, around the world. God willing, that goal will be achieved."

"Thank you and good night."

When the President stops talking, the worried looks on Mom and

Dad's faces speak more than words. Dad's eyes are frozen on the screen as the Cronkite guy comes back on. Mom sits back on the couch, lets out a gush of air, but says nothing. This is one of those occasions where, if you tried, you could cut the air with a knife. Mom's jaw seems to drop lower and lower the longer she sits there. Finally, Dad breaks the silence by turning off the television. "Don't anyone worry," he says. "Everything will be all right."

But notwithstanding Dad's assurances, I remember this moment as ushering in a very scary time. All of a sudden, discussions around the water fountain, overheard by us kids, are not about the weather or this coming weekend's events, but "the realization," one of the nuns says, "that all of civilization could be wiped out and made extinct—much like the dinosaurs!" For the first time, millions of ordinary people—not just the fringe doomsday lunatics—seriously think the world might come to an end through a Soviet-U.S. nuclear holocaust.

The Collinwood neighborhood, however, admittedly takes a different twist on this theme than the broadcast media and the papers. We are fighting mad—ready, willing, and able to kill any and all Commies who might have the foolish balls to invade our neighborhood. And I'm sure we have the firepower to do it, keeping in mind that the mob rules the area that will one day be known as "Bomb City U.S.A."

Put another way, any Commies who might have dared to step foot in our neighborhood would have been killed in an instant. That's the America I was growing up in in 1960s Collinwood.

Mom gathers herself and stands up, ready to back up Dad's remark. "That's right. No reason to worry. Boys, Cheryl, why don't you show your dad your Halloween costumes." We run into our bedrooms, and five minutes later, with Mom's help, come out booing and shrieking in our Frankenstein, Dracula, and Cinderella costumes.

The next day at school, a thick atmosphere of doom-and-gloom hangs in the air. It's evident in the way the Sisters are acting—getting distracted during class presentations, gathering together and talking in groups in the hallway between classes, and fidgeting nervously more than usual. In a word, the cool-as-a-cucumber Sisters are rattled to the core. In fact, everyone seems to be on edge, including the students and, in particular, a fellow by the name of Dan Kemper.

Dan lives on the Euclid side, but he doesn't live in one of the nice houses. He lives in the low income project that was built right after World War II to provide housing for returning soldiers who had no place else to turn. The Euclid Projects, as they are called, are considered by almost everyone else as an eyesore.

With everyone already on edge, the nuns practically have heart attacks when they find Dan flashing a knife around the other kids. Who knows whether it's a military weapon or something else, and who cares, because a knife is a knife, and for a knife, it is big. For once, I'm not the one who gets the paddle. However, this knife incident from grade school does bring up another interesting story, reminding me that in Collinwood, being ever-vigilant becomes a condition of survival.

One day, not long after the troubling incident with Dan, I'm playing basketball after school with some of the other guys in the neighborhood at Nottingham Playground, where recently a new kid to the area had also started hanging out. Apparently at the nearby public school—which, of course, my brother and I do not attend—he's already made a reputation for himself by bullying people around. Rumor has it that he's fresh out of a detention home and is feeling the wild oats of his newly acquired freedom.

After finishing several games, we decide to call it quits. I'm preparing to leave when I notice that the new kid is stumbling toward me with an odd look on his face and an odder, cock-eyed gait to his walk. It looks like he's carrying a near-empty whiskey bottle in one hand and something that looks like a long knife in the other. As he gets closer, I realize that the knife is, in fact, a long-blade machete.

When he is almost upon me, he suddenly cocks his arm and swings the machete sideways at my neck. Because he's intoxicated, I'm able to duck and avoid the blade. He swings again, and luckily, he misses again, practically falling to the ground. Shocked by what's assaulting me, I start backing up fast on my heels as he throws yet another swipe of the sword out of pure frustration of me side-stepping his prior two swings so easily. This time he falls to the ground and passes out, lucky not to have cut off his own head.

Though I have the choice of just walking away, I'm thinking this guy needs to be taught a lesson. Let's just say I leave my calling card on his face in hopes he'll notice something when he wakes up and won't be dumb enough to come after me again. Then, having doled out some Collinwood justice of my own, I decide to take the machete so he won't try to hurt anyone else when he comes to. A few blocks from home, I toss the machete into the crik in hopes it will wash out into the lake when the next big storm hits.

Why he chose to come after me I do not know. But it was my first experience with what I've come to call the small man syndrome or the classic Napoleon complex, since this kid was very short for his age and seemingly very troubled by it. Or maybe he was just messed up from the whiskey or a rough home life. Who knows?

In any case, it seems that the state of the nation, being on edge, has spilled over into our everyday lives. Fear and anger are the emotions of the day.

EXERCISE:

Despite our individual skills or success, most things take team work. List ways that team work has and could help you achieve your life's goals.

_____

_____

_____

_____

_____

The mood of a country can be positive or negative, and that mood can affect your ability to overcome adversities in your life. List ways you can embrace a positive mood or turn a negative mood into a positive one.

_____

_____

_____

_____

_____

Crazy things happen in life, sometimes with a violent edge. Make notes of how to handle these episodes if and when they occur so as not to throw you off your game.

_____

_____

_____

_____

_____

Chapter 15

HALL OF FAME & DEATH OF A PRESIDENT

"We have no government armed with power capable of contending with human passions unbridled by morality and religion.... Our Constitution was made only for a moral and religious people. It is wholly inadequate to the government of any other."

— John Adams (signer of the Declaration of Independence and the Bill of Rights and our second U.S. President)

Built 50 miles from Collinwood, in Canton, Ohio, the Football Hall of Fame opens on September 7, 1963, not long after I turn 11 years old. The 19,000 square foot museum honors American professional football which, coincidentally, was founded in Canton in 1920 as the American Professional Football Association. The Hall's mission is written across its walls: "Honor the Heroes of the Game, Preserve its History, Promote its Values, and Celebrate Excellence EVERYWHERE!"

Similar to my own, as well as athletes and coaches everywhere, the Hall's five core values are: "commitment, integrity, courage, respect, and excellence." *No coincidence that these same values go to the core of being an American.*

CONQUERING YOUR ADVERSITIES

The charter members are a who's who of football at the time, some with better known nicknames: Sammy Baugh, Bert Bell, Joe Carr, Earl "Dutch" Clark, Harold "Red" Grange, George Halas, Mel Hein, Wilbur "Pete" Henry, Robert "Cal" Hubbard, Don Hutson, Earl "Curly" Lambeau, Tim Mara, George Preston Marshall, John "Blood" McNally, Bronko Nagurski, Ernie Nevers, and Jim Thorpe. I mention this only because this kind of fame has a way of filtering down to young kids, and of instilling laudatory values. Indeed, the proverbial winds from the museum blow wide and with prodigious effect.

That same year I enter fifth grade. At 11 years of age, finally I'm old enough to play the game being celebrated everywhere. Locally, football games are organized by the Catholic Youth Organization, or CYO, as we call it. Dad says I'm a natural quarterback, so I'm looking forward to taking the helm of my first team with the strong arm that I've developed by playing baseball and throwing the football a gazillion times in the park.

Then the bombshell. The pastor (Father Herman) announces that the church will be discontinuing CYO football. I'm bummed out beyond belief. All of the hours that Dad, Dennis, and I had practiced will go for naught. My football career seems to end before it ever starts. The irony is that the number eleven—my age and the year my football career seems to end—will eventually be the jersey number I take with me from high school to the pros.

In turns out that 1963 will also be a tumultuous and transformative year, not only for me, but for the nation. On the one hand, George Wallace is sworn in as governor of Alabama with a pledge of "segregation forever," as San Francisco real estate developer Marvin Sheldon refuses to sell any of his new Golden Gate Heights homes to "negroes." He even rejects an impressive $39,950 offer by Wilt Chamberlain, the African American star center of the San Francisco Warriors. Racism is nationwide, and it is rampant. On the other hand, the Reverend Martin Luther King, Jr., begins the first non-violent civil rights campaign in Birmingham, Alabama, and President Kennedy declares segregation morally wrong, beseeching Americans that it is "time to act" to eliminate racism and prejudice everywhere.

But the scariness of the times goes beyond racism. Despite backing down in the Cuban Missile Crisis, Soviet Premier Nikita Khrushchev claims the Godless USSR has developed a 100-megaton nuclear bomb that can sink half the world, thereby asserting Soviet superiority among superpowers. Ironically, a few weeks later, our own Supreme Court decides 8-1 to bar the reading of the Lord's Prayer or any biblical verses in public schools.

At St. Paul's, we hear the Sisters talking about this among themselves. "No more prayer in school? That's blasphemous," I hear one Sister say in exasperation.

"Well, no more prayer in the public schools," the other replies.

"So, we're safe here?"

"Yes, we're a private school."

"Oh."

In fact, I notice a small change in the Sisters over the coming weeks. Rather than shrink back with fewer prayers, the Sisters double-down and do more. Looking back, it's as if they were in their own quiet way expressing a form of religious defiance.

That summer, Reverend King marches on Washington, preaching equality, jobs, and freedom. With television becoming a bigger and bigger part of every American household, including our own, King's protest enters the privacy of our home with great stridence. Mom and Dad seem to appreciate his stance. They are not bigots, but we do live in a highly bigoted neighborhood.

Standing before 250,000 demonstrators at the Lincoln Memorial in the nation's capital, Reverend King delivers his famous "I Have a Dream" speech. The speech is replayed many times on television from the moment it is given, unlike the speech ending World War II. King is calling for equality and peace among all people. But the year ends in tragedy. On November 22, 1963, our beloved man from Camelot, John Kennedy, the first ever Catholic President, is assassinated by Communist sympathizer Lee Harvey Oswald while riding with his wife in a motorcade in Dallas.

The assassination enters my world at school in the late morning, when the Sisters abruptly stop class. We know something big is brewing because the nuns are huddling in the hallway and bawling their eyes out. Finally, Sister Mary Margaret, followed by the school principal, comes on the PA system to tell us the President of the United States has been shot and killed. She asks us to bow our heads in prayer, and we do.

That Sunday's Mass is devoted to President Kennedy. Many women in the congregation break into tears. Several times, Mom wipes her cheek with her handkerchief. A certain numbness permeates the church and our house for weeks. It is a very sad time for Catholics and all Americans, as the collective consciousness seems to fear we're coming to some kind of end.

Predictably, Christmas at the Polke house that year is a forlorn one. The killing of Kennedy hits my parents harder than anything has ever hit them before. For devout Catholics, die-hard Kennedy Democrats, and unmitigated Kennedy supporters, the death of the President who visited our home many times via television is like losing a loved one.

The innocence of America following the Allied victory in the Second World War is now gone—for a nation, for our family, and for me personally. Our President is dead, our Catholic leader has been assassinated, and I will not be playing football. But then, surprisingly, football comes to the rescue, making its first profound appearance in my life. It happens when the *Plain Dealer* holds a contest for all of its paperboys: we have one month to add as many new subscribers to our paper routes as possible, with the winners getting a big prize.

For the next month, I knock on a thousand doors and make my pitch, "Please subscribe. If I win, I get to go to the nation's capital," to every person I pass. Then the tally is in. I and a few of my hardworking paperboy colleagues win an all-expenses paid trip to Washington, D.C., where we will tour the city, visit the campus of the U.S. Naval Academy, and see the Navy Midshipmen play a real college football game at a real college football stadium.

As it turns out, the Navy's quarterback at the time is the great Roger Staubach. In 1963, Staubach becomes the second Naval Academy football player in four years to win the Heisman Trophy. The team is on fire and so is he. Known as "Roger the Dodger," as a junior quarterback he leads Navy to number two in the country and a berth in the Cotton Bowl, where he sets Bowl records for pass completions (21 of 31) and yards passing (228). That year, the Midshipmen also post impressive wins over West Virginia, Michigan, Notre Dame, and Maryland. Staubach completes 106 passes in 161 attempts for 1,474 yards, while earning honors as an All-America player, as well as winning the Maxwell and Walter Camp Memorial Trophies.

I learn that Staubach is also a baseball player, which at that time is more my sport than football because I am allowed to play on the baseball little league teams (baseball not being deemed such a rough contact sport). He will letter in baseball three straight years in a row (1963-65), as an outfielder and as a pitcher. In1963, he hits .420, and in 1965, he will be named team captain. Even before achieving all of this, with this visit, he quickly becomes my first ever sports hero from a college team.

For me, watching the Naval Cadets play the Duke Blue Devils is the highlight of the trip. It is the first college football game I have ever seen in person, and what a game, I don't know whether I ever got his stats for the game, but I do know that he will go on to win the Heisman Trophy in 1963, the year of our visit.

When I return home from D.C., for the first time in my life I know exactly what I want to be when I grow up: I want to be a professional baseball or football player. If I play baseball, I want to be the next Mickey Mantle or Roger Maris or Rocky Colavito (the star player for the Cleveland Indians that my Dad loves). If I play football, I want to be the next Roger Staubach. And when I go to college, which I now know I must do, I want to attend the U.S. Naval Academy and serve my country while playing quarterback for the midshipmen.

EXERCISE:

Heroes can play such an important role in our lives, providing us with inspiration and hope. Name your heroes.

_____

_____

_____

_____

_____

_____

How have your heroes inspired your life and helped you conquer your adversities?

_____

_____

_____

_____

_____

_____

How can the values of your heroes help you achieve your ambitions and life goals in ways they have not already done?

_____

_____

_____

_____

_____

_____

Chapter 16

1963-64: CHANGING TIMES

"Never doubt that a small group of thoughtful, committed, citizens can change the world. Indeed, it is the only thing that ever has."

— Margaret Mead

The assassination of John Kennedy creates such shock and injury to the American psyche that it allows the new President from Texas, Lyndon Johnson, to usher in massive new social programs, as if to put salve on our wounds and heal America's pain. In his State of the Union Address, the man who was marginalized by Kennedy only weeks earlier, declares a bold new war, but not one against Communism. The war he declares is against ourselves. He calls it the "War on Poverty."

Johnson takes America in a very liberal direction versus Kennedy. His War on Poverty is a stab at fighting a politically-correct war, not one we can win in the traditional sense of winning a war due to the countless factors and rules of engagement involved. Today, I think Kennedy might even be dubbed a conservative Republican in many respects, versus Johnson or the Democrats of today.

Also soothing the American soul in these painful times is a revolutionary shift in popular music. The British sensation, the Beatles, takes the U.S. by storm. Twenty-five thousand cheering fans meet the fabulous four at La Guardia Airport in New York to view their first steps onto American soil, as if they were landing on the moon. Soon afterwards, they make their historic appearance on *The Ed Sullivan Show*, where Ed introduces the mop-haired foursome into the bedrooms of millions of Americans. We in the Polke family do not become big Beatles fans, but we are music lovers, and the excitement is infectious, helping to sooth our own pain at the death of our beloved Catholic President.

In June, the Civil Rights Act of 1964 survives an 83-day filibuster in the U.S. Senate, finally gaining approval by a wide 73 to 27 vote margin. For the first time in U.S. history, Congress has passed an Act that guarantees the right to vote for everyone regardless of color and that expressly prohibits segregation in public places, thereby overriding the Jim Crow laws that accomplished the opposite. Discrimination on the basis of gender is added to the Act to make it more complete, thereby outlawing sex discrimination in the workplace. For a moment, it seems that racial and gender prejudice might be behind us.

Ironically, it is the Democratic Party that fights mightily to defeat the Civil Rights Act, just like it was the southern wing of the Democratic Party that fought for slavery during the Civil War, thereby splitting the Democratic Party into halves and allowing the lone Republican, Abraham Lincoln, to win. Am I the only one who sees the hypocrisy and irony in all of this?

But despite the lofty words of the Civil Rights Act, the reality couldn't be further from the import of the words. A law does not alone quell the hatred of racism or prejudice that has festered and been embraced for generations. Only a few weeks later, three young civil rights workers disappear in Mississippi. Their car is found burning, without them in it. Forty days later, their bodies are discovered buried in an earthen dam near Philadelphia, hundreds of miles away. Ultimately, eight Klansman are convicted of conspiracy in relation to their deaths, but none serves more than six years in prison. Murder charges are never brought. The event will later inspire the 1988 motion picture, *Mississippi Burning*.

In August, the U.S. begins carpet-bombing North Vietnam, Congress having passed the Gulf of Tonkin resolution, thereby giving President Johnson broad powers to engage U.S. air and ground forces and advance another war. Before the month is up, Johnson signs the centerpiece to his "War on Poverty," a budget largess called the Economic Opportunity Act, committing nearly $1 billion to anti-poverty programs, an Act that by most accounts will utterly fail. The next month, he signs the Wilderness Act and designates nine million acres as places "where the Earth and its community of life are untrammelled by man, where man himself is a visitor who does not remain."

Honestly speaking, the Economic Opportunity Act does not make anyone in our house feel any better. We are a family struggling to survive, economically and emotionally, with two parents working and three children in private Catholic school. That's what matters to us, despite all the lofty aspirations of the Act and its well-deserved passing.

By October, anti-war sentiment is getting traction, and the Free Speech Movement has launched in Berkeley, at the University of California. Mario Savio, a UC Berkeley physics student, begins the student civil rights movement, boldly and radically protesting the war, capitalism, racism, and sometimes even America itself. On the heels of this, Dr. Timothy Leary and Dr. Richard Alper, both fired from Harvard University for experimenting with the hallucinogenic LSD, speak to huge crowds in San Francisco, urging all of their student audiences to forthwith take LSD weekly to increase their intelligence and perceptiveness.

And, of course, in 1964, a curly-haired, bushy-browed musician named Bob Dylan warns our Congressmen to heed the call of change. So true his words are. Of course, I'm only 12 years old and thus distanced from the direct impact of these changes, but the unrest of the times is beginning to filter down to the lives of ordinary Americans and their families, including the Polke family and the poor kid from Collinwood who would ultimately need football, faith, and determination to save his life.

~ ~ ~

By the mid-1960s, television is considered the most important source of news for the American public and, possibly, the most powerful influence on public opinion itself. Throughout the Korean War, the television audience was small. In 1950, only 9 percent of homes owned a television. By 1966, however, this figure had ballooned to 93 percent. By 1972, most Americans receive their news primarily from television, while those relying primarily on newspapers drops to 50 percent. Thus, as the Vietnam War drags on, more and more Americans turn to television as their primary source for war news.

The reality of television is that it is a business with a profit motive; very often profit comes first, before it functions as a public service. As a result, producers and reporters attempt to make the news more entertaining by airing stories that involve conflict or morality, as these topics naturally draw a greater audience. However, it isn't until July 1965 that television news finds material dramatic enough to gain a highly profitable audience. The news that drives that profit is war. President Johnson, exercising his executive powers, increases the number of American troops in Vietnam to 175,000 boots on the ground.

1963-64: CHANGING TIMES

Combat coverage, interviews of American soldiers, and nail-biting helicopter scenes all provide television news the dramatic tension it needs. On many occasions at the Polke house, we find ourselves huddled around the television, watching the war unfold. All three networks establish permanent news bureaus in Saigon, dispatching hundreds of correspondents there throughout the war. From 1965 through the Tet Offensive in 1968, a cool 86 percent of the network nightly news programs are covering the war, focusing mostly on ground and air combat.

At the beginning, the news coverage is mostly supportive of the U.S. involvement in Vietnam and of the brave young men fighting there. Put another way, the media is generally characterizing the conflict as the "good guys shooting Reds," democracy fighting Communism. It fits nicely into the ongoing narrative of the Cold War. The American soldier is thus seen as a hero, even as the war itself comes under criticism. One striking example is TV correspondent Dean Brelis's interview of Marine Colonel Michael Yunck while he was having his leg amputated:

> I said, hell, they can't be right around in there. So I didn't call bombs and napalm on these people. But that's where they were. I'm sure that's where they were. God damn it. I hate to put napalm on these women and children. I just didn't do it. I said, they can't be there.

Predictably, of course, when the tide of public opinion starts to turn against the war, and opposition to it mushrooms, the news coverage shifts. And though the Polke family are following the Democratic party line, we are becoming as frustrated with everyone else as to how the war is being fought. It seems more like a political battle than a soldier's war with the defined objective of winning.

Friends and neighbors who served are coming back from Vietnam complaining bitterly that their hands were tied behind their backs, and that they were essentially precluded from fighting to win. Word starts to spread that it is the politicians who are fighting the war, and not the greatest military in the world. The phrase "rules of engagement" is first employed in open forums, as if war were an athletic competition with rules of sportsmanship, not a fight for freedom and survival. Mom starts to be concerned that her sons will be sent off to fight in the jungles of Vietnam if the war is not ended soon.

Opinions are changing. Incredibly, my parents are so affected by the times that they vote for Richard Nixon for President—a Republican!—in hopes that he will end the war. He is the first Republican they ever voted for, and ultimately, the last. So unpopular has President Johnson become at home and in the polls that he decides not to run for another term.

1963-64: CHANGING TIMES

EXERCISE:

War can take the wind out of your sails, even if you and your loved ones are not on the battlefield. Describe tools you use, or could use, to succeed in achieving your life's goals in the face of such an adversity.

_____
_____
_____
_____
_____

When times around you change, you are presented with an opportunity to adapt and change yourself and your own goals and priorities. Name some new goals and priorities that current times might inspire.

_____
_____
_____
_____
_____

Conquering your adversities does not occur in a vacuum. What are you currently doing to conquer your adversities, notwithstanding the negativity around you?

_____
_____
_____
_____
_____

Chapter 17

CRAZY 1965

"Abandon hope all ye who enter here."

— Dante's *Divine Comedy*, inscription on the gates to hell

If 1964 was disturbing, 1965 is downright crazy. Can you imagine if CNN and Fox had covered the events of the '60s in a modern, 24/7 digital news cycle? But before I get to the crazy happenings of 1965, I do want to discuss three positive things that blossom within my life that year.

The first relates to music—and in particular, a new song by the Righteous Brothers, hands down one of my favorite acts of all time. In 1965, the Righteous Brothers release their smash hit, "Just Once in My Life." I love this song when it comes out. It speaks to me, and though I am not yet a teen, I'm close. Girls are starting to enter my radar field. I'm thinking for the first time about kissing a girl and having a girlfriend.

"Just Once in My Life" says it all for a Catholic schoolboy soon to enter high school, especially one born on the wrong side of the tracks (that being the Collinwood Railroad tracks). Like the song, I don't foresee a rags to riches story in my future, but "just once in my life" I've got to have the girl of my dreams even if all else fails! It is amazing how love can make fools of even the strongest of men. The tale of *Samson and Delilah* immediately comes to mind.

In my world, though I'm no Samson, I'm wondering how someone like me could ever score points with the likes of Marrieta Massiello, Linda Fatica, Georgia Slava, and Rita Shea—the hottest babes in my eighth grade class, all of whom come from proper backgrounds and have already begun to evidence the wonders of estrogen.

The second relates to football. In football this year, it's all about Joe Namath—later dubbed "Broadway Joe"—the record-breaking quarterback who will take the Alabama Crimson Tide to the NCAA championship under Coach Paul "Bear" Bryant. This year, a total of twelve lettermen from Alabama will be drafted into the NFL.

As for Joe himself, at the end of the year, he will sign to the New York Jets for a whopping $427,000 per year, which is $421,500 more than the $5,500 per year paid generously to Don Shula in 1952, the year I was born. In other words, it appears that superstar quarterbacks like Joe now have the potential to receive 77 times more in compensation than their brethren received a mere 13 years earlier. Talk about an oil gusher. Talk about a gold rush. Talk about a dream for a poor kid with a strong throwing arm.

All of a sudden, the potential lure of the streets—a life of exciting crime, hot cars, hotter women, and unlimited riches at a price— pales in comparison to my dreams of becoming a sports superstar. Though I've never seen it put this way before, guys like Joe Namath, by virtue of their hero status, might have done more to quash the false hope of a life in crime than any other single factor in America. If the possibility of becoming the next Joe Namath (or now, Stephen

Curry in basketball or Helen Maroulis in wrestling) couldn't provide an incentive for a young kid growing up in poverty or on its margins to strive to become a pro football player, I don't know what would. The dream of big money, fame, fortune, and respect is now available on the right side of the law.

The third relates to baseball. As I've said, Dad is a diehard Cleveland Indians fan. In 1964, Indians legend Rocco Domenico "Rocky" Colavito, Jr., returns in time to play the entire 1965 season. He is Italian, so it's not surprising that all of the Italians in the neighborhood love him. That year (as well as 1966), he makes the All-Star team, places fifth in the MVP vote after leading the league with 108 RBIs and 93 walks, and finishes among the American League's top five in home runs, hits, and runs scored. He also becomes the first outfielder in American League history to complete a season with a perfect 1.000 fielding percentage.

"Not one error the entire season!" Dad exclaims. "He hustles onto the field, he's ready for every play, and he keeps his eye on the ball. Always remember that," he tells me and my brother, as if delivering words from the Mount. And to this day, I do just that. While the world of sports instills discipline, team work, and values, it also teaches the virtue of hustle. Even to this day, when I enter onto a field, I don't walk; I trot or run out onto the field.

For me, what that boils down to is this: When I head onto our neighborhood streets each day—whether I'm riding my bike, hanging out at the high school, or playing ball in the park—who do I want to be like: Danny Greene or John Scalish, on the one hand, or the Righteous Brothers, Mickey Mantle, Roger Maris, Whitey Ford, Rocky Colavito, Roger Staubach, or Joe Namath, on the other hand? In the nitty gritty of reality, that's the kind of choice facing millions of young men every day in the rough and tough streets of America. And faced with that choice, the decision is usually obvious.

At the same time that football players are making more money than ever before, the government is giving away more money than ever before. President Johnson's War on Poverty has now become a mere cog of his Great Society. Expanding like a balloon being filled with helium at the state fair, the Great Society programs now offer low interest student loans and financial assistance for the needy; Medicare and Medicaid (health insurance) for the elderly, poor, and disabled; and a host of welfare and assistance programs costing Americans more money and giving away more benefits than any time since President Roosevelt's New Deal.

My family, with two working parents and three children in private Catholic school, are certainly in need. This is especially so when you consider that my brother and I easily consume—as around-the-clock athletes and eating machines—between 7,700 and 10,000 calories of food every day. But for our parents, the very thought of applying for welfare or assistance is anathema to their core American values. Not to beat a drum, just to tell it like it is in the Polke family growing up in Collinwood.

Adding to the new financial burden of the Great Society, President Johnson has become a virtual hawk on the Vietnam War. Empowered by Congress to act, he dramatically escalates America's commitment in terms of manpower and resources, and he's soon to institute a mandatory draft that will put thousands more soldiers in harm's way in the Vietnamese jungles. Before the year is over, the 175,000 soldiers mentioned earlier arrive at the battlefront, making it the third largest deployment of American ground troops in history...all with very little support or opposition from the average, oblivious American.

All the while, and notwithstanding the new Civil Rights Act and the passage of 100 years since General Robert E. Lee surrendered to General Ulysses S. Grant at the Appomattox Court House, our country is buckling asunder from an explosion in racial tensions. As 1965 gets under way, 18 Southern whites—reputedly connected to the Ku Klux Klan—are arrested in Mississippi for the murder of those three civil rights workers. That summer, state troopers break up a march of 600 civil rights demonstrators in Selma, Alabama. In response and in outrage, the black community of nearby Marion marches to protest the earlier killing by a trooper of one of the demonstrators.

The response of whites in Selma reaches the White House, prompting President Johnson to dispatch 4,000 National Guardsmen to protect the mostly-black marchers. Unlike only two decades earlier when World War II ended, the television networks splash everything across our screens on a daily basis—if it's not the violence of war on the Vietnam battlefields, it's the violence of civil rights marches in America's streets. Only days later, Reverend King, sensing an opportunity, leads another 3,000 civil rights demonstrators on the 50-mile march from Selma to Montgomery, the state's capital. He follows this by leading another 25,000 protestors to the capital to protest the denial of voting rights to blacks, notwithstanding the abolition of poll taxes by the recently-ratified Twenty-Fourth Amendment. The battle for civil rights is mushrooming into a national storm of epic proportions.

Before the year is over, the arrest of a black motorist for drunk-driving in the Watts District of Los Angeles, coupled with a minor roadside argument that escalates into a fight, will lead to one of the biggest race riots in American history. Six days of looting and arson, especially of white-owned businesses, follows. To contain the violence, the Los Angeles Police Department enlists the aid of 4,000 California Army National Guard members. Ultimately, 34 will die, 857 will suffer injury, over 2,200 will be arrested, and over $200 million in property damage will be inflicted and suffered. Initially, unemployment is fingered as the cause, but a later investigation points to police racism and police brutality—hot button issues to this very day.

On the international front, the Cold War is far from thawing; to the contrary, it's downright frigid, bordering on below freezing. In March, the U.S. performs a nuclear test at an unidentified Nevada test site. In response, the Soviet Union performs its own nuclear test in Eastern Kazakhstan. The arms race thus takes on a new, potentially apocalyptic agenda: for the first time in its history, the two most powerful countries in the world are battling for dominance in the creation of bombs that, if fully unleashed, would decimate the planet and potentially exterminate the human race.

But that's not all. Just when you thought it was safe to go out at night, organized crime rears its ugly head. Mafia crime boss Edward "Teddy" Deegan is found dead in an alley in Chelsea, Massachusetts. A week later, the FBI fingers six men, including Vincent J. Flemmi and Joseph "The Animal" Barboza as Deegan's killers. Barboza becomes a star witness in the ensuing trial, breaking the silence of *omerta* but, it turns out, provides false testimony to convict four innocent men so as to save his own skin. In retaliation, the New England Mafia hits Barboza in San Francisco. And in the course of the next three decades, over 20 FBI informants in Boston will be murdered because of it.

The widespread killing that defines 1965, however, is not over. On December 11, a white motel manager in Los Angeles shoots and kills legendary R&B singer Sam Cooke after a prostitute steals his clothes and money. Cooke's chart-topping hits included, "You Send Me," "Cupid," "Chain Gang," and, of course, "A Change is Gonna Come," the theme song performed in duet by rocker Jon Bon Jovi and Bettye LaVette at President Barack Obama's first inaugural. I love all of these songs, being much more an R&B man than a fan of the electric rock and roll music that will sweep the Western world in the '60s and '70s.

Also that year, the Supreme Court in the case of *Griswold vs. Con-*

necticut invalidates Connecticut's legal prohibition on the use of contraceptives. The court says the state cannot regulate a married couple's use of birth control. Sexual promiscuity is thus a hop, skip, and a jump away, a phenomena that helps to define the 1960s. Of course, even in the '60s, to a 13 year old boy, any mention or discussion of sex is *verboten*. (By the time I reach college in 1970, I must admit that this development will have its rewards. Indeed, in 1972, the ground-breaking book, *The Joy of Sex*, will be published, the first ever frank discussion of sex where sex is put in a positive light, with a certain "loosening up" soon evident on college campuses.)

My own neighborhood of Collinwood is by no means immune from the aforesaid national conflagration, though the worst is still a year away. According to an article in the *Cleveland Plain Dealer*, "with the passage of each year, the western fringes of the Collinwood area [are] being occupied by the Negro overflow from Glenville." This change in demographics, coupled with the caustic atmosphere of civil rights demonstrations, causes racial tensions to intensify in Collinwood, particularly at nearby Collinwood High School.

Why the escalation in racial tension? Certainly much of it can be traced to forced busing. For the first time, blacks and whites are forced to attend school together. Typically, black children are bused from poor neighborhoods without adequate education to wealthier white neighborhoods whose residents do not want them and are, frankly, opposed to the busing due to fear and/or racist beliefs harbored for generations. The consequent mix becomes volatile and destabilizing in many neighborhoods such as ours. Being told what to do by an elite group of politicians and policymakers in Washington does not go over well in hard-knocks places like Collinwood.

Collinwood High School is located smack dab in the middle of Little Italy, and the Italians don't want the blacks moving into or even entering *their* neighborhood. Many, if not most, of the Italians in our community are—there is no other way to put it—died-in-the-wool racists. And those who aren't racists are concerned that Negroes moving into the neighborhood will lower their property values. As much as most wish no harm to come to any particular black person, even non-racist residents are terrified of having to move so as not to lose the hard-earned equity in their homes. For many, their home equity represents their life savings, without which they will not have enough to survive on retirement.

Given the volatility of the times, this is juncture in *the rest of the story* where I'd like to offer another one of my humble opinions. Many liberals look back on the '60s as good times, hippies grinning ear-to-ear with flowers in their hair, peace signs spray-painted on their Vee-Wee vans, new civil rights laws flying out of Washington like hunter's buckshot from a 22 gauge, a romantic time of acid-dropping and expanded conscience, Timothy Leary, and all that rock 'n' roll jazz.

But for most Americans—for most middle Americans like our family—the times are utterly tragic. Young kids from the cities, not old enough to vote (the Twenty-Sixth Amendment recognizing the right of all 18-year-olds to vote has not yet been proposed), are dying left and right in a war not calculated to be won. Racism is rampant, putting the nation on fire. And in neighborhoods like ours, the war zone and racism will soon spilleth over. Sadly, that's the real truth.

EXERCISE:

It is impossible to imagine a life without music. What music gets you through the day, enabling you to overcome the daily challenges of life and ultimately conquer your adversities?

_____

_____

_____

_____

_____

When the world around you seems to be going up in flames, what do you do to keep your mind on life's positive things?

_____

_____

_____

_____

_____

Attitude is everything. How can you use music and other sources of inspiration to achieve your dreams?

_____

_____

_____

_____

_____

Chapter 18

HIGH SCHOOL, TANKS & FOOTBALL

"When I went to high school, an all-boys' school, a Catholic
school, I tried out for football, and I didn't make it. It was the
first time, athletically, that I was knocked down."

— Mike Krzyzewski, Head Basketball Coach, Duke University

For me, 1966 is a watershed year. It's my first year in high school,
my first year playing organized football, and the first time I ever see
with my own two eyes a military tank churning down a neighborhood
street—mine.

I'm 14 years old that memorable summer—memorable because the
violence exploding within our community is constantly being covered
in all the media—newspapers, radio, and television—for all to hear
and see. It is also a running subject of discussion between Mom and
Dad.

Though my parents are not racists, they are concerned about the
violence reaching our community, and like others on our block, the
impact on their property value should whites start exiting Collinwood

in large numbers. My parents are good people, but they feel they must be honest about the realities of the times. To this day, I wonder how I would have felt if I had been walking in their shoes. Would I have moved or stayed?

The proverbial "you know what" finally hits the fan on July 18, 1966, when a sign reading, "No Water For Niggers," is posted outside the Seventy-Niners' Bar at East 49 and Hough Streets, which is the heart of Collinwood's Old Hough neighborhood. A mere seven miles south-west of Collinwood High School, Old Hough runs ten miles from my house. In those days, it's a regular bike ride for me and my buddies.

To complicate matters, the bar manager at Seventy-Niners and a hired hand, both white, patrol the front of the bar with shotguns to back up the mandate of the sign and show they mean business. Hough's population of 90,000, however, consists of 78,000 African-Americans, an overwhelming majority. All live in the area stretching from East 55th to East 105th Streets, bordered on the north by Superior Avenue and the south by Euclid Avenue. In a matter of minutes, a crowd of over 300 African American adults, teens, and children gather at the crossroads.

The Cleveland Police Department (consisting of mostly white offi-cers) arrives in force to diffuse the boiling tensions. But rather than help, their presence only makes things worse. The crowd reacts with anger to the aggressive police presence. Rocks and bottles start to fly. Someone fires a shot or lights a firecracker or yells an epitaph, and the police react by shooting overhead into the sky to disperse the angry gathering. This tactic only serves to backfire, setting off a wave of fire-bombings and arsons that spread west to 71st Street and as far east to 93rd Street.

When firefighters arrive to douse the flames, snipers from the neigh-borhood scare them off. Sporadic shooting from the windows of nearby apartments and houses causes most of the first responders to retreat to protect their lives. As a result, the uncontrolled fire inflicts heavy damage and losses to nearby property, both public and private. Police redouble their determination to secure the area, busting into homes and apartments in what residents describe as Gestapo-style search and seizure tactics.

On the streets, police deliberately shoot out streetlights to create a blanket of darkness that provides them some modicum of cover and enables them to respond in kind to the snipers. In the melee, a young mother of three is shot dead when she yells out her window, merely fearing for the safety of her children. The neighborhood resembles a war zone.

Though Dennis, Cheryl, and I normally walk to school, Dad loads us into the car early each day and takes us all the way into Euclid before dropping us off. For six straight nights, the violence and upheaval continue. Mom requires us to play in the front yard or near the house; she bans us from going to the park without parental supervision, and even then, urges against it. On Tuesday night, the arsons increase. Looting, which began the night before, spins out of control. Vandals strike businesses along Hough, Wade Park, and Lexington Avenues. Finally, Cleveland Mayor Ralph Locher calls in the National Guard, initially dispatching 1,000 guardsmen to the Hough area alone.

Killings, gunfire, lootings, police clashes, and fires continue all week. On Tuesday, July 19, a sniper shoots 36-year-old Percy Giles in the back of the head. Early Friday morning, July 22, a 54-year-old Sam Winchester is fatally wounded, bringing the death toll to three. The same day, 24-year-old Benoris Toney becomes the fourth to die. Others are wounded but do not lose their lives, and now the disturbances and arsons have spread south as far as Kinsman Road and north as far as Saint Clair Avenue. In the nearby Murray Hill area, which borders our neighborhood, armed white vigilante groups have been formed and now roam the streets unchecked. Rumors of black marauders invading the neighborhood begin to spread, prompting the FBI to be on the lookout for outside agitators.

When the dust finally settles, four lives (all black) have been lost, hundreds of individuals (black and white) have been injured, some critically, and police have made 275 arrests. Literally blocks and blocks of homes, apartments, and businesses along the same route of Hough, Wade Park, and Lexington Avenues have fallen into ruins—the target of over 240 fires—as if pounded by munitions dropped by war planes. Thousands of residents are displaced, their homes uninhabitable. Because utility workers are banned from the area during the week, tens of thousands of homes and businesses go without power or phone service. Weeks pass before everything is restored, a death blow to many businesses in the neighborhood that lack insurance coverage for this kind of risk.

Though "the Hough uprising," as it is called, eventually starts to wind down and go into recovery, the battle continues. Racial tension spreads to nearby communities, including the Murray Hill-Mayfield Road area, then much of "Little Italy" and South Collinwood where we live. Expecting the worst, Collinwood residents arm themselves and form patrols. Dennis and I watch them from our bicycles. We see armed patrols everywhere on our way to and from school since Dad has stopped taking us all the way. A rumor starts to circulate that a sniper is shooting people from someone's roof right outside the neighborhood. When two kids accidentally hurt themselves with a shotgun, it's not reported as the accident that it is; instead, it's reported as "two white boys shot by Negroes," though clearly no Negro was involved.

The next thing we know, military-style tanks are rolling into South Collinwood, grinding up and down our normally quiet neighborhood streets. The curfew is reinstated, keeping our whole family in the house at night; but during the day, my friends and I are more curious than ever. We ride our bicycles all over the place to see the soldiers and the tanks, disobeying Mom's orders not to leave the block.

The premonitory point at Collinwood High School allows us to see everything—the hordes of National Guard troops dressed in camouflage uniforms, the green and black camouflage-colored Army flatbed trucks half covered by green canvas tops, and, of course, the dark green tanks grinding up and down the streets. It's the closest in my life I've ever come to a war zone, reminding me of TV shows like *Combat*.

Heavy rains on July 24 help douse the violence, though the rain does nothing to end the animosity between residents, blacks, and police. While Dad normally helps me with the Sunday paper because it is so large, he now makes an effort to help me during the week as well, no doubt concerned for my safety. I remember him commenting, "The Police Chief says the Hough area gangs are building bombs. What is the country coming to?"

As shocking as all this seems to our small neighborhood, the truth is that Collinwood is merely a microcosm of the nation. Everywhere across the country, cities are on fire, marches and protests are begetting bloodshed, and racism is locked with cries for equality in a fight for life or death.

~ ~ ~

Talk about an atmosphere in which to start high school, huh?

As if things are not bad enough in our neighborhood, I remember the first day I walk onto our football field as a freshman. Here I am, a young guy with a heck of an arm by all accounts, but I've never played organized football, never been on a team, never learned a playbook, and never played in an official game with a game clock, penalties, first downs, and referees.

First and foremost, this means that no one knows who I am. Everyone else—except for a few others like me—have been playing organized ball for many years in one of the many nearby grade schools or youth leagues. Always wanting to see who's coming up in the ranks, the St. Joseph coaches have been watching and scouting the leagues for years, sorting out likely starters and positions. By freshman year, the coaches have long since honed in on their favorites. Needless to say, that gives all these players a huge edge over a virgin player like me.

I do have something that most freshman quarterbacks do not have. I have an arm—a big arm. Despite never having played organized ball, I can whip the football in a perfect spiral fifty-plus yards down the field on one knee—virtually unheard of for a freshman. Through unrelenting practice, and due to some good athletic Polke genes, I have mastered the technique of throwing the football from my ear à la Joe Namath (known for his quick release) in a snapping and curling motion. But that is far from enough.

Lacking the needed experience to be a quarterback, I'm relegated to the position of punter. In addition to a good arm, I guess I have a good leg and foot. On more than one occasion, I get the offense out of a tough jam with my long, well-directed punts. But I am only a freshman, and freshman punters can only deliver so much.

Eventually, a host of factors conspire against me. A few weeks before winter officially sets in, we're leading 6-0 against the very tough Chanel Cardinals (a crosstown, arch-rival Catholic school). The field is a mud bowl; it is raining cats and dogs; and the freezing Lake Erie winds are howling at gale force. Taking the ball from center, Mike Campelletti, our starting quarterback, moves right and hands off to Bill Centa, who cuts hard right and slides into a pile of muddy defenders. Now it's fourth and six.

"Polke!" the coach yells. I slosh over and stand there, awaiting instructions. "Punt that ball as far as you can kick it. Get us out of this jam."

"Yes, sir," I say, and sprint onto the field, snapping my chin guard as I run. I call the play in the huddle and take my place ten yards behind the center. That puts me on my own 30 yard line. "Ready, set, red, forty-three, blue, hike!"

The ball wobbles back, a greased pig in howling wind and rain. I brace my cleats in two inches of mud, rain pelting my helmet and face in the torrential downpour, then wing my foot against the ball with all my might. As I do, my left foot slips out from under me, and when my right foot connects with the ball, I'm already cartwheeling backwards.

The ball rises into the air like a rocket blast, and for a second, it looks like it will be a whopper. Then the brutal, howling wind grabs it, suspends its forward motion, and hurls it backwards. The ball lands literally five yards behind me, and the other team takes over on our 20. Three plays later, they score, and we're darned lucky they miss the extra point, causing the game to end in a 6-6 tie.

It's the only game we don't win that year—indeed, it's the only game we don't win in all four years of high school. How's *that* for a freshman year.

CONQUERING YOUR ADVERSITIES

EXERCISE:

The world around you, even your own neighborhood, can be a crazy place. How do you take your mind off the negativity to focus on your daily tasks, in the pursuit of your dreams?

_____
_____
_____
_____
_____
_____

Sometimes circumstances conspire to make your wishes and dreams seem impossible. In those times, things can be done to persevere. List what things those might be.

_____
_____
_____
_____
_____
_____

What moments from your childhood embarrassed you to death that you laugh about today? Believe it or not, recalling these precious memories will help you conquer your adversities.

_____
_____
_____
_____
_____

Chapter 19

TET OFFENSIVE, PEANUT BUTTER & JELLY

"Crack the Sky, Shake the Earth"

— Message from National Liberation Front, ironically known as the NFL, to Viet Cong forces as they were "about to inaugurate the greatest battle in the history of our country."

By the fall of 1967, 90 percent of the evening news is devoted to the war, and roughly 50 million people are watching television news each night. Our family fits the mould. Until this time, the war has enjoyed strong support from the media, the public, and Congress. The military continuously reports that the U.S is making excellent progress and that the American people should be encouraged with our imminent victory.

Gradually, however, when victory is not imminent, support for the war begins to diminish. Because no military censorship is in place, journalists are free to follow the military into combat and report their observations unfiltered and as they see fit. Thus, as journalists are exposed to the horror of war, most for the first time, they present the public with shockingly graphic descriptions and imagery that seem to get worse over time, not better. Also, for the first time ever, soldiers interviewed in the battlefields and stateside begin to reveal serious reservations and angry frustrations with the true progress of the American war effort.

Media support for the war begins to deteriorate in the fall of 1967. But the major turning point, the point from which there will be no return, is the television coverage of the Tet Offensive. This phenomenon of war and media coverage diverging—of reality being one thing and media coverage another, perhaps a first in the annals of modern American history—profoundly impacts the American public.

On January 31, 1968, the day of the lunar new year known as Tet, the Tet Offensive unfolds across 100 towns and villages across South Vietnam. It is a surprise attack, not unlike the Japanese attack on Pearl Harbor, except it is by ground, not water. Seventy-thousand Communist North Vietnamese soldiers and Viet Cong forces spring a succession of synchronized offensives on the South Vietnamese that will change the war, and Americans' perception of it, forever.

South Vietnamese forces, finding support from President Johnson's previously-mentioned *boots on the ground*, somehow manage to repel the surprise attacks, killing in the process in excess of 40,000 Viet Cong. Far fewer South Vietnamese and American soldiers are killed. Thus, from a purely military perspective, America could have claimed a decisive victory. But it doesn't.

News coverage of the offensive presents the outcome in a diametrically opposite light. Television news portrays Tet as a resounding defeat for U.S. troops. This news fuels the burning perception at home that America is losing a war that is killing young Americans over what, the right to thump one's chest atop a cliff in the jungles of Vietnam?

General William C. Westmoreland, commander of the American forces, doesn't even claim victory despite clearly having the battlefield stats to do so. Instead, he blinks, comparing Tet to the *Battle of the Bulge*, Nazi Germany's last major drive in World War II, meekly asserting, "Advantage, but Defeat," because of the media's pervasive adverse coverage. But the most compelling words come from the "most trusted man in America," CBS news anchor Walter Cronkite, who earlier in my life had given us the "first transcontinental television broadcast...[of] the President of the United States, Harry S. Truman, addressing the welcoming ceremony of the Japanese peace conference...."

In a CBS special seen by millions of Americans, Cronkite observes: "To say that we are closer to victory today is to believe, in the face of the evidence, the optimists who have been wrong in the past. To say that we are mired in a bloody stalemate seems the only realistic, yet unsatisfactory conclusion."

After Tet and Cronkite's commentary, the news coverage of the war does a 180-degree flip. Before Tet, war journalists described 62 percent of their stories as victories for America, versus 28 percent defeats and 2 percent inconclusives. After Tet, it changes. Victories reported drop to 44 percent, and defeats rise to 32 percent, with a full 24 percent being inconclusive. The imagery portrayed also changes. Pictures and video footage became far more graphic, pushing the line of what ordinary Americans are willing to accept in their living rooms. Not to mention, the media reverses its perspective on soldier morale, now focusing on drug abuse, racial conflict, and disobedience within the ranks.

The dagger in the heart comes from the television news coverage of My Lai. Initial news coverage reports American soldiers have killed 100 enemy soldiers at My Lai, a hamlet near the DMZ in South Vietnam. Then the media reports that First Lt. William Calley and his men killed, in fact, not enemy soldiers, but 500 innocent South Vietnamese men, women, and children, many of whom were put in a ditch and shot point blank or blown up with hand grenades. Dubbed the *My Lai Massacre*, the killings result in the court-marshal and conviction of Lt. Calley for murder. Initially, he is sentenced to life in prison, although his sentence is reduced on appeal.

~ ~ ~

Despite Tet saturating the media on a global scale, and entering our home for months in what seems to be nonstop morning, evening, and night via television's daily news cycle, my focus as a junior in high school is playing football. My junior year, beginning in the fall of 1968, will be my first experience playing on the varsity squad. Our starting varsity quarterback is Jim Stevens, a senior, while I am third on the depth charts of quarterbacks.

Bob Bobrowski, a junior like myself, is the number two man. Although, technically, we are all three vying for a starting position, the team's style as a running team gives both Stevens and Bobrowski a decided advantage over the kid who never played an official game of football before his freshman year, and whose biggest weapon is his arm.

Head Coach Bill Gutbrod is a three-yards-and-cloud-of-dust style coach in the vein of legendary Coach Woody Hayes of the Ohio State Buckeyes. Coach Hayes preached a rock'em sock'em playbook, and Coach Gutbrod took every page from that playbook, relying mainly on a massive offensive line and big strong bodies to carry the ball. This is Bob Bobrowski and Jim Steven's *forte*, especially when Coach Gutbrod embraces the Veer offense. Put another way, passing is an afterthought, barely on the radar.

For those of you not familiar with the Veer formation, the College

Football Hall of Fame credits Bill Yeoman with its invention. It's a powerful and versatile offense that he first used when coaching the Houston Cougars back in the mid-1960s. The Veer's hallmark is the so-called "triple option." The "triple option" provides the offense with a three-running back attack option, whereby one player dives down the middle, one swings wide for a pitch, and one serves as lead blocker on the perimeter.

For me, the problem with the Veer is that it is primarily a running offense, while my skill lies in passing, which, in my opinion, is far superior. Look at what Staubach and Namath and all those guys did with the passing game. Consider it this way: If you have a piece of lumber you need to cut, why would you take a handsaw to cut the board when you can use a power saw? But that doesn't matter to Coach Gutbrod, and he certainly isn't listening to me. So naturally, as between me and Bobrowski, when it eventually comes to that, Bobrowski is the easy choice to run the offense.

Now, that said, obviously many high school coaches do not see eye-to-eye with Hayes and Gutbrod. In fact, many of our opponents rely more heavily on the passing game than the run game—passing games that our mighty defense must be prepared to address. As a solid passer with a bullet arm, now I've become the perfect candidate to play the role of scrimmage quarterback.

Scrimmage quarterback is the guy tasked with learning and executing our next opponent's offense against our starting defense. Needless to say, I get my bell rung and clock cleaned every day in practice. I am literally a whipping boy for our doomsday defense, which boasts some of the biggest and best defensive linemen and linebackers in all of high school football. Mincemeat comes to mind—me being the mincemeat at every practice.

But in many things, there is a silver lining. For me, that lining is survival, i.e., learning how to survive as a quarterback against a formidable defensive line. To survive, I must get off the ball with great speed, instantly read the defense, and then release the ball (whether by handoff, lateral, or pass) before being crushed into a bloody pulp.

To this day, I remember the visual image of getting pummelled so hard one day that my helmet flies off together with a mouthful of my teeth. Coach Gutbrod is standing a few feet away, watching and laughing, then screams at the top of his lungs: "Polke! Throw that ball…," which is when I roll over and fall out of bed. I wake up from my nightmare as I hit the floor and smash into the wall, realizing I'm at home and not on the field. But that is the emotional tipping point—the point in high school when I first come to grips with a huge reality: Given my situation, should I quit football, do something else, maybe take a job and make some money like all those Italians do, or tough it out?

Digging deep, thinking of my heroes, and having faith, I choose to tough it out. And it pays off. By sacrificing my body in these daily scrimmage games for an entire season, I learn how to read the defense while preparing our team for each and every opponent. Because few if any third string quarterbacks could ever execute as I did, our defense becomes the most prepared and feared defense in the conference. And when the season is over, we go undefeated yet again, proving my value and contribution to the team's success.

Notwithstanding my quiet, brutal contribution, at the annual varsity football team banquet in December I'm not expecting any kind of special recognition for all my sacrifice. A third string scrimmage quarterback does not warrant that. But I'm certainly not expecting what is about to come, either. Never before have I been so humiliated in front of such a large crowd. If I had entertained doubts about toughing it out before, now I want to cover my face, walk out of the room, and turn in my helmet tomorrow. Here's how it plays out.

TET OFFENSIVE, PEANUT BUTTER & JELLY

Having gone 12-0, all wins and no losses, our St. Joseph Vikings squad has a lot to celebrate at this year's annual team banquet. In that spirit, Coach Gutbrod and his staff go to great lengths to procure individual trophies for each and every man on the team. I remember sitting there in the large auditorium filled with revelling players, parents, and guests, proud to be a member of one of the top high school football teams in Northern Ohio, if not the country, patiently waiting for my name to be called and my little trophy to be handed to me.

Coach Gutbrod commences with the starting line-up for the offense, defense, and special teams. He hands each and every player a solid silver trophy with a proud inscription of one kind or another etched on the front, the inscription suited to that person's individual skills and contribution. Each time the audience stands and claps; it's a proud and joyous occasion. Oddly, my name is the last one called. I jump up from my chair and hustle to the stage, chest puffed out and as honored as I could be to be part of this team.

Then the unthinkable happens. Rather than a trophy, I'm given a glass jar of peanut butter and jelly, the kind with the swirls. The coaches, players, and audience roar with laughter. I don't even smile. I'm stunned. By the look on my face, you might think I've been shot between the eyes with the bullet of an AK-47. I didn't get the joke then, and I still don't get the joke. What peanut butter and jelly had to do with me or my contribution to the team that season was and is beyond me. To this day, you wouldn't want to hear the words that I wanted to speak.

Going into the holidays, the humiliation I experienced takes me to a new low. It depresses me for weeks, well into the new year. I mope around and feel as bummed out as a teenager can feel, even reluctant to show my face at school and face potential ridicule. For the first time in any sport I've ever played, I really feel like quitting; that's the direction toward which I'm leaning. *Maybe it's time to get a sum-*

mer job, I think, *rather than attend summer practice. Though Dad lets me use his car, I could really use a car of my own.* In fact, for the first time in my life, I feel like quitting sports altogether. *Why waste my time on this nonsense?*

Fortunately for me, the season is over. I don't have to get pummelled every day, and I don't have to make a hasty decision. The team will not officially get together again until late in summer, and informally, not until June. In the meantime, I must make a decision. What I will do—quit or carry on and conquer my adversities?

EXERCISE:

Recall all the times in your life when you had the choice of quitting or toughing it out, and list them here.

_____

_____

_____

_____

When and if you quit on any of these occasions, consider whether it was the right or wrong decision and why.

_____

_____

_____

_____

When and if you toughed it out on any of these occasion, consider whether it was the right or wrong decision and why.

_____

_____

_____

_____

How can you use any of the tools you used to make the right decision—whether quitting (and doing something else) or toughing it out—to achieve your goals and dreams today?

_____

_____

_____

_____

Chapter 20

"BROTHER, CAN YOU SPARE A DIME?" & THE 1968 DEMOCRATIC CONVENTION

"There's a lot of things wrong with this country, but one of the few things still right with it is that a man can steer clear of the organized bullshit if he really wants to. It's a goddamned luxury, and if I were you, I'd take advantage of it while you can."

— Hunter S. Thompson, *Fear and Loathing in America: The Brutal Odyssey of an Outlaw Journalist, 1968-1976*

In 1968, I'm 16 and about to get my driver's license. My brother is 15, and Cheryl is 13, so we're all in high school. Dad's in his late thirties, as is Mom. For the three of us in high school, looking good, despite having to wear a Catholic uniform, is everything.

We boys have girls to impress, and Cheryl has boys to impress. Some things in high school never change. But remember, we have five people living in a tiny house and sharing one bathroom. If that visual still doesn't make you laugh…it's only because you haven't thought it through.

Every night, as girls do, Mom and Cheryl hog the bathroom—taking long baths, washing their hair, rolling on curlers, applying face masks, looking at themselves in the mirror, doing what women do and taking all night to do it. It's so bad, sometimes we "men" have to go into the backyard to relieve ourselves.

What that means for the typical weekday morning is that that same bathroom is chaos. In a single hour, all three Polke guys are scrambling to shit, shower, and shave, like thirty clowns in a circus; get dressed for school or work; eat breakfast; and get out of the house by 7:00 a.m. Need I say more.

~ ~ ~

On March 31, 1968, the man who brought us the Great Society—President Lyndon Johnson—announces that he will not seek re-election. With popularity for the war plummeting, his favorability rating with the American people drops to an all-time low, somewhere in the 30 percent basement range. The announcement jolts the anti-war factions, for they have planned to use his dismal war record as a rallying point. Already, many anti-war activists have thrown their support to men like Senator Robert Kennedy, Senator Eugene McCarthy, and Senator George McGovern, all of whom oppose the war.

By early April, however, Johnson's Vice President, Hubert Humphrey, gives indications he will officially enter the race. This reinvigorates the anti-war crowd and keeps the planned demonstrations on track. Couple this with other events preceding the 1968 Democratic convention and you have another powder keg ready to ignite.

That ignition occurs on April 4, with the assassination of Reverend Martin Luther King, Jr., who will later be compared to India's Mahatma Gandhi and South Africa's Nelson Mandela. Riots break out across the country. All the gains made for civil rights in Johnson's Great Society seem to vanish overnight, with the single shot of the assassin's bullet. To many, it's John Kennedy all over again.

"BROTHER, CAN YOU SPARE A DIME?"

In Chicago—the city chosen for the Democratic Convention later in the year—things are so bad that Chicago Mayor Richard Daley gives a "shoot to kill" instruction to police trying to control the angry demonstrations welling up in the streets. On June 3, two months later, artist and cultural icon Andy Warhol is shot. Two days later, Senator and presidential candidate Robert Kennedy, priming to carry forth his brother's liberal agenda and return a Catholic to the White House, is assassinated after winning the California primary. Countless protests against the Vietnam War fill the streets and campuses of America. Freedom is not ringing; it is buckling asunder from the weight of death, protests, rioting, and violence.

How soon we forget.

Efforts to move the Democratic Convention away from Chicago fail. Mayor Daley promises America and the Democratic Party operatives that he will enforce the peace and permit no outrageous demonstrations. He also asserts the power and influence of the great Daly political machine, threatening to withdraw his support for Humphrey, the likely nominee in the wake of Kennedy's death, should the convention be moved. And Humphrey needs his support more than ever, as he is seen by many as Lyndon Johnson's man.

Mayor Daley, who had previously stood behind Kennedy, caucuses with his state's delegates the weekend leading into the convention and convinces them to stay "uncommitted." Eventually, delegations from 15 states try to unseat Humphrey's delegates and seat anti-Vietnam delegates instead. Humphrey's forces prevail. Politicians behind the scenes maneuver to launch Bobby Kennedy's surviving brother, Ted Kennedy, into the race, but he declines. He has issues of his own. In the end, Humphrey wins with a romp, leading by more than 1,000 votes.

Mortified by Humphrey's nomination, over a period of five days hundreds of anti-war protestors marching and milling outside the Convention Hall lock horns with nearly 12,000 heavily-armed Chicago policemen, 7,500

U.S. Army troops, 7,500 Illinois National Guardsmen, and 1,000 Secret Service agents. Battlefields in war often involve fewer combatants.

The violence begins on Sunday, August 25, when the city refuses permits to the protestors who want to sleep in Lincoln Park right outside the convention hall. When protesters won't leave the park, the Chicago police assault them with canisters of tear gas. Smoke filling the air, the police then beat the disoriented and recalcitrant protestors with billy clubs in an effort to run them out. The images of bloodied protestors and news reporters enter the homes of millions of Americans via their televisions, again bringing the nation to the edge.

Immediately, the police are perceived as the enemy, engendering countless clashes, including the so-called "Battle of Michigan Avenue," at which the police engage tactics so violent that many innocent bystanders, reporters, and doctors offering medical help are swept up in the melee and beaten to within an inch of their lives.

When the convention is finally over, and the smoke dissipates, Chicago reports 589 arrests with 119 police and 100 protesters claiming injuries, though the numbers could be higher. A study commissioned to determine the cause of the violence will place most of the blame on an abusive Chicago police force, and the next year, a Chicago grand jury will indict eight police officers and eight civilians for crimes committed in relation to the protests.

Ironically, eight private citizens, dubbed the "Chicago Eight," will be the first individuals in history charged for violation of the criminal provisions of the 1968 Civil Rights Act, which made it a federal crime to cross state lines to incite a riot. In the November 1968 Presidential elections, Humphrey loses. Americans instead elect Republican Richard Nixon, who is sworn into office in January 1969.

~ ~ ~

"BROTHER, CAN YOU SPARE A DIME?"

Meanwhile, as we move into 1968, I'm twisting in the wind, wondering whether after the humiliating banquet experience, I should continue to play football or not. If I continue to play, I will continue to get my tail kicked in every practice scrimmage and may well be humiliated at the year-end banquet; but I will save face. If I quit, I may be humiliated even more every day I go to school, which will also impact my brother and sister. Being a quitter will certainly expose me to ridicule by teammates and friends. As a proud young man, I'm not sure I can live with that. The proverbial horns of a dilemma block my path.

But the more I think about it, the more I realize that getting a football scholarship is my only real chance of attending a four year college. My parents simply do not have the money to put me through school, and no one has any confidence in or understanding of the educational loans that might grow out of Johnson's Great Society initiative. Plus, despite the fact that I do not start, St. Joseph's has Coach Gutbrod, who runs one of the best high school football programs in the state, if not the country. And Gutbrod has a reputation for getting scholarships for starters and non-starters alike. So, I have a fighting chance, I think, although it seems to be a long shot.

I power my way through the second semester of my junior year with my life in balance. Sometimes I can't tell whether my tension is spilling over to the household, or whether the tension of the household is spilling over to me. One Friday evening, I come home late from school. When I enter the house, Mom is assembling the card table in the living room. Every Friday night, she plays contract bridge or pinochle with her sisters and/or her brothers and their wives well into the wee hours of the night. The moment I walk through the door, she barks at me: "Ken, where have you been?"

"I...I...I'm sorry, Mom. We had game films today, later than usual."

"Well, I needed some help around here. Your sister is sick and your father is playing softball. I can't do everything by myself, you know."

"I said I'm sorry. I forgot to tell you this morning."

"They do have something called the telephone, you know."

"I know. Next time I'll call if I'm going to be late."

"It just worries me, Kenny."

At this time, the door pushes open and Dad walks in with Dennis. "Grabbed him at the park," Dad says.

"What's for dinner?" Dennis asks, food always the first thing on his mind as he's sprouting toward his 6' 7" frame.

Mom puts her hands on her hips, her hair tussled with an "I've-had-enough" look on her face. "Men, please come into the living room and sit down."

We do, albeit with trepidation.

"I need some help around here," she states. "Cheryl is sick in her bedroom; she needs some medicine from the store. I'm trying to get to dinner, and I have my sisters coming over for cards tonight. Yet you three are nowhere to be found."

"You know I have softball every—" Dad stops mid-sentence. "Sorry, Lois. Boys, let's help your Mom, can we? Ken, you run to the store. Get her whatever she needs. Dennis, go with Ken or stay and help your Mom around here."

"I'll stay," says Dennis.

"Where's the keys, Dad?" I ask.

"Lois, giving it some thought, after Ken goes to the store for you, how about I take the boys out of the house. We'll grab dinner at Larry's and I'll keep them out of your hair for a while."

"Thank you, but how can we afford that?"

"I have a few extra dollars," Dad says as he fishes some loose bills and change from his pocket.

"Me, too, Mom," I say, grabbing for my wallet.

"Money does not grow on trees," she says.

"Of course not, honey," Dad says.

"I married you, Gene, to save you from your family," Mom says.

"What does that have to do with anything?" Dad says with an edge of anger.

Mom gives him a steely look.

"Boys, grab your things," he says. "I'll drive you to the store for Cheryl's medicine."

"It has to do with everything," she adds. "It has to do with family being here for each other."

Out the door we head, Dad slamming the door behind us.

~ ~ ~

As summer approaches, I overhear the seniors at school talking about receiving their draft cards and anticipating going off to war—an ever more unpopular war—upon graduation. Rumors abound of kids from the neighborhood getting killed and coming home in boxes, or having their limbs blown off, or suffering mental and emotional trauma. Apparently one kid even stuck a gun in his mouth and blew his brains out.

Later on, I remember learning about Joey Andrey, a kid who was on the St. Joseph track team. He was a popular kid who would play a main role running for our 1969 cross country team that would go on to win the Ohio

State Championships. After finishing the championship season, he gets drafted and sent to Vietnam, where he loses a leg. How tragic, a runner losing a leg, not to mention that Joe was one of the best guys around, a real stand-up individual, both on and off the track. And adding fuel to the fire, soldiers were no longer coming home heroes. A growing part of America wanted to place blame on guys like Joey for losing a bad war.

The logic escapes me as to why our brave soldiers risking life and limb for this country are being treated like common criminals upon returning home. Like many others, I am weary of this lingering war, but in the same vein, there is no need by citizens of this country to spit on those returning soldiers who have fought so bravely in the name of freedom and country…and many of them had no choice, as they were drafted. A line from the movie *A Few Good Men* comes to mind: "They stand on the wall and say, 'no one will hurt you. Not on my watch'." To disrespect our fighting soldiers is like having a bad day at the office and then coming home to kick the dog. How pathetic.

In summary, the '60s were a tumultuous time. We had war raging in the streets here in America between whites and blacks, and protestors and police, and we had the same occurring in the rice paddies of Vietnam between the Vietcong and our GIs. But as our football locker room banner stated, "Tough Times Breed Tough People," and so we must weather the storm.

And then there's the other reality, the one that's closer to home. If I quit football, don't go to college, and somehow avoid the war, what will I do? Do I follow the road taken by guys like Danny Greene—join the union, break some kneecaps, rise to power, and become a well-heeled gangster? Those guys sure live a good life on the surface—no hard work, lots of money, fine cars, power and, most importantly to me now in light of the peanut butter and jelly fiasco, respect. For once, I'm thinking, *I* would get respect. Nobody messes with the mob. Isn't that what Uncle Eddie and his brother did? Eddie even starred in movies, rubbed elbows with the stars, guys like Frank Sinatra and Dean Martin…and he got to live in Las Vegas, the entertainment capital of the world.

What will I do?

EXERCISE:

We all have crossroads in our lives, as teenagers, young adults, and older adults. Identify the crossroads you have faced, or are about to face, in your life.

_____
_____
_____

With respect to each of those crossroads, write out how you addressed the decision you ultimately made, what factors you considered, what seemed to matter, and what didn't.

_____
_____
_____

Now, examine the decisions you have made and ask yourself whether, in hindsight, you think you made the right decision or wrong decision and the lessons to be learned from each. Those lessons should help you today in overcoming any adversities you face.

_____
_____
_____

Chapter 21

TOUCHED BY AN ANGEL

"Hang in there. There may be hard times ahead. But you're gonna get through them, and He'll be with you all the way."

— Tess, CBS Television Series, *Touched by an Angel*

The summer is fast approaching, and I know I will soon have to decide whether to quit football altogether or continue playing on the team. Official practice cannot start until August under high school football rules, but beginning in June, anyone who wants to play on the team better be working out in shorts offsite every Tuesday and Thursday night. On those nights, we will do push-ups, sit-ups, jumping jacks, sprints, 220s, and the like. Technically, it is not mandatory, but for all intents and purposes, anyone who wants to make the team must attend.

With the school year coming to a close, and unofficial practice imminent, I wake up every day with a gnawing knot of indecision in my gut. Then one day, I find myself again kneeling in the pew of St. Paul's Church after Sunday Mass. A few candles and the recessed lights are lit, but otherwise, I'm alone. I shut my eyes, fold my hands in front of me, and again ask the Lord for divine guidance. *What should I do, God?* I ask myself, repeating it again and again. Though he does not speak directly to me through words in my head, I do feel a presence. *Have faith in the Lord, my son.*

A few days later, I'm doing homework at the kitchen table after school when the phone rings. "Hello," I say.

"Ken Polke, please," the deep male voice on the other ends says.

"This is Ken," I say, wondering who it is since I don't recognize the voice and immediately breaking into a nervous sweat and thinking, *Did I do something wrong?* Funny how living in Collinwood conditions the soul to immediately think, "What did I do wrong this time? Every time the phone rings! Much like Pavlov's ol' dog.

"Hi, Ken. This is Dick Modzelewski, Mike's uncle." Mike plays with me on the Vikings, same last name as Dick, and his uncle Dick is Assistant Coach for the NFL Cleveland Browns. "I was out at St. Joe's the other day and saw you and Mike practicing. Pretty impressive arm, I must say. You can sure whip that pigskin. I'd like to invite you both down to work out with Ryan and Warfield."

I cannot believe my ears. "Frank Ryan and Paul Warfield?" I say incredulously.

"Yes, come on down after school about 3:30 next week. Fleming Field."

Fleming Field is home to the Case Western Reserve University football team, and the field is shared offseason by both the Cleveland Browns and CWRU.

"You know where it is?"

"Yes. Yes, sir. I sure do."

"Great. That's where we practice. Just go into the locker room. They'll meet you there."

Apparently, Mike had told his dad, who played for the Browns in their heyday, that I was a crack quarterback with a great passing arm. His dad, in turn, had told his brother, Dick, who must have gotten my phone number from Mike, who was one of my favorite receivers during our brutal scrimmages.

I can barely speak, but I manage to thank him several more times before I hang up. And the moment I do, I know that the football angel has answered my prayers, and that my prayers are actually starting to pay off.

~ ~ ~

Little does Coach Modzelewski know, but I have studied Frank Ryan carefully. He is another of my heroes. When he played at R.L. Paschal High School in Fort Worth, Texas, Ryan was recruited by college coaches from across the country, including Alabama Crimson Tide Coach Bear Bryant, from Joe Namath's *alma mater*. He declined Alabama and Yale University and chose to major in physics at Rice University. The most important thing to him was the physics program. Ryan totally dispelled the "dumb jock" myth. After his NFL career was over, he went on to teach mathematics at his *alma mater*.

Given his desire to obtain his Ph.D., Ryan initially declined to play professional football even though the Rams chose him in the fifth round of the 1958 NFL draft. He only changed his mind because the Rams' coach allowed him to enroll at both UCLA and the University of California, Berkeley, in pursuit of the advanced degree he wanted. Ryan then transferred back to Rice, where he studied during the off-season.

Ryan spent the first four years of his NFL career primarily in a reserve capacity, making $12,000 per year. However, in 1961, he and future Hall of Famer Ollie Matson connected on a 96 yard touchdown pass, establishing a new team record. Then, as rumor has it, after sitting on the bench for the last four games of the 1961 season, Ryan stormed into the dressing room and threatened General Manager Elroy Hirsch with quitting football if he was not traded. His wild antics led to him being packaged into a multi-player deal with the Browns.

Acquired by the Browns to back up starting quarterback Jim Ninowski, Ryan moved into the starting slot in October of his first year when Ninowski broke his collarbone in the game against the Steelers. More than rising to the challenge, Ryan secured his leadership position and kept the starting slot for most of the next six seasons. In 1963, his first full season as a starter, Ryan threw for 2,026 yards and 25 touchdowns with only 13 interceptions, aiding the Browns to a 10–4 win-loss record. He tossed 13 of those touchdowns to Gary Collins, who ended up tying the league for first place in touchdowns received that year.

In 1964, Ryan established himself as one of the league's best passers. He tossed for 2,404 yards and repeated his 1963 performance by successfully completing 25 touchdown passes, sufficient to lead the league. Of course, he had one heck of an offense, with Jim Brown at fullback, Collins and Warfield as receivers, and Lou Groza and Gene Hickerson at offensive line, both of whom would become Hall of Famers.

Throughout the Browns' 10–3–1 season, Ryan was a huge contributor, especially in the final game against the New York Giants. They needed that one to clinch a spot in the NFL title game. Ryan took the game by storm, completing 12 of 13 passes for five touchdowns. He also ran for a sixth, making the final score 52–20 Browns. In the championship two weeks later against the Baltimore Colts, he tossed three TD passes to Collins, winning the title 27–0.

I'm following Ryan every week in the newspaper and asking Dad a zillion and one questions about everything from college to pro ball. While not a huge football fan, Dad does follow the Browns and redoubles his effort to keep up on the latest Ryan details and statistics so he can answer my questions.

After the Browns won the championship, Art Modell raised Ryan's salary to $25,000 per season, up from about $18,000 the prior year. Despite the raise, Ryan's numbers dropped in 1965, where he only threw for 1,751 yards with 18 touchdowns. After his shoulder healed, he hurt himself again. In training camp, he developed a sore elbow that was compounded by an arch injury in the regular season, all contributing to a lackluster passing year.

But Ryan was no quitter. In 1966, he came back with a fabulous season, and despite playing with enormous pain, led the league with 29 touchdown passes and came in second with 2,976 yards. I have several of his bubble gum cards from that time and am always looking for more. Ryan's output helps alleviate the absence of Jim Brown, who retired prior to the start of training camp to pursue his film career, thus crushing many of us Browns fans. Ryan's 29 touchdown passes in 14 games that year ranked second in Browns' franchise history, only less than Brian Sipe, who threw 30 in the Browns 16 game 1980 season.

So, yes, this is the man who a few weeks later will be giving me a technical clinic at Fleming Field on how to be a better quarterback. And when I say I am touched by an angel, I mean it. For I'm not just getting the opportunity to clinic with the amazing Frank Ryan. Mike and I also are also going to work with legendary wide receiver and future Hall of Famer, Paul Warfield.

~ ~ ~

When that angelic call comes in, as I've said, Paul Warfield—who, like Ryan, is only ten years older than me—is playing wide receiver for the Browns. He's known for his speed, fluid moves, grace, jumping ability, and hands. He's another one of the many great football players to hail from Ohio, having played in 1960 for the Warren G. Harding High School Panthers. For the Panthers, he played running back and defensive back, starting varsity as a sophomore in 1957. In 1958, he ran for 810 yards and scored 15 touchdowns. How amazing is that?

Warfield graduated from Ohio State University, where he was a two-time all Big 10 halfback in the 1962–1963 season, as well as a star track team sprinter, jumper, and hurdler. He started with the Browns as a wide receiver in 1964, but as the good Lord would have it, both he and Ryan would leave the Browns soon after they practiced with us. In 1970, Warfield would trade to the Miami Dolphins for a draft pick, which the Browns would use to acquire Purdue University All-American quarterback Mike Phipps.

Warfield will ultimately become a major factor in the Dolphins' championships in the early 1970s. And before he retires, he will make the Pro Bowl eight times, and be named All-League six times. An incredible receiver by any standard, and a receiver to whom any high school quarterback would love to throw the football.

When throwing the football to Paul Warfield that summer, it became apparent to me that there is something different about this man. A clearly defined aura of greatness cloaks our surreal time together, magical moments to a young high schooler that defy words. His beauty and grace while performing his athletic skills is so unparalleled as to be profound, in a religious sense. He is a mere mortal, but he is in a class by himself, so much so that his talent inspires me to take my God-given talents to the next level.

This experience becomes more than a "Kodak moment." With the power of prayer, this moment reverses my fortunes for the rest of my life.

~ ~ ~

The day finally comes, and I borrow my dad's car, the '64 Chevy Biscayne, to drive to Fleming Field to work out with Frank Ryan and Paul Warfield. I either pick Mike up on the way or he meets me there, but either way, we both arrive early and walk into the locker room— two high school juniors—having no idea what to expect. Though we are football players, in this place, we are fish out of water.

In these days, the NFL is not yet big business. Guys like Broadway Joe are a rarity. Teams, coaches, and players have a vastly different philosophy and outlook on the game. Salaries are still relatively low, requiring most players to take offseason jobs to make ends meet. Work precludes most of them from working out days during the summers except when their employment schedules permit. So we walk in, and somehow they spot us. Imagine that! "Ready to play, guys?" one of them asks. And we say, "You bet."

For the next two hours, Mike and I take the practice field with Frank Ryan and Paul Warfield. Since I'm the quarterback, Ryan at first works with me, and since Mike is a wide receiver, Warfield at first works with him. Ryan starts with the basics, showing me how to hold the ball, how to take the hike from center, how to spin and turn, the need for setting up quickly, how to use the correct footwork, how to read the defense then release quickly, and so forth. Ryan is 6' 4" and 220 pounds, but for a junior, I'm not far behind him at 6' 1' and 205 pounds. He acknowledges the power of my arm, instilling in me an enormous confidence.

After they each school us in our respective positions, we all come together. I throw to Warfield and Ryan throws to Mike. Just throwing to a guy with the speed of a Warfield is out of this world.

"Always throw to a spot," Ryan tells me. "Never throw to the man. If a receiver is open, it is already too late."

He tells me I must know where my receiver is going. "In our world," he says, "we often look away from the place we plan to throw the football to trick the cornerbacks. Those guys are so fast they will rob you blind with interceptions if you tip them off as to where you intend to throw the ball."

To our good fortune, that day a bunch of sportswriters are hanging around the locker room looking for a story. In the quiet of summer, all of them are digging for an angle. With us, they find it. A few days later, a big spread comes out in the *Plain Dealer*, telling the story of how a couple of high school juniors from St. Joseph High School showed up and practiced with two of the best pro ballplayers in the game.

Before we are through that summer, Mike and I have the honor of doing three or four practice sessions with Ryan and Warfield. To my total amazement, I later find out through the sports world grapevine that both Ryan and Warfield separately and without solicitation predicted to the Cleveland sports reporters that I will make it to the NFL.

"Ken's arm and natural passing talent," they apparently said, "will take him all the way."

Unbelievable. In fact, at the time so unbelievable I can't even make myself believe it, especially given my history. But these remarks, and the amazing grace of working with Ryan and Warfield, do more to salvage my sunken ego than anything the St. Joseph coaches could ever do by way of encouragement. My experience with these two great men becomes the go-to, self-help talk I give myself whenever times get tough. If moments like this ever occur in your life, stash them away for a rainy day. They will get you through the hardest of times.

Later, the thing I will be most proud of in my life is to become part of the great fraternity known as the NFL Alumni Association. Other than my wedding day, playing in the NFL will be my dream come true, the pinnacle of my life. Even becoming a doctor (a high point for many other individuals in their lives) will not mean as much to me, and will happen on what I consider to be a downward slope of my life. Seemingly sad but true—so much so, that immediately upon graduating from dental school, I will know I've made a big mistake.

However, I expect that slope to start going back up when I publish this book and Urban Myers calls me to help coach the quarterbacks at *the* Ohio State University. Urban? What's your address so I can send you a courtesy copy of the book? But again, I get ahead of myself.

~ ~ ~

The sessions with Ryan and Warfield teach Mike and me the mechanics of playing football the way it must be played. Nothing against Coach Gutbrod, but the truth is that this is the first time in my life as a player that anyone has ever shown me the correct techniques for doing the things I need to do as a quarterback. My advice to college and high school coaches alike is make sure you are learning the right techniques to take not only yourself but your players to the next level. Sometimes the coaches have the knowledge, but often they do not. Mastering the right techniques for athletically qualified players is the key to success. Coaches, please remember that.

Unfortunately, until I meet Coach Don Shula a few years later, I will not have that special coach for someone like myself blessed with a God-given talent to throw the football.

When the sessions are over, I have football fever. I also have a plan to get out of Collinwood and escape a life of hard knocks, financial struggle, the Mafia, crime, or all of the above. The reality is that the peanut butter and jelly humiliation created doubts in my mind, thereby leading me to prayer and to seeking guidance from God about what I should do. I could never have conceived that my prayer would be answered in such a profound way. For the first time, I fully realize that football will be my way out of Collinwood.

But what I do not foresee are the battles and tests still to come…and exactly how faith and football will once again come together to save my life.

EXERCISE:

Have you, or has anyone you know, ever been touched by a magical moment, as if touched by an angel? List any examples you can think of, whether big or small.

_____

_____

_____

_____

_____

Examine carefully the circumstances leading up to that magical moment, describing all the things you were doing and thinking that might have impacted that moment's occurrence.

_____

_____

_____

_____

_____

Think about what you can do today to embrace those things so you can enjoy another magical moment and achieve your goals, dreams, and happiness. Then write them down here. It may be as simple as never giving up, discipline, hard work, and prayer.

_____

_____

_____

_____

_____

Chapter 22
R&B MUSIC

"Once you're a Motown artist, you're always a Motown artist."

— Smokey Robinson

In the midst of all this craziness, I am dead set on developing my own singing group. This is my backup plan to make it out of Collinwood should football fail me. Not the Mafia, not the union, and not being a doctor or dentist. Yeah, baby, music.

I had always been a singer in the school choir, and both the Sisters and the Brothers frequently complimented me over the years on my strong singing voice. Unlike many of the white youth of the day who love rock 'n' roll, I'm not such a big fan. What I love is Frankie Valli & the Four Seasons, the Righteous Brothers, and Motown. Vocal groups like the Four Tops, the Temptations, and Smokey Robinson & the Miracles—these are the artists that catch my fancy and float my boat.

I listen to Dad's phonograph whenever I can. Dad often played his 33 rpm records on his big stereo console, the Vic Damones and such, but the moment he leaves the house, I snap on the little plastic adapter to allow 45 rpms to be played. If you happened to walk by our house when I was spinning, you might hear "December 1963," "Ask the Lonely," "You've Lost That Lovin' Feeling," "Baby I Need Your Lovin'," "My Girl," "Papa Was a Rolling Stone," "Get Ready," "Tears of a Clown," and "Ooo Baby" at any time of the day or night.

In fact, going back just for a moment to make my point, I'm so taken by becoming a professional singer that in the summer of 1968, with race riots and racial tension all around us, I convince my dad to run an ad in the *Plain Dealer* seeking a vocalist to join my acapella group. My vision at the time is to create a racially-mixed vocal group, giving it the unusual sound that I can hear playing out in my head. (Looking back after several decades, I realize I did not appreciate then how innovative that concept really was. I was definitely ahead of my time on this one.)

And if I might indulge in a small digression before telling the *Plain Dealer* story, I'd like to interject my humble opinion that Motown Records and professional sports did more to improve racial relations than any other thing this country ever tried, including voting for a black President.

I also credit my father for not espousing racial hatred in our home and allowing it to trickle down to our young, impressionable minds. Given the circumstances of the times, it would have been easy for both of my parents to have become bigots, but they didn't. Instead, what I learned from my father was a true love of sports and a true love of competition.

In that process, I sensed from him that anyone, whether black or white, or red or purple, who loved what he himself loved was not all bad. So, for a black man to play to the level of my dad's baseball skills and enthusiasm for the game, meant there was true value in that individual, regardless of color. That's a lesson for all of us. Is this not what Martin Luther King, Jr., proposed we all do—judge a man or woman by their character and not by their skin color? Martin Luther King, Jr., and his ideas will ultimately stand the test of time!

Back to the *Plain Dealer*. At the moment, the group only consists of me (the Bill Medley) and my buddy, Bobby Childs (the Frankie Valli). We need a third with an R&B voice like David Ruffin of Temptations fame. Given the racism in the neighborhood, however, this presents no small challenge. Ever creative, Dad takes the approach of advertising for a singer in the *Plain Dealer* without specifying our location or race, just that we're looking for an R&B singer. Within hours of the paper hitting the streets, the calls start pouring in. How we will proceed from here is now the question.

We know a black person cannot openly drive or walk into Collinwood at this sensitive juncture in time. It would be dangerous and someone would get hurt or killed. Not to mention, the neighbors would talk. So, Dad comes up with another plan. I will call the prospects and pick whoever I think best fits the bill. We will then drive together outside the neighborhood to pick the candidates up and drive them back to the house. When we enter the neighborhood, the prospect will duck under a blanket in the backseat until we get to the house. Then we will quickly slip him inside the house via the side door.

We do this a number of times, and get lucky with some really good prospects. But then football season kicks in and we put everything on hold until the season is over in December. What we don't plan on is the military draft. It starts officially on December 1, 1969, and all the guys we select get drafted—every single damn one of them. As a result, we never hear from any of them again.

Bobby, by the way, is reluctant from the start to bring black vocalists into the group for fear his buddies might find out and chastise him.

To be honest, I too have my doubts, but for different reasons than Bobby. My fear is that the black vocalists will reject us for being white. A piece of the Janis Joplin story if you will. But to our amazement, what Bobby and I learn is that, whether an individual is black, white, yellow, purple, or what have you, we all share the ideal of the American Dream. And for these young black men meeting with us, it is R&B music. Or, you could say, once R&B, never back.

But we aren't the only ones who learn a lesson. What the black guys learn from us is that two white boys in Collinwood can sing and dance and aren't looking to bring baseball bats to their heads. We can all get along and, more importantly, we must if America is going to be the land of opportunity for all.

EXERCISE:

It's always a sensitive subject, but this is your book and you can write and say what is on your mind. Describe any forms of prejudice and/or racism you have experienced or witnessed up close.

_____
_____
_____
_____
_____
_____

How did you deal with it, or observe it dealt with?

_____
_____
_____
_____
_____
_____

Inflicting or receiving prejudice can be debilitating. How can you embrace the power of equality and non-prejudice to conquer any adversities in your life?

_____
_____
_____
_____
_____
_____
_____

Chapter 23

1969: MY SENIOR YEAR & THE DREAM TEAM

"You're five-foot nothin', 100 and nothin', and you have nearly a speck of athletic ability. And you hung in there with the best college football team in the land for two years. And you're gonna walk outta here with a degree from the University of Notre Dame. In this life, you don't have to prove nothin' to nobody but yourself."

— Fortune, from the movie, *Rudy*

As the summer of 1969 lingers on, I find myself working harder and practicing more football than ever before, truly inspired by the lessons of Ryan and Warfield. Every day, I work on setting up quickly, getting my footwork right, and mastering my quick releases. I throw thousands of passes to Mike, Dennis, and my dad. When running patterns with Mike, I anticipate where he will be before he gets there. Timing, timing, timing. Pop, pop, pop.

Though the movie *Rocky* will not come out until 1976, when I see it for the first time with Rocky fighting against all odds but believing in himself, I practically break into tears. It reminds me of the summer of 1969, when I am a young man on a mission.

Given the amazing grace of my summer, and the subsequent news-paper article heralding our good fortune, you might be surprised to learn this: I still don't have a fighting chance of starting at quar-terback my senior year. Why? Because our current starting quar-terback, Bob Bobrowski, has never lost a game as a freshman or sophomore; because Bob held the second slot on the varsity team the year before behind Jim Stephens, on a team that didn't lose one game; and because Bob is a master at running our heralded Veer running offensive.

Why would Coach Gutbrod fix the team strategy when it is not bro-ken? Why would he reverse course and change from a dynamic op-tion offense that has delivered the team three undefeated seasons and many championships over the years, to a never tried and never proven passing offense led by a guy who has never started a game as quarterback in his life? It would mean changing the whole offense with no basis for doing so to advance the personal career of the kid jokingly known as Poke Salad. That's simply not going to happen.

~ ~ ~

Things are also not always hunky dory at home. In my senior year, my parents' situation is that they have three children in a private Catholic high school. Needless to say, public school is free; private school is not. It is very expensive to put three children through Cath-olic school at the same time. As a result, Mom and Dad argue about money. A lot.

One night in late October, Dad bursts into the house with a wide grin on his face, holding up a handful of tickets. Dennis and I are in the living room doing homework and shooting the bull. He slams the door behind him and looks over at us, wild-eyed. "Hey, boys, I got 'em," he says enthusiastically. "I got third base tickets to next week's Indians game."

Dennis and I look at each other and yell in unison, "Hell, yeah!"

Mom grabs a handful of papers from the kitchen table and walks over to Dad, gives him a pointed look, then shoves the papers in his face. "I don't know how much you spent on those tickets, but you better take a close look at these, Mr. Bookkeeper."

Dad studies the papers for a moment, then says, "What's the big deal?"

"Tuition for three is the big deal, Gene. Cheryl's in high school now. And here you are spending money on those, those, those, ball bat tickets."

Dad puts the tickets into his coat pocket, adjusts his hat, then looks at Mom. He says nothing, though it's obvious he's fuming.

She says, as if to poke him with a sharp stick, "Think about that the next time you spend our money on your dumb ball tickets."

"Shut up, Lois. Just leave me alone."

He pulls the door open, slams it shut, and leaves. We all listen as the car spins out of the driveway and backfires down the road.

"I'd be more than happy to quit school for a few years, Mom, to take the pressure off," Dennis says deadpan.

I put my hand to my mouth and feign a cough, fighting back a laugh, as it's obvious that Mom is in no mood for humor.

Mom looks at Dennis and me, then puts her hands to her face and starts bawling. I stand up, uncertain of what to do. "Why are you crying, Mom?" I ask.

She sobs for a moment, wiping her cheeks with her apron as the tears flow. I start to walk over to comfort her, but she puts up her hand to stop me.

"I'm okay, Kenny. I'll be fine."

"Why not just work it out?" Dennis says. "You know, you joist, he counter-joists, and in the end, you compromise."

"This is family, honey; it's not a sword match, game, whatever, and it's a simple matter of money we don't have. When it comes to money, there is no compromising."

~ ~ ~

Of course, our financial situation has serious, immediate ramifications for me. This being my senior year of high school means it's my last chance to get the attention of the college scouts and somehow attract a scholarship offer. Not an easy task, considering I haven't started *or* played in a single season football game since my freshman year when I punted the ball backwards, leading to our only non-win in three years.

But the angels have not flown south, at least not yet. About halfway through the season, I get my break. We're in Parma, Ohio, playing the tough Padua Franciscan High School Bruins. The game is tight. We're doing what we do best: three or four yards and a cloud of dust, rock 'em, sock 'em running football, bone-crushing blocks and tackles. But halfway through the third quarter, we're only ahead 7-0. Victory—and ending our undefeated streak—is within reach of the Bruins. We run Veer left and Bob Bobrowski goes down, hurting himself badly. The game comes to a halt, and they have to carry him off the field.

"Polke!" Coach Gutbrod booms. "You're in for Bobrowski." For a guy who's never played or started a varsity football game, this is like winning the lottery, or jumping out of an airplane. My heart skips ten beats and there's a lump in my throat so big I can barely swallow. But as my stomach joins the chorus and does somersaults, I whip my helmet on and run over to the coach, never in a million years expecting to play in this game. *Then it hits me: if you blow it, you'll never play again.* "Sheet," I whisper under my breath.

"What, Polke?" Coach says.

"Nothing, Coach."

"Okay, Veer right. You got it?"

"Yes, sir, of course." I race onto the field, heart pounding again, knowing that finally I have my chance, but that everything is on the line—my future and the team's winning streak. But right away I feel the football angel is with me, as I march the team down the field… for the first time in my life. I throw for a first down…for the first time in my life. My line collapses, and I scramble for fifteen yards…for the first time in my life. Then I score…for the first time in my life.

Getting crushed in scrimmages week after week finally pays off. I take the team down the field again after a quick turnover, running right, then left, then up the middle, praying not to fumble and turn over the ball. We score again. Our defense holds them scoreless, and we win the game 14-0, our undefeated season intact. Thank you, God! And thank you football angels.

"Bob will not be returning next week," Coach Gutbrod says to me sternly on the field at Monday's practice. "Polke, you'll be starting next week against our nemesis, Notre Dame-Cathedral Latin. The Marionettes are tough, as you know. And I don't have to tell you it's a rivalry game and we cannot break our streak and lose. Can you be ready?"

"Absolutely, Coach," I say, but I would be lying if I didn't admit I feel the pressure. Not only is it a big game, not only will I be blamed if we lose and end the winning streak, but it's my first game starting as a high school quarterback (first game starting *ever*) and my first real chance to prove myself to college scouts. Literally *everything* is on the line.

That week in practice I'm on fire, hitting on all cylinders. I remember all the great advice that Ryan and Warfield had given me over the summer—that I have been practicing in the front yard, at the park, on the field and in my mind ever since. I remember all the crushing blows I have taken in the weekly scrimmages. And I remember the peanut butter and jelly jar that made me the laughingstock at last year's banquet and for weeks following it. All of that needs to change, and this is my chance.

Boy, oh boy, does God need to come through for me now, I think one day after practice since it is late in the season and the weather can be very iffy this time of year. Thoughts of the "Mud Bowl" flash back into my mind, the hurricane game where I kicked the ball backwards, thereby ruining what would otherwise be a three-year winning streak with the potential of a four-year winning streak.

What I'm praying for is a few days of Indian summer, common in this part of Ohio at this time of year. Fortunately, God blesses us with exactly that. It's a perfect practice week and a warm sixty-six degree Saturday night for football in Northeast Ohio—ideal for passing.

The weather going into the game has boosted my confidence to a new level and, to quote that great American philosopher, Al Bundy, and despite my musical preferences, I just had to say to my teammates before game time: "Let's rock!" And boy, do we, catching Cathedral Latin totally off guard with an unprecedented passing attack à *la* Frank Ryan to Gary Collins for the Cleveland Browns '64 NFL National Championship.

We carbon-copy the Browns like nobody's business. I throw two long touchdown passes to Ward Hill, my speedy split end—both of them absolute bombs, both putting the crowd onto their feet with cheers so deafening we might have disrupted the whole state. I throw another touchdown pass to my speedy tight end, Greg Leib. Then I run for a long touchdown just to show the recruiters I have the mobility and versatility to pass and run.

Hysterically, just like Al Bundy's famed four touchdowns in one game at Polk High—yes, I am not joking, Polk High—I deliver four touchdowns that night as we go on to win by a large margin. Even to this day, I remember parts of that game like it was yesterday, and on warm balmy nights during the fall season, I can't escape the flashbacks as if certain synapses were being uncontrollably and unconsciously triggered.

That weekend, the *Plain Dealer* does its weekly write-up on local high school football and names me to its weekly "Dream Team." My prayers have been answered, but the dream is a short one. Bobrowski's injuries are healed.

Our final game of the season is against cross-town rival, the St. Edward Eagles. I have been demoted back to the bench after my 40 minutes of fame. However, because we are still working on three undefeated seasons in a row and an undefeated four-year record, the *Plain Dealer* has been able to arrange for our final game, and the City of Cleveland Public High School championship game, both to be played the same night—billed as a double-header—at what is now known as the old Cleveland Municipal Stadium.

Little did I know that I would be playing in this same stadium a mere five years later in a Cleveland Browns uniform. *How on God's earth did that ever happen?*

EXERCISE:

Sometimes you get a break, and the opportunity you've been waiting for presents itself. Discuss any such moments in your life.

_____

_____

_____

_____

_____

_____

Luck is one part serendipity, nine parts preparation. When that amazing opportunity presented itself, what had you done beforehand to be ready for it?

_____

_____

_____

_____

_____

_____

Discuss situations in your life where preparation and determination have paid off, and how you might use those values again to achieve your current goals and dreams.

_____

_____

_____

_____

_____

_____

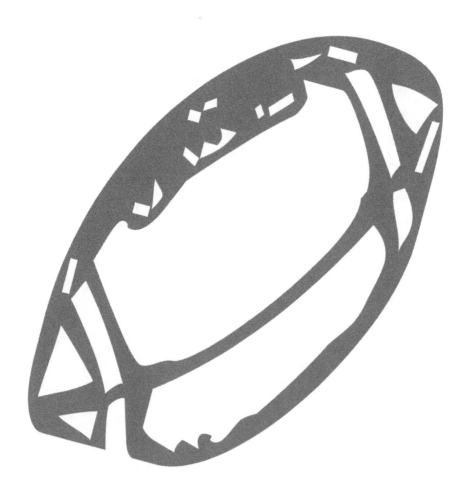

Chapter 24

A LARGE HEART

"Life is a series of experiences, each one of which makes us bigger, even though sometimes it is hard to realize this. For the world was built to develop character, and we must learn that the setbacks and grieves which we endure help us in our marching onward."

— Henry Ford

We finish our 1969 football season undefeated. In fact, except for that single tie in our freshman year, my high school football team wins every single game it has played in four years. We are so good that we have to play the best teams from other states just to face some decent competition. Many people consider us one of the best high school football teams in the nation, and one of the best in our high school's storied history.

But for me—for a guy who starts only one game at varsity or, for that matter, who starts only one game in his entire life to date—the verdict is out. Whether I will play football in college or, for that matter, ever play organized football again or even attend college, is in God's hands.

At this year's team banquet, the coach does not mock me with another joke trophy. Instead, I receive a real trophy that restores my dignity. More importantly, after the season is over, Coach Gutbrod redeems himself in my eyes by putting together a game reel for me—using footage from the two games in which I played, plus the coverage in the newspaper of my working with Ryan and Warfield—that he sends to a handful of impressive universities and colleges. To be sure, he does this for every member on our team. But that's okay. Him sending a package out for me means I still have a fighting chance to get an athletic scholarship and attend college.

Coach Gutbrod is a story unto himself, and his influence on college recruiters is not insubstantial. I know this as I'm holding my breath in hopes that at least one good team will show interest in me. In his 40 years at St. Joseph, from 1950 to 1990, Coach Gutbrod will compile a 268-107-17 record, winning or tying about 71 percent of all season games played—while cranking out NFL players such as Brian Stenger, Richie Moore, Ken Novak, Tom Schoen, Mike Zele, Bob and Mike Golic, Elvis Grbac, and Desmond Howard to name just a few. His teams will earn seven Crown Conference titles, enjoy five unbeaten seasons (four of which are ours), a 25 game winning streak from 1962 to 1964 (my freshman class was 1966), and a Division II state championship in 1989. He is a virtual force of nature.

Notwithstanding this phenomenal record, however, most of us remember Coach Gutbrod more for his passion for the game than for his winning streaks or technical coaching ability. What we remember is his motivational speeches, his tough coaching style, his sense of values, and how he galvanized boys to become men. He adds deeply to the values taught to me by my parents and the Catholic Sisters and Brothers. These values are team work, hard work, discipline, hustle, and toughness.

When we are young, sometimes we worry more and sometimes we worry less than we should. In my case, I should have been sleepless, worrying about my chances of getting a football scholarship for all the reasons I've previously laid out. Cathedral Latin had been my so-called "15 minutes of fame," and now all I have is the reputation and credibility of Coach Gutbrod working for me...and, of course, the power of prayer and the good Lord above.

Over the Christmas holidays and into January 1970, I wait patiently for the college scouts to contact me. Most days, I wake up to a nervous growl in my stomach and nothing more. But some days, I wake up mad, recounting the unfairness and disrespect heaped on me over the years—the CYO's elimination of organized football before I even got started; the financial struggle of our family, with Mom's shredded and bloody hands; the humiliating peanut butter and jelly jar; and my inability ever to gain a starting quarterback position notwithstanding my talent. If not picked up on a scholarship, my new Plan B is to be a football walk-on and hope for a scholarship—one in a million odds for sure, since few walk-ons make the team, much less get a scholarship...and if that fails, I can always try to put that singing group together. Sure.

~ ~ ~

Second semester classes commence, but I still have not heard anything from the college scouts. I do know the scouts are out looking for new recruits, however, because I can see it happening with my own eyes. If a scout is interested in a player, typically a coach will stick his head into the middle of a class and pull one of the senior players out. This has already happened for many of the players, but not for me.

"Brother Mark," a coach says one day after poking his head into homeroom, "may I please have Bob Bobrowski for a few minutes?"

"Of course, Coach," he replies. "Mr. Bobrowski, please return as soon as you are done."

When the door shuts behind Bob, my buddy Pete Appicella whispers, "Polke, whattabout you?"

I shrug my shoulders and wag my chin before I recover and wink. "I'm next."

Bob returns a half hour later, grinning from ear to ear. Everyone knows he's been called out to meet with another college scout and that he's been offered another scholarship. Ultimately, he will go with Purdue University and be drafted in 1974 to the Baltimore Colts.

Years later, in June 2013, northeast Cleveland media company Cleveland.com will name Bob to its list of finalists for the greatest northeast Ohio high school football players of all time. Other notable players making that list will include Stow's Larry Csonka in the '60s, St. Edward linebacker Tom Cousineau in the '70s, Desmond Howard from our own St. Joseph High in the '80s, St. Ignatius quarterback Dave Ragone in the '90s, and Glenville quarterback Troy Smith in the 2000s, to name a few. Needless to say, I will not be among them.

On top of that, the *News Herald* will name ten of Coach Gutbrod's football teams to the Top 50 greatest Ohio high school football teams of all time, including both my 1968 and 1969 teams. Despite it all, that's still a source of great pride.

My big day finally comes in mid-January 1970, following our return to school from the holidays. Getting more nervous by the day, I give a big sigh of relief when our offensive coach pushes open the door of my chemistry class and says, "Brother John, Kenny Polke, please," nodding his head toward me. Before Brother John can say a word, I've jumped up from my seat and am halfway to the door.

As Coach and I walk down the hallway, our steps echoing in the empty halls, I think: *Thank, God.*

A LARGE HEART

"Who is it?" I ask.

"The Naval Academy wants to talk to you. This way," he says as I start to turn toward the locker room. "Recruiter's in the gymnasium."

When the rapid beating of my heart slows down, I feel a rush of adrenaline. The Naval Academy is my absolute first choice, having been a Navy and Roger Staubach fan since visiting the Naval Academy after winning that newspaper competition as a kid.

When we walk into the gymnasium, a clean-cut man in his Navy service uniform—pressed Navy blue pants and hat, light brown khaki shirt—stands up from a chair located behind a foldout table. "Good morning, Mr. Polke," he says with a military formality that quickly dissolves to a welcoming smile. "Have a seat."

Coach and I sit in the two chairs opposite his, the air of anticipation amplified by the cavernous gymnasium ceiling and the off-red tile basketball floor (also known as the Purple Palace). The sound of my heart beating returns to my ears, causing me to miss the man's first few words.

"I'm sorry, can you please repeat that?" He starts over.

"Yes, of course. As I was saying, we are a special place where the scholar-athlete is constantly raising the standard of excellence. Only special people choose to become these athletes. At Navy, in both the sporting arena and the classroom, and as part of the family of midshipmen and women, over 3,000 strong, he or she prepares to be a combat leader of tomorrow. Past members have excelled in service to our country and beyond. Others have become Rhodes Scholars. All are lifetime members of one of college athletics' most distinguished, elite orders."

When he finishes, he puts his hand on a letter that's lying on the desk in front of him, pushes it forward, and spins it around. "We'd like to extend you a letter of interest, Mr. Polke." I stare down at the paper as I see my dreams unfolding before me. Despite my coolness on the outside, I'm frozen in shock in the inside. He says, "This is a full, four-year scholar-athlete scholarship, all tuition paid, room and board, with your commitment to the Navy."

I lean my head forward to read the typed print, hardly believing my own two eyes. I turn my head toward Coach, who nods his head and smiles. "Yes, sir, I say," as the man stands, followed quickly by me and Coach. "The Navy is my first choice."

"Excellent, Mr. Polke. Please follow me over here. We put you through a short physical and, assuming you pass, which I'm sure you will, we'll talk further details."

Now I'm practically giddy with excitement. I'm 6' 1", 205 pounds, and the epitome of good health. So, when I take and pass this physical, a no-brainer, I'll be returning to class with a letter of intent to my number one choice, the Naval Academy. Tonight, I'll be celebrating the biggest achievement in my life.

A nurse in a white and blue uniform approaches and administers various tests that constitute my physical, takes blood, and returns to a nearby desk. The recruiter and I engage in small talk for a few minutes, whereupon the nurse walks back over to us. At once, I notice a look on her face that is disconcerting, making me break into a small sweat and wonder what is wrong.

The recruiter looks at the test results. His eyes flit up to me and back down to the paper. "I'm afraid, Mr. Polke," he says solemnly and directly, "that you have not passed your physical."

The world in front of me flashes black, and I almost pass out. I must not have heard him correctly, I think. "There must be a mistake," I say. "I'm in perfect—"

"No mistake, Mr. Polke; we've seen this before. It's something that sometimes afflicts athletes. Your pulse is very low, off our charts for military service. I'm so sorry."

Barely able to comprehend what I'm hearing, I start to get dizzy. After a wave of nausea hits me and passes, my mind connects the revelation to my dad. He suffered from a heart defect that kept him from playing sports or being drafted into World War II—which prevented him from achieving his dreams. *It must be the same for me*, I think. *Like father, like son.*

When I return to class, everyone can see the devastated look on my face. No one says a word. I skulk around the rest of the day. When I see Mom after school and tell her what happened, including my belief that it's related to Dad's heart condition, she gives me a hug and says it will be all right. When I tell Dad, he breaks down and cries. "I'm sorry, son," he says. "I'm truly sorry."

Ironically, I will later learn that there was nothing wrong with me. I was in perfect health. What put my pulse and other measurements off the charts was my enlarged heart. I had what is now known as athletic heart syndrome (AHS), also known as athlete's heart, athletic bradycardia, or exercise-induced cardiomegaly. It is a non-pathological condition commonly seen in sports medicine, in which the human heart is enlarged, and the resting heart rate is lower than normal, resulting from extreme exertion and exercise, i.e., excellent conditioning. So, in a harsh moment of irony, it was my escalated training following my sessions with Ryan and Warfield that ended up working against me, not for me.

I'm not going to lie. After flunking the physical, I'm utterly and totally devastated. In the next 48 hours, I'm thinking my days playing football are over and that I will be getting a union job or attending community college or, shit, maybe it is time to roll into the Mayfield area to see what opportunities exist.... Not to mention, I'll still be living at home, so I'll have to do something else with my life.

The next night, Mom asks me to go to the store to grab some things she needs for dinner.

"Keys are in my jacket pocket," Dad says from the living room.

I grab the keys and head to the local grocery store. On the way, I pass the Nottingham Bar. A group of young Italian guys are leaning against a hot Roadrunner with hot babes on their arms. I tap the brakes and contemplate stopping and going inside. When I recognize one of guys as Tony Milano, the punk who robbed me on the paper route, I have second thoughts. Given my state of mind, who knows where it might have led me if I hadn't seen Milano and succumbed to my emotions by going inside.

Thankfully, my agitation and confusion does not last. The next day, Coach returns to my class, sticks his head in, and again says, "Kenny Polke, please."

My mouth drops and I hustle to the door, looking back at my buddy with wide eyes.

As we're walking down the hall, I say, "But, Coach, I won't pass the physical."

"Didn't I tell you? Only the Navy does those physicals. Well, maybe all the military schools. None of the other schools have that requirement."

"You're kidding?" I say.

"No, sir."

That day and over the ensuing weeks, I get visits from some incredible schools, including Colgate (an Ivy League school), Columbia University (another Ivy League school), and Syracuse University. Since I didn't start, Coach Gutbrod probably sent out my package toward the end, I figure. But after talking to the recruiters, I learn that, with my strong academic record at a Catholic school known for its high quality of education, and a decent football package, I have a fighting chance. My prayers are still being answered.

As part of the recruiting process, I'm invited to visit all of the colleges that give me a letter of interest, at their expense. I remember when I arrive in Hamilton Village, home to Colgate University. Colgate is an historic place, its roots going back to 1817. The campus itself covers over 500 acres and is surrounded by another 1,100 acres of undeveloped forest lands. It is truly one of the most beautiful campuses in America, invoking images of America's history going back to the Revolutionary War. *I could really go here,* I think to myself.

But that's when I get my second major setback. Neither Colgate nor any of the other schools are willing to offer me a full, four-year scholarship covering tuition, room, and board. I learn that Ivy League schools never even give tuition scholarships. They merely help students obtain education loans. And the other schools only offer me partial scholarships. Given my parents' financial condition, I cannot afford to go to any of these schools. So I'm back where I started with no hope of playing football again or attending a four-year university.

Thankfully, Coach Gutbrod has also sent my recruitment package to his own *alma mater*, University of Dayton. UD is a Division I school and only several hours driving distance from my house. It is considered a top-tier Catholic research university, so its academic status is also alluring. After I receive my UD letter of interest, Dad drives me to the campus to check it out.

Though nothing like the Colgate grounds, the UD campus is impressive. Most of the buildings are brick edifices with pitched roofs capped by ornamental spiral peaks and surrounded by old growth trees in a setting not unlike most of the Ivy League schools. Founded in 1850 by the Society of Mary (Marianists), it is one of three Marianist universities in the nation and the largest private university in Ohio. The university's campus is located in the city's southern portion and covers 388 acres on both sides of the Great Miami River. The campus is noted for the Immaculate Conception Chapel and the University of Dayton Arena.

Not bad, I think, and given my circumstances, I really don't have a choice since UD offers me a full athletic scholarship—tuition, room, board, the whole works. That solves all of my financial issues with the added benefit that it is much closer to home. It's also a smaller school and thus presents a real opportunity for me to start at quarterback. *Imagine that*, I think. I tell the recruiters on the spot that I'll accept their offer.

On the ride home, I say to Dad: "For a guy who started only one football game in his life, I will soon be a freshman quarterback on full athletic scholarship to a Division I university. Not bad for a kid from South Collinwood."

Dad reaches over and offers me his hand, which I take and shake vigorously. "Son, I'm so proud of you. Your mother will be beside herself."

And she is. The tough redhead breaks down in tears and hugs me with all her might. Of course, her only reservation is that I will still be playing football—because if I am playing football, I might get hurt. "But if that's what it takes to get a good education," she says, "then so be it."

EXERCISE:

Regardless of whether you are religious, perhaps you have experienced events in your life that seem to have resulted from a Higher Power. Recount any religious or other experiences that fit this scenario from your own life.

_____

_____

_____

_____

_____

_____

Persistence and faith in yourself can pay off. Describe where these qualities have worked for you.

_____

_____

_____

_____

_____

_____

How can you take your prior experiences and apply them to the goals and dreams that you now want to achieve?

_____

_____

_____

_____

_____

_____

Chapter 25

MORE RIOTS

"All great changes are preceded by chaos."

— Deepak Chopra

Collinwood High School is located at 15210 Saint Clair Avenue East, at the intersection of East 152nd Street, exactly 2.4 miles from my house. To get there, all we have to do is ride our bikes northwest on Nottingham Road for several blocks, then take a left and pedal southwest down Saint Clair Avenue until we reach 152nd. Twenty-five minutes later, we reach the knoll on which the high school is perched.

The knoll provides a spectacular view of everything below. We can see Lake Erie and the Lake Erie Islands, which are playground to thousands of families on summer holiday; many major Cleveland landmarks, places like the James A. Garfield Memorial, Case Western University and the surrounding medical complex, and the U.S.S. Cod Submarine Memorial; and, of course, the busy hub of Five Points, which lights up like a Christmas Tree as the sun sets and darkness falls.

In the heart of Little Italy, and a long-standing commercial hub of Collinwood, Five Points gets its name from the intersection of Saint Clair, E. 152nd, and Ivanhoe Road, which come together to form a star. Italians have been settling here since 1910. It thrives from a combination of students, workers, and neighbors all mixing and coming together in one place. Apparently, there are lots of Italians who want to live together to preserve their traditions brought over from the old country.

By 1970, the flight of white homeowners from Collinwood has taken off, while the blacks are moving here in greater and greater numbers. One group of white merchants has recently formed the Collinwood Better Business Association. Its mission is to reverse the flight of white families, fight for better city services, and restore home and business values. Five years later, in 1975, Collinwood will receive $100 million of Title I money to refurbish Five Points and other sections of the neighborhood, but that isn't even on the board yet, and people are getting desperate as property values and business profits fall.

On the morning of April 6, 1970, only two months before I graduate, nearly 400 angry white students gather outside Collinwood High School. Their pent-up frustration prompts them to pelt the school with large rocks, ultimately breaking some 56 windows. It's a school day, so teachers usher the 200 black students to the third floor cafeteria for their protection. At 10:30 a.m., the whites enter the school and head straight to the second floor.

Fearing for their lives and safety, the black students begin breaking the legs off of chairs to arm themselves. Some bravely block the stairs leading to the third floor with tables and chairs. Fortunately, tensions somehow defuse themselves. The white students withdraw from inside the school, and the black students rush to the safety of their buses. To keep the whites from attacking, teachers, staff, and policemen form a protective line that blocks what is now an angry mob.

MORE RIOTS

Clashes at the school actually began back in 1965, when I was an eighth grader still one year away from high school. Though Mom never said so, I am certain this impacted her decision to put all of us through private Catholic high school, despite the crushing expense of paying the tuition for three children at the same time, the hardship of having children one year apart.

To be sure, what is happening in Collinwood is not an isolated incident. As the Supreme Court's 1954 desegregation decision of *Brown v. Board of Education of Topeka* finally starts to take hold, hundreds, if not thousands, of schools have become places of white protest and racial violence.

According to the *Plain Dealer*, "with the passage of each year, the western fringes of the Collinwood area [are] being occupied by the Negro overflow from Glenville." The change in demographics in Collinwood, coupled with civil rights demonstrations nationally, combine to boil racial tensions to the surface, causing them to spill into our neighborhood with great intensity.

(Recently, I happened upon Gerald Phipps' blog, posted in November 2015, in response to Heidi Fearing's article, "Collinwood High School Riots, Cleveland Historical." Here's what Phipps, who is African-American, had to say—sentiments I agree with and which capture the true atmosphere of Collinwood at the time:

It was a difficult time growing up and going to school in the Margaret Spellacy Jr. High and Collinwood High School 70's era. I was an eyewitness to some of the most painful and brutal occurrences of those times, from stabbings to rioting to murder. I could not understand why people hated us so much and tried so hard to hurt and injure us just because we didn't look like them. These were some of the worst and best years of my life. Mostly they were the worst years. I will never forget them; their scars remain etched upon my mind and seared upon my heart. Whenever hatred reigns as openly as it did during these Jr. high school and high school years (1970 through 1976) you never really ever get over the things that you learn that people are capable of when they become a frenzied and hysterical mob, and that very mob is after you. I can only imagine what a lynching must have been like, but on the worst days, walking along as a lone Black in a neighborhood with a high concentration of angry whites was a constantly fearful and unnerving experience that I know and recall ever so well with intricate clarity.

On May 4, 1970, now only about four weeks before I graduate from high school, the winds of violence endemic to Collinwood drift 44 miles south to Kent State University. A *Newsweek* article will later joke that "the most vicious outbreak of violence" prior to May 1970 was "a 1958 panty raid launched against two women's dormitories, which resulted in the prompt dismissal of twenty-nine students."

Though I am no news junkie, what happens this day will saturate all of the news channels, newspapers, and magazines for weeks. The May 18, 1970, edition of *Newsweek* captures it best:

The bloody incident shocked and further divided a nation already riven by dissent over the war in Indochina. More than that, the shots fired at Kent State were taken by some…that the U.S. might be edging toward the brink of warfare…on the home front….

William Fitzgerald, a 29-year-old graduate student in history, felt it was no accident. 'It was butchery,' cried Fitzgerald. And a correspondent for campus radio station WKSU told his editor, via walkie-talkie: "I'm coming back. I'm sick…disgusted."….

Beyond that there was little left but to bury the dead. In New York City, nearly 5,000 mourners joined the family of Jeffrey Miller at services addressed by Dr. Benjamin Spock, who declared that the Kent

MORE RIOTS

State killings "may do more to end the war in Vietnam than all the rest of us have been able to do.".... There were smaller, simpler services for Allison Krause, but emotions ran just as high in her hometown. "I can't blame 18-year-olds for not wanting to go to Cambodia and be killed," said Krause's mother. "Look, I had a daughter and now she is dead.".…

Allison's father was even angrier. "May her death be on [Nixon's] back," he snapped. His daughter, he said, "resented being called a bum because she disagreed with someone else's opinion." "Is dissent a crime?" he asked. "Is this such a reason for killing her? Have we come to such a state in this country that a young girl has to be shot because she disagrees deeply with the actions of her government?"

"That's one heck of a sending off party," I say to Dennis one day when discussing the Kent State headlines.

"Hell," he says, "who needs to go to Vietnam to get killed? We can do it right here in our own backyard without even holding a weapon. Much more convenient when it comes to the funeral."

As I said earlier, people often romanticize the 1960s and early '70s as the era of social meaning, free love, and spiritual awakening. I beg to differ. For those of us growing up in America's heartland, it was total hell. The race riots that brought tanks into our streets in 1966 when I started high school had not gone away. Now, nearly four years later, I'm about to graduate high school in the wake of more race riots and the tragedy at Kent State College.

From my viewpoint as a teenager, not much has changed in the last few years. As a consequence, I couldn't possibly be more ready for college than I am.

EXERCISE:

Sometimes in life it's time to move on, to take a big step like going to college or taking a job across the country to a place you've never been. Describe experiences in your own life where this has worked for you.

_____
_____
_____
_____
_____
_____

Describe experiences where this has not worked and the lessons learned.

_____
_____
_____
_____
_____
_____

Have you ever made any great changes in your life that were preceded by chaos? Describe the chaos and the resulting change, including whether it was good or bad.

_____
_____
_____
_____
_____
_____

Chapter 26

FRESHMAN FUN, TRAGEDY & *WE ARE MARSHALL*

"Nobody here wants to go home either."

— Movie, *We Are Marshall*

It's the summer of 1970, the summer before my freshman year in college, and I'd be lying if I didn't admit I was filled with anxiety and anticipation. And because I'm broke and want to arrive on campus with some money in my pocket, I have to work a full-time job all summer.

As soon as my shift ends at Euclid Chemical (two doors down from Mom's job at Jergens), where I pour solvents into large canisters for treating concrete, I race home to borrow Dad's car and head to football practice. If I'm ever going to start in college, now is the time for me to hone my skills and be in the best shape of my life. I pull up to the practice field with a jerk and hop out of the car. For the next two hours, five days a week, I throw footballs to anyone who will catch them.

The anticipation comes from the simple fact that, in less than 60 days, I will be leaving Collinwood with all my limbs attached *and* heading to college. Apprehension from race riots, thugs, and crime will no longer greet my day when I wake up each morning. To be sure, I hate to leave my family, but for the first time in my life, I will be living away from home—300 miles southeast, to be exact. And that's every blue-blooded teenager's dream.

The big day finally comes.

"Ready, son?" Dad yells.

"Coming," I reply as I force the zipper of my overstuffed bag. "I love you, Mom," I say, a whirlwind of motion as I gulp down the remainder of a quart of milk and give her a parting hug and kiss.

"Be careful," she replies.

"Mom, it's college, not a race riot," Dennis wisecracks from the living room. "Don't let the books bite, Kenny," he says chuckling.

I wink to Dennis and charge out the door. Dad's got the trunk up and car started. I toss the bag inside and slam the lid. All my other worldly possessions are jammed into the backseat—clothes, a mini-refrigerator, my stereo, and a bunch of albums.

"Ready, Dad!" I say, and off we go. Before I know it, we're pulling up to the UD dorms—Founders Hall in particular—after making only a few wrong turns.

All the jocks on scholarship are assigned to Founders Hall, which is located in the middle of the campus and houses 400 students. Within the hour, I've met my first roommate ever, other than my brother. He's Mike Luczak. Mike is also from Cleveland and, ironically, played for the Chanel Cardinals, the only team to put a blemish on our entire four-year football odyssey at St. Joe's. We joke about the Mud Bowl, have a bunch of laughs when he learns I was the punter, and with that the ice is broken.

We toss our bags onto our beds and head out into the hallway. The hallways are deliberately huge, thereby encouraging students to hang out and study or goof around outside the confines of our dorm rooms. We take full advantage of that. Before we know it, we're talking total trash—football feats of glory, hot girlfriends from high school and even hotter co-eds, and food—yes, we have our own cafeteria and can eat all the food we want.

Mike and I feel like kids in a candy store now that we're attending a co-ed campus for the first time, both having attended all-boys Catholic high schools. The running joke is about neck pains, not from football practice, but from sudden jerks of our heads to check out the passing co-eds.

Over the ensuing years, we will throw some legendary parties. Many of them will get started in the double-room housing Smitty (Bob Smith) and Matt Dahlinghaus. Both play defensive tackle, so these guys are massive. Matt has a zest for life that is incomparable, and everybody loves him; but boy does he get crazy. One thing he does is cover himself in water, then squirt lighter fluid all over the water and light it. He goes up in flames but, because of the water, he never gets burned except for a few crispy eyelashes.

On one occasion, Matt crawls onto the ledge of our window and looks three stories down. Fearless, he puts a pillow to his behind and leaps, landing in a squat position. Everyone screams, no doubt thinking he will injure or kill himself. But he lands square on his feet, pops up like a jack-in-the-box, and yells, "Okay, who's next?" No one answers, not surprisingly. Nor is it uncommon to see him walking on stilts or crouching and barking like a bulldog. Needless to say, each and every time we laugh our heads off.

Sadly, in two years (the '72 football season), Matt will suffer a freak injury. Fast forward to our game against Bowling Green. We're at Doyt Perry Field, and I'm watching from the sidelines. Matt's chasing the

279

runner with the ball and tackles him; then both roll over on the ground. Nothing out of the ordinary. When Matt doesn't get up, those of us on the sidelines start to worry. An ambulance screams onto the field and whisks him off to St. Elizabeth Medical Center.

At the next practice, we learn that Matt broke his neck at the spinal cord's fifth cervical vertebra. We're told the break is so serious it has left him paralyzed from the chest down. Many of us drop by the hospital to wish him the best. But the doctors can't control the complications that follow. He succumbs to a blood clot in the lungs, dying three days after Christmas.

His death knocks the wind out of all of us. A foundation is later set up in his honor, which to this day is still going strong. We football players are like elephants; we never forget, and we will never forget Matt and his soaring free-spirit. For many years after Matt's death, when things get stressful, I remember Matt and think to myself that things can always get worse, so enjoy the ride, for someday we are all going to die. Even to this day, it is hard for me to accept Matt's early demise. It is still so surreal. Matt, I know you've got all the angels in heaven laughing and in stitches. Love you and miss you, brother.

~ ~ ~

My freshman year also brings with it something else that's new. For the first time in my life, I'm getting respect. Because I'm a quarterback playing at UD on a scholarship, I am, as they say, a "big man on campus." Whether I'm grabbing drinks with other guys on the team at a local watering hole, walking around campus and hanging out, or just sitting in a classroom, all of the girls know who I am.

Indeed, when I reach my junior and senior years, my name will keep popping up in the newspapers week after week, generating for me a virtual celebrity status. This celebrity status, I will find out, is a double-edged sword. I will learn a valuable lesson as I become the victim of a stalker. While extremely flattering at first and putting me on an ego trip, I begin to realize that this particular co-ed needs deep psychological help. When I decide to break it off, suicide attempts as well as death threats over the phone become very troubling to deal with.

It is also during my freshman year that I experience my first infatuation with an "older woman." Let's refer to this as my *Summer of '42* experience since Joan resembles Jennifer O'Neill from the movie with the same title. Joan is working on her Master's degree and assisting one of the math professors as a student teacher. She is tall and naturally beautiful, with long brown hair. She has just the right spread of freckles sprinkled around her nose, giving her a sense of innocence mixed with raw sex appeal. She leaves me broken-hearted as I experience for the first time the bad side of "catching someone on the rebound," since she turns to me after breaking up with her long-time boyfriend.

Meanwhile, on the practice field, UD freshmen players are far from being big men on campus. We are the smallest players on the team and the biggest targets. Many of the varsity players are very "big turkeys," as my center Steve Siewe often says, who want to make us pay our dues dearly, just as they did when they were freshmen. (Five of them will eventually make it to the NFL.) When they come at us, there is no mercy. In fact, we occupy the unenviable position of being so-called "tackling dummies," a drill where everyone lines up, hands behind our backs, and gets crushed by varsity players charging straight at us. There's also the "B and B drill," which is short for "bend 'em and brand 'em." Believe me, you don't want to try it.

Then tragedy strikes. About midway through the season, on the evening of November 14, 1970, Marshall University's charter plane, while returning from a loss at East Carolina, does not make it. One mile short of the runway at Tri-State Airport in Ceredo, West Virginia, the plane clips the trees on the ridge as it tries to land. The impact causes the plane to crash into a nearby gully, killing all 75 people on board. The deceased include all 37 members of Marshall's varsity football team, their head coach, Rick Tolley, and five members of his coaching staff, as well as Charles E. Kautz, their athletics director, Jim Schroer, the team's athletic trainer, Donald Tackett, his assistant, 25 boosters, and five crew members.

In the wake of the tragedy, Marshall's President, Donald Dedmon, initially leans toward suspending the football program indefinitely; but the pleas of Marshall students; Huntington, West Virginia, residents; and especially the few football players who didn't make the flight, cause him to reconsider. Dedmon hires a young new head coach, Jack Lengyel who, with the help of Red Dawson, the sole surviving member of the previous coaching staff, manages to rebuild the team, despite losing many of its prospects to West Virginia University.

Faced with a team shorn of its varsity squad, Coach Dedmon travels to Kansas City, where he pleads with the NCAA to waive its rule prohibiting freshmen from playing varsity football (a rule which had been abolished in 1968 for all collegiate sports except football and basketball, and will be permanently abolished for those sports in 1972). Dedmon returns victorious. The new Marshall team will be composed mostly of the 18 returning players (three varsity, 15 sophomores) and walk-ons from other Marshall sports programs.

Marshall being only three hours southeast of Dayton (166 highway miles), the tragedy strikes very close to home for us. Many Dayton players and students have friends or relatives who died in the crash or attend Marshall. After the disaster (later memorialized in the movie *We Are Marshall*), I remember our whole team huddling together in a large group and praying for the downed team. Many of the guys, 200-300 pounders, are bawling. There's no question about it. The Marshall crash makes my freshman year bittersweet. I left Collinwood hoping to escape death and disaster, but it follows me to UD. When will this end?

EXERCISE:

New beginnings can change your world. Describe the new beginnings in your life that have changed yours.

_____
_____
_____
_____

What is it about these new beginnings that you loved and hated the most?

_____
_____
_____
_____

Do you see a "new beginning" in your future, and if so, what is it and how do you see yourself accomplishing it?

_____
_____
_____
_____

Chapter 27

THE DRAFT & *ANIMAL HOUSE*

"Conscription without representation is tyranny."

— Dr. Kenneth J. Polke

"Well, as of this moment, we're on double, secret probation."

— Movie, *Animal House*

The '70s bring with them more than Watergate, bell bottoms, and disco. Over the years, the La Cosa Nostra—or Mafia—has surreptitiously insinuated itself into every facet of American society—from mom-and-pop grocery stores and labor unions, to neighborhood drug dealers and prostitution, to bank robberies and extortion. And by the '70s, it reaches a zenith not known since Lucky Luciano first conceived of the idea of organizing crime in America.

There's also the military draft. Up until now, conscription hasn't existed in America in my lifetime—or the lifetimes of anyone residing in Founders Hall. By now, all American men born between January 1, 1944, and December 31, 1950, have received their draft cards, with many more to come, including me. Being born in '52 means I barely escaped the first wave the previous December. But I know in my sophomore year I will not be so lucky.

For me and all the other freshmen, the prospect of getting drafted and going off to fight in the jungles of Vietnam is a sobering reality. At UD, we're seeing upperclassmen not much older than us getting caught on the horns of the war dilemma. Should I graduate and volunteer for the service, should I join the war protesters but honor my draft notice, or should I skip to Canada to dodge the draft as an expression of conscience or cowardice? Those are the gritty, real-life questions many of us are asking ourselves. In other words, am I for the war, or am I against it? And with the anti-war movement sweeping the country, no one wants to fight in an unpopular war only to come home in a box.

~ ~ ~

The year leading up to our sophomore football season is a strange one. *All in the Family* with Archie Bunker commences, Charlie Manson and his "family" are found guilty in the 1969 Tate-Bianca murders, and Frazier beats Ali in the "fight of the century." As my freshman year ends and summer arrives, *The New York Times* publishes the Pentagon Papers, thereby proving we are losing the Vietnam War, for which I now hold a draft card. The Doors' frontman Jim Morrison overdoses, mob boss Joe Columbo is assassinated, and the voting age is lowered to 18 across the land.

Only weeks before returning to UD for August football practice, I remember celebrating the Fourth of July with my parents. We're all standing on the sidewalk in front of our house—me, Dennis, Cheryl, Mom and Dad, as well as Christine, our new baby sister who is swaddled in Mom's arms—as fireworks explode across the neighborhood. I'm thumbing a square card that's sticking out of my front shirt pocket. It's my draft card. I pull it out and study it.

"Did you see this?" I ask as I hand it to Dad. He takes it and studies both sides of the card. It's a "Selective Service Registration" card, all typed except one place, recording name, date and place of birth, weight and height, eye and hair color, any special marks, and Social Security number. The only information not typed is the draft number. In the upper right corner, that number is written in by hand. Back in those days, of course, we did not receive any email and there was no online confirmation or support.

He hands it back to me. "At least you can vote now. In my day, we could get drafted before we were even eligible to vote. We had to fight for our country and die without having an official say on anything. Count your blessings, son."

"America ratified the Twenty-Sixth Amendment yesterday," Dennis says.

A Roman candle shoots into the air and explodes, brilliant colors showering in every direction against a moonless, star-filled summer night.

"What did you say?" Dad asks.

"America ratified the Twenty-Sixth Amendment yesterday."

"Oh, really. That's—"

"The amendment that lets us vote before we're sent off to war to die for no reason," Dennis says. "We've been following it in our government class."

"Yes, I know," I say. "But yesterday it was ratified? I didn't know that."

"Too many pillow fights with the co-eds," Dennis says with a snort.

Dad holds up this morning's *Plain Dealer*, where the headlines proclaim that 18-year-olds conscripted to fight in Vietnam, who previously could not vote, now have that right.

I start to rip up the draft card, then stop. I don't believe in the Vietnam War. But like my entire family, I am a proud American. "It's about time. And you can guess who will be exercising his right to vote in the 1972 election."

Dennis shakes his head in agreement. "Amen."

Dad's chin is nodding in the affirmative, too.

~ ~ ~

In late August, I pack my bags, walk out the side door, and jump into my new '64 Mustang hardtop that I bought from working a job over the summer. "New" of course is a misnomer. "New" to me is more accurate since it was so trashed I had to take it to Earl Scheib for his highly-advertised $29.95 paint job special. Earl painted her white and she almost looks new, except for the "small" matter of rust. Again, "small" is a misnomer. She's a rust bucket, no question about it, but I had a plan. I bought a gallon drum of roof tar and gave her a complete undercoat.

After cranking the engine and letting her warm up, I head over to Nottingham Road. From there, I power north, humming Al Green's new hit single, "I'm Still in Love with You," thinking of Joan, on whom I still have a huge crush, despite the fiasco of driving all the way to New Jersey to see her the day after my car was painted and learning the hard way that her feelings were not reciprocal. Finally, I hit the onramp for the Lakeland Freeway, roll west to Interstate 90, then cruise south until I arrive in Dayton.

Once I figure out my new parking, I head straight to Founders Hall, where I meet my new roommate, Ted Zukowsi, a big kid from Lansing, Illinois, with Elvis sideburns and who plays offensive tackle. Ted is a hoot, and we will have many laughs over the coming months. (Mike Luczak, my freshman roommate, had suffered a career-ending back injury during the season and left the team, never to play football again.)

When my sophomore season starts, I'm second string varsity but vying tough for starter. It's not like high school, and by now, my passing arm has taken on a whole new level of expertise. With nearly four years of practicing the tips passed on by Ryan and Warfield, I'm deadly. I set up, read the defense, and spot my passing target with lightning speed. Hours and hours of passing practice at UD gives me a sixth sense of when and where to throw the ball, often before my receiver cuts and looks back, just like Ryan taught me. I'm inches away from securing the starting position, and I can feel it in my bones.

With building confidence, of course, comes cockiness off the field. When the guys from our floor head out to the bars, we make our presence known. We are jocks, full of ourselves, and don't take lip from anyone. This can lead to trouble, and one night it does. Many of us are at The Pit, which is on the UD Campus. We're goofing off, talking trash and doing what young men do when sowing their wild oats. A couple of students from the northeast get smart with us, making fun of us being "dumb jocks" and suggesting we aren't the sharpest blades in the drawer.

Big mistake, especially when some of those blades are over six feet tall and approaching 300 pounds. Before we know it, someone throws a punch, which quickly escalates into a bar brawl. Chairs, bottles, and bodies are flying everywhere. When the dust settles, people are bloodied and hurt. The police arrest a dozen culprits, and the rest of us, yours truly included, are lucky to scat back to the dorm without being cuffed.

Rumors spread that I led the brawl on behalf of the players. That isn't true so no witness steps forward to substantiate the false accusation. I'm interviewed, tell it like it is, and the furor subsides. However, several players get kicked off the team, and a few of them get kicked out of the school. Looking back, I'm not denying I was *not* quiet. I spoke my mind, but I didn't throw a punch. The last thing I wanted to do was blow it after all those years of struggle. But it was a very close call.

Perhaps this is just as good a place as any to admit I would be lying if I claimed to be a choir boy my *whole* life. Many stories I could share with you, especially during my bachelor days, would ruin the clean-cut image I worked hard to build up over the years. And, of course, there are some stories that I'm ashamed to share with you. But there are some stories I can share that won't threaten me if I should ever decide to run for public office again. Like the time the whole dorm, or what seems like the whole dorm, holds a Black Mass when Dave Hout's pet owl died. Dave is a tough, hard-nosed defensive nose tackle from Massillon, Ohio, who descends into a severe state of depression when his pet owl dies. Responding to Dave's plight, we dub our offensive guard from Westlake, Ohio, known only as James, our irreverent mock-priest, Father Janosek. Father Janosek, a fake name of course, then decides to lead a funeral procession through the entire dorm before finally burying the pet owl out on the practice football field next to the dorm hall—borrowing (a polite word) for authenticity's sake a few priest garments and Catholic instruments normally reserved for Catholic funerals, the crowning touch coming when we also "borrow" a tombstone from the City of Dayton grave-yard.

All of this in honor of the dead pet owl seems totally logical and nec-essary at the time. Father Janosek's prayers for the dead owl, uttered with aplomb from the third floor balcony to hundreds of students, brings new life to Dave, one severely depressed nose tackle. There is nary a dry eye in the house, but this is more from laughing than crying as we show our support for Dave's tragic loss.

Looking back, it makes me wonder what lunatic ever called college a place of higher learning. Because little did we know, but all of this would literally come back to haunt us. No, seriously, I mean literally come back to haunt us. Our efforts to console our teammate comes with a stiff price, as the ghost from the borrowed tombstone of David Gray comes to haunt us every year. Halloween is never the same in Founders Hall after that; many residents swear they witness very strange happenings on the third floor from that time onward. And the coaches could never understood why, in one particular area of the football practice field, we always made the Sign of the Cross coupled with an occasional giggle just as we stepped on one distinct, bare spot.

Every team needs a Father Janosek, and usually has one to lift its spirits. For many of us, a college semester is the longest we've ever been away from home, so our longing for familiar comforts begins to wear on us as the season drags on. Morale for the team dips, and at one all-day practice, we're dragging lower than usual. Father Jano is off for a few days due to injury, but the rest of the lowerclassmen are getting beaten to death.

Our practice field is right next to Founders Hall, and unbeknownst to us, someone has placed huge concert speakers on top of the building. As sweat pours down our faces, and I have the offensive unit in a huddle to call the next play, music starts blasting from these speakers. "I'm Your Captain (Closer to Home)" by Grand Funk Railroad starts booming across the courtyard and onto the practice field.

This song is just what the doctor orders. The remainder of the practice takes on a whole new life, as guys start moving to the bassline of the song and spirits are lifted. And as the end of the song crescendos with a loud haunting violin, accompanied by an even louder crashing of football helmets and pads down on the practice field, it's as if heaven and earth had combined into one.

To this day, we don't know who was responsible for this grand, funky act, but if I were a betting man, I'd put all my chips on Father Jano, who was secretly given credit. No question about it, music can tame the angry beast.

Despite the way I've made it sound, living in Founders Hall is not all fun and games, as evidenced by the relationship of that same Father Janosek and his roommate, one Patrick Hayden, a defensive tackle from Louisville, Kentucky. If you did not know any better, you would have sworn that Father Janosek and Pat Hayden are an old, grouchy married couple of 50 years, judging by the way they fight and carry on.

One evening, Pat comes flying out his dorm room with Father Jano hot on his tail. It seems that Jano was having his usual evening verbal battle with his high school sweetheart, Sandy, monopolizing the only dorm room wall phone. I guess Pat wanted to use the phone to call his sweetheart back home in Kentucky, but Jano's fight with Sandy was an unusually long-winded one this night.

Lacking in patience, Pat did the only reasonable thing that anyone in his position could do: he stabbed Jano in the thigh with a long butcher knife. The next thing we know, we're witnessing Jano chase Pat out of the room with the knife stuck in his leg and blood gushing everywhere. Jano stops running only long enough to pull the knife out, before yelling to Pat that he better not return or he will be killed in his sleep. Jano then turns around and returns to the phone, where we can hear him continue to argue with Sandy for another hour, saying nothing about the stabbing. Such is life in the hallways of a jock dorm.

Did I say it is not all fun and games? Well, if I did, the focus has to be on the word *all*, because certainly it's often fun and games, and practical jokes *are* the order of the day. Two freshmen students assigned to our third floor at Founders Hall who were not jocks learn the hard way. Being non-jocks, they are quickly chosen as easy marks for one of those unusual happenings deriving from the ghost of David Gray.

During one late night of studying, when everyone instinctively meets out in the hallway during the occasional break, our young freshmen students are told about the returning ghost of David Gray. In particular, they are warned to be especially careful when alone in the dorm. The trap is set; now it is only about execution.

Enter the Radzik twins, all 6' 5" and 250 pounds of them, showing off their new ski masks from Christmas. This is when the genius strikes me full throttle. I recall the movie *Psycho*, where the pretty blonde is slashed to death in the shower, and re-enacting that scene becomes the plan. Sparing you the gory details, you have never seen two soaking wet, fully-naked freshmen run so fast out of the dorm's community showers as when one of the twins walk into the shower room, completely naked except for a ski mask over his face and a big butcher knife in one hand.

Why we have so many butcher knives handy on the third floor baffles me, but we laugh about it for weeks, and the two freshmen are quickly taken under our wings for being good sports about it afterwards (and, of course, not getting us all tossed out of school). They earn their stripes and feel special for being accepted into the jock fraternity. Nowadays, we'd probably be considered bullies, or an investigation would be commenced, but I can guarantee you this: Those two freshmen never considered themselves nerds again, thereby gaining a whole new level of confidence by befriending us jocks.

Truth be told, it wouldn't surprise me one bit if the person who conceived and wrote the movie script for *Animal House* had lived in Founders Hall. Motorcycles being driven through the large hallways, beer kegs being thrown out of windows and rolling down a flight of stairs or two, toga parties, road trips, and we jocks "streaking" in front of the girl's dormitory—were nothing new to us.

"Streaking," for those who are new to the concept, is when a slightly intoxicated college co-ed runs completely naked, usually from one dorm building to another, or maybe even across the football field during halftime. It would land you in jail today, but not then. In fact, on one stellar evening, we jocks—all of us on the third floor—decide to do this in front of one of the girl's dormitories. And since one depraved, totally classless act deserves another, the girls figured they'll hold up signs with scores on them. I mean really? One to ten? How crass. And because I only received a score of eight, I never spoke to any of those girls for the remainder of the school year. Moi, Poke Salad, now on scholarship to UD, only an eight? How could that be?

EXERCISE:

It is easy to forget the wild and crazy times of youth. Recall some of your best times.

_____

_____

_____

_____

_____

Lasting friendships are made from the bonds of college or earlier times in our lives, from simply friends to fraternities to classmates. List five individuals whom you have not connected with in years.

_____

_____

_____

_____

_____

Think about how old friends might fit into your life today, enabling you to conquer your adversities and achieve your dreams. Make notes here. Then reach out to them via social media or otherwise.

_____

_____

_____

_____

_____

Chapter 28

FIRST STRING QUARTERBACK, BABY

"We're not asking you to be perfect on every play. What
we're asking you is to give a perfect effort on every play
from snap to whistle."

— Coach Bob, Movie, *When the Game Stands Tall*

"If lessons are learned in defeat,
our team is getting a great education."

— Murray Warmath, Head Coach, University of Minnesota

My junior year is my most fun year to date. For starters, my pals and
I always go to the front of the line at Timothy's Bar. Timothy's is the
number one off-campus hot spot, the place where all the hot babes
hang out, and the place where we often drink for free. How cool is
that?

Of greater importance than Timothy's, however, is the great friendships I make this year with jocks of all kinds—seven-foot tall basketball players, short, skinny wrestlers, and massive football players all
occupy the same dorm terrain. Though still five years away, the *Star*

Wars cantina scene could have been inspired by the diverse looks and crazy antics that take place on our third floor.

But the most important friendships I'll make are with members of my offensive line. Playing tackle on both sides of center, the Radzik twins whom I mentioned earlier—Glenn and Gary—and guard Steve Jaye (Gary and Steve always covered my blind side) all warrant special mention. They are so imposing that, at first blush, they seem like three monsters coming at you. The 6' 5" tall twins push past 250 pounds and are all bone, muscle, and sheer might. Steve Jaye nips at their heels at 6' 4", 240 pounds. I'm not *de minimis*, either, at 6' 2" inches and 210 pounds. God bringing nearly a half ton of raging football prowess together off-field—all with a penchant for weird and perverted humor—leads to some crazy escapades.

Add to the mix, Gerald McFadden. Unlike us, Gerry is not attending UD on a sports scholarship; in fact, he doesn't play any organized sport. He's a non-jock from Philly who, due to a glitch in the school registrar's system, is assigned to our notorious jock-only third floor (like the two other freshman nerds mentioned earlier). Well, despite him being a fish totally out of water, somehow he quickly endears himself to our "little" click, becoming a focal point for many of our shenanigans. What's the glue binding this motley crew of jocks and non-jock together? Yes, that mutual penchant for weird and perverted humor in the vein of Jonathan Winters and Robin Williams.

Being flat broke and poor college students left little opportunity for us to wine and dine the college co-eds, so we actually filled many weekend nights with all-night Pinochle games and impromptu comedy routines. The characters on that third floor of my junior year could have given some stiff competition to the cast of *Saturday Night Live*. The disparate senses of humor blended well into many laughs and memorable nights, from sneaking college co-eds into the dorm after hours and putting black shoe polish on the receivers of wall phones, to exploding envelopes filled with shaving cream and beating each other up out on the football field.

~ ~ ~

But putting hijinks aside, my junior year presents me with my first chance to show my stuff on the field. And that's why I'm here at UD in the first place. Though I knock heads with Head Coach John McVay, he at least recognizes my passing skills and, despite always wanting to employ a running game, at least he is willing to embrace more than an occasional pass (the first coach ever to do so with me on the team).

On September 1, 1972, the Friday before our first season game, our school newspaper—*Flyer News*—describes the way everyone feels about the upcoming game. It boasts that this year's "campaign of UD football promises to be exciting. The coaches and players are bristling with the confidence and enthusiasm that every new season brings...." And indeed we are.

Later in the article, the *Flyer News* accurately describes the particular pressure being put on me as the new starting quarterback—yes, I am starting as quarterback for the season opener—a first! "POLKE TAKES COMMAND," it says. "Quarterback, as always is the key. At this writing *Ken Polke* has taken command of the team and should open the year. Ken's long suit is passing and with Nickels and Bierdeman to receive Flyer fans should expect a lot of passing. *The team will win or lose on Polke's performance...*" [emphasis mine].

Talk about pressure. I remember my center, and our team co-captain, Steve Siewe, showing me the paper the night before the game. For a long minute after I read it, I can't stop smiling. Then it hits me: Everyone is relying on me. Our first game of the season, set for September 9, is against the Youngstown State Penguins. Its quarterback

CONQUERING YOUR ADVERSITIES

is none other than Ron Jaworski, soon to be nicknamed "The Polish Rifle," who will spearhead its pass-oriented offense.

So, to put it another way, it's Polke vs. Jaworski in my first starting game as a college varsity player...and my second game starting in my life. Yes, the same Ron Jaworski that many predict will be the first quarterback taken in next year's NFL draft. (Ron, to this day, is featured in many ESPN shows and often cited as a commentator for the NFL. He had a very successful career with the Philadelphia Eagles after being first drafted by the Los Angeles Rams.) Needless to say, the stadium stands for our first season game are filled to the gills, with NFL scouts chomping at the bit to see Ron perform.

But I won't mince words. Before this game is over, I will kill it. Jaworski and I will throw more than 50 passes each, but mine connect. I throw for three touchdowns and we beat the Penguins 18-13. If you were there and saw this game, you would agree with everyone that I beat Jaworski hands down at his own game. No question about it. When this game ends, I'm pumped; I'm on fire. In my mind, and for many who saw that game, there is no doubt who the better quarterback was, as evidenced by the many NFL scouts coming into the locker room to meet me, the new sensation they never expected to see. For the first time in my life, I'm looking and feeling like a winner. That winning spirit carries me forward, as if I've grown the wings of Pegasus.

By mid-season, I'm leading the nation in several offensive categories. Coincidentally, so is my former St. Joe teammate, Greg Leib. Big, strong, and fast, Greg has switched from playing tight end in high school to playing defensive safety at Ohio University. Like me, he's leading the nation in several categories, except he's on the defensive side of the playing field. (Later, in our school reunions at St. Joseph, I will tell Greg that I always thought he could have and should have gone on to the NFL, even though he didn't; he was that talented.)

FIRST STRING QUARTERBACK, BABY

We go on to have a decent but not great season largely due to the friction between Coach McVay and myself. This friction results from vastly different philosophies concerning offensive strategies. It is a similar story to what I faced in high school: a head coach who doesn't understand the depth of my passing talents and who fails to embrace the revolution that's changing football forever from a running game to a passing game.

Especially after the very first game against Ron Jaworski, when it becomes apparent not only to me but to my teammates that putting the ball in the air is the best way to beat most if not all of our opponents, the key to success should have been clear. This conflict over run versus pass reaches a climax during a special team meeting on Monday following our loss to Southern Illinois where they ran a Box 8 running defense that totally shut down our running offense.

A Box 8 defense is designed to stop the run and dares you to throw the ball. Rather than spreading our offensive formation out and going to a controlled, quick-hitting passing attack, which is where we excel, we stick to a traditional running game and never adjust to their highly-effective Box 8. The coaches then blame the team for not putting out enough effort to win the game, when in actuality we were just plain outcoached. It's during this meeting following this game that I defend our team's performance and tell the coaches point blank to look at themselves in the mirror if they want to pin the blame on someone.

In my humble opinion, the sign of a great coach is adjusting the offense and defense to embrace to the team's talents and skills rather than trying to make the team fit into a predetermined offensive or defensive mould, and of course, then adjusting to the opposing team's strategy. But because of the flagrancy of my opinions, my Mom's genes ironically shining through, I am benched for the next three games for speaking my mind. As a result, I fall out of the national rankings.

With me at second string, the coach starts his own son, Jim McVay, at quarterback, but the team does poorly—so poorly that I am quickly reinstated back into the starting lineup. But it is not until the last game of the season against East Carolina that my humble opinions are finally vindicated.

Still sticking to a running attack, for which we do not have the talent, we find ourselves four touchdowns down going into the last quarter. Out of complete frustration, and feeling that he has nothing to lose, Coach McVay allows me to call my own plays for the rest of the game. Immediately, there is a sense of hope on the team, and the momentum of the game turns around. We march up and down the field almost at will by throwing the football and scoring three touchdowns.

East Carolina walks off the field feeling very lucky to have won that game, and if time hadn't run out, they would have lost. Afterwards, it's obvious to everyone in the locker room that we could have achieved a much better win-loss record that season had we adopted a passing offense all year. We had the talent to run what would later become known as the West Coast offense, but we never did have the bruising running attack needed to succeed with a running game. If the coaches had summoned the courage and vision to run a shotgun-style offense, I truly believe we could have beaten most major colleges that season. Our talent was that exceptional.

I'm later vindicated by the coach himself when he apologizes to me after the East Carolina game, both for not believing in my passing talents more and for not embracing a consistent passing offense throughout the year. Unfortunately, he's a day late and a dollar short, as the saying goes.

Nevertheless, by year's end, people are saying that, if I continue on the same course, I'm bound to break a bunch of school records next year. After all those years of sitting on the bench and being disrespected, my determination, hard work, and discipline is starting to pay off. I am finally getting my due.

EXERCISE:

Sometimes all your hard work starts to pay off, but adversities, obstacles, and conflicts still challenge your journey. Recount some of these experiences in your own life.

_____
_____
_____
_____
_____

When faced with these adversities, obstacles, and conflicts, what did you do to overcome, conquer, and resolve them?

_____
_____
_____
_____
_____

Looking back, are there other things you could and should have done, and looking forward, how might you apply these lessons to achieving your goals and dreams?

_____
_____
_____
_____
_____

Chapter 29

SENIOR YEAR & THE RECORD BOOK

"When you win, nothing hurts."

— Joe Namath, legendary Quarterback, aka Broadway Joe

The great Yogi Berra once stated so eloquently—and humorously—that something "seemed like *deja vu* all over again."

After our junior year, Coach McVay is promoted to Athletic Director and is replaced as Head Coach by Ron Marciniak. Unfortunately, our offensive playbook does not change with the new coach. All we do is go from a stubborn, dye-in-the-wool, old school running game philosophy to a non-creative, old school military drill instructor attitude.

Coach Marciniak believes in the same general running attack as his predecessor, the acclaimed Veer, but this time, he wants us to work harder in practice. Yes, before the season starts, he's already setting up the team for blame. If we work harder in practice, he avers, we can master the Veer running game and have a great season. We'll see.

Addressing our season opener against cross-town rival Youngstown, Dayton's leading newspaper, *The Journal Herald*, runs an article that's much like the *Flyer News* article the previous year. It states with optimism: "Flyers Primed for Youngstown." Then it puts the spotlight again on me. "All eyes will be on Flyers quarterback, Ken Polke, to see if he has what it takes...." Next to the article is a large profile picture of me. I keep a copy of the paper and later give it to my parents.

We beat Youngstown handily, and in our second game of the season, go up against the Bowling Green Falcons. This time we get beaten soundly, and frankly, I'm pissed at our new coach for reverting to the Veer. Our team talents do not lend themselves any more to a running game this year than they did the year before.

Again, the coach and I do not see eye-to-eye. When the game is over, out of sheer frustration and knowing we could have beaten this team under different circumstances, I don't follow our players into our own team locker room. Instead, I peel off to the Falcons' locker room to give them a pep talk on beating our common nemesis, Miami University of Ohio, whom they will soon face.

My center, Steve Sewie, later tells me our coach grabbed him by the shoulder pads in our locker room, mad as a hornet, and asked him, "Where in the hell is Polke?"

"I believe he's in the Falcons' locker room," Steve replies sheepishly.

"What? Are you kidding me? Would you please do me a favor and get the hell over there and bring me back my quarterback?"

"Sure, Coach," Steve says, then runs over to the Falcons' locker room. When he arrives, I see him out of the corner of my eye. I'm standing on a table in the middle of the locker room, socks on but helmet and shoulder pads in my hands, haranguing at the top of my lungs how the Falcons can beat University of Ohio at Miami. The entire Falcons' team, coaches included, are riveted to my every word. It's clear that an opposing quarterback has never entered their locker room after a game *they* won and told them how to beat an upcoming joint rival.

"When you play those Redhawks, I want you to kick their asses," I yell, channelling Coach Gutbrod. "Watch out for this…. Don't do that…. Kick their asses through the goal posts of life."

"Ken!" Steve yells to me. "Coach wants you right away. Get off that table and let's get over there. He's about to blow a gasket."

I stop for a moment, say, "Tell him to cool his heels. I'll be right there," and then I proceed to give the Falcons a few more sage words of advice.

I must admit, Steve and I see the universe differently. He tells me he's never heard of anyone doing what I'm doing—giving the opponents and winning team a pep talk in their locker room after a game. And surely he's right. But things like that do not deter me. If nothing else, I speak my mind, *in my humble opinion*. In fact, Steve once accused me of speaking "everything" that's on my mind. While I wouldn't agree with that entirely (he is, after all, only my center), I'm sure that from time to time it must have seemed that way. If he only knew that, to me, it was actually the opposite: I rarely spoke what was really on my mind.

As the season nears the end, the headline to the *The Journal Herald's* November 12, 1973, Monday paper captures the glory of our Saturday victory against Louisville, where we prevailed in a squeaker 10-9. It reads: "Polke sets three records; Flyer defense impressive." That victory brings our season record to 5-4-1 going into our last game against Marshall State, now three years as a team following the horrific plane crash. Unfortunately, our performance against Louisville was lackluster. I completed only *twelve* of *twenty-two* passes for a total of only 127 yards. But when my game totals are added to my previous season totals, I break three school records. The article states:

Kenny now has the most total yards in a season (1,461) and the most pass attempts in a year (241) and career (457). He needs nine completions and 97 yards to match Frank Siggins' UD season marks, and 15 receptions and 174 yards to catch Frank's career totals.

Also, Polke is 186 yards away from tailback Gary Kosins' UD career total offense figure of 2,831.

The next week, we beat Marshall for the final game of my college career. Despite butting heads with the coach, and totally disagreeing with his use of the Veer offense, I did turn in a very solid college career performance. For that reason, when the Sunday night annual UD Football Banquet takes place, I expect to be recognized for my many accomplishments and multiple school records. Instead, I am shunned, invoking the humiliation and disrespect that I thought I had long left behind with the peanut butter and jelly jar fiasco.

The Review Journal's, November 19, 1973, Monday morning edition captures the essence of our banquet night. First it congratulates "Steady Eddie" Zink for walking away with two major awards—MVP and Flyer of the Year. My buddy, offensive guard Don Daily, receives the scholar-athlete award, and three more players are named to play for the West in the Second Ohio Shrine Bowl.

As for me, the article states:

Ken Polke, the senior quarterback who broke seven school records this season, including Gary Kosins' career total offense mark, did not win an award.

But the Flyer record book will be shattered with these Polke records: Season—Total Offense (1,689 yards); most pass completions (110); most passing yards (1,517), and most pass attempts (274).

Career—Total Offense (2,873), passing yards (2,696), and pass attempts (490).

In a way, it's the story of my life. Now I go into the post season wondering whether I will be picked up in the NFL draft...or whether I will be finished with football forever...and return to the ghosts and goblins of Collinwood.

EXERCISE:

Sometimes we break records or win awards that have been a long time in coming. Name and describe some of your award-winning moments.

_____

_____

_____

_____

_____

What do you believe enabled you to conquer your personal adversities to reach each of those award-winning moments?

_____

_____

_____

_____

_____

Often the record or award is not as important as the journey to get there. Does that observation apply to any of your special moments?

_____

_____

_____

_____

_____

Chapter 30

DON SHULA &
THE WORLD CHAMPION MIAMI DOLPHINS

"Winning can be bittersweet."

— Dr. Kenneth J. Polke

Despite being shunned on awards night, as a college quarterback who set seven school records, I have my eye on the NFL. I want to go pro, it being a dream of mine ever since I won the paper route competition as a kid. In my mind, the notion that football is my only way out of Collinwood has only gotten stronger. While majoring in Pre-Med, I'm on track to graduate with a 3.2 average out of a possible 4.0, and am slotted to receive a B.A. in Chemistry. Sports is my first love, and I've never been so sure that I want to make it to the NFL: the dream of playing in the NFL burns in my soul.

In 1974, my college graduation year, the NFL draft is held in January in New York City. When I'm home for the Christmas holidays, I'm on pins and needles hoping against hope that I will get a call. Back then, we didn't have mobile phones and most college players did not have agents, so we literally waited by the phone, jumping every time it rang.

Unfortunately, the holidays come and pass without a peep. I return to school and focus on graduating. On many occasions, I take off on a walk late at night, mulling over in my mind my various options. Mom and Dad are at home taking care of my little sister—Christine is only three. Dennis and Cheryl are both still in college, which costs my parents a fortune. There's no way in the world they can pay for me to attend dental or medical school, but that is my only real option other than returning home and seeing what shakes out in the neighborhood, soon to be dubbed "Bomb City, USA."

The year ends and I graduate without so much as a feeler from any NFL recruiter. Packing my things at the dorm evokes strong mixed emotions. With college came the best times of my life. I made countless friends who would remain so forever, and, of course, I did well on the football field, finally gaining some modicum of respect. But not being drafted to the NFL is the most painful thing ever to happen to me. It means the likely end of something I truly love: the all-American game of football.

For the first few weeks after returning home, I catch up with old friends, falling back into some old neighborhood habits. I'm over 21 now, of course, so I can go to all the bars and drink hard liquor. Ohio has always been easy when it comes to booze, allowing 16-year-olds to buy and drink 3.2 percent beer, which is indistinguishable from any other beer in the darkness of most bars.

One Saturday afternoon, my dad and I are sitting in the living room watching a Cleveland Indians game. The previous year, the Indians had come in last place in the AL East, a miserable 71-91 record, but as a diehard fan, Dad is optimistic they will rebound in 1974. "That John Ellis is having a hot bat so far," Dad says. "If Lowenstein can start to connect, we have a fighting chance."

The phone rings and Dad gets up to answer it, his eyes glued to the television as Ellis faces a three and two pitch. "Hello," he says, barely catching it in time. "Yes, this is the Polke residence. Yes, he sure is."

"Son," he whispers as he covers the mouthpiece with his hand, "it's Coach Don Shula of the Miami Dolphins."

I roll my eyes and say, more to myself and to him, "Sure it is, Dad. Tell those jerks to buzz off, will you?"

Dad pushes his hand harder on the phone mouthpiece and raises his voice several octaves. "Son, listen to me. I'm not kidding. It sounds like Coach Shula. He wants to talk to you."

I climb off the couch and head toward the kitchen, thinking he might be in on it and muttering, "I'm going to kick some ass when I find out who's messing with me." I reach out and jerk the phone from Dad's hand. "Hey, you guys—"

"Is this Ken Polke?" an older male voice asks. My heart almost stops.

"Ah, ah, ah, yes," I say slowly.

"Hi, Ken. This is Coach Don Shula, Miami Dolphins."

"Yes, sir, Coach Shula. How are you, sir?" I look over at Dad, my eyes growing as my voice rises so high I could be singing soprano in the Cleveland Philharmonic.

"Excellent. Ken, we'd like you to play for the Dolphins. Would you be interested in that?"

For a solid minute, I cannot breathe. When air finally returns to my lungs, I say, "I sure would."

"I'll have my recruitment guy call you with his travel plans and get your address. He'll probably call you Monday, and then make it to your house next week to sign the paperwork."

"I look forward to it," I say.

"Excellent. See you soon."

I hang up the phone, numb with shock. The coach for one of the greatest professional football teams ever assembled has just called me directly at our tiny prefab home in Collinwood and offered me a spot on his team. And on top of that, I already know he hails from Cleveland and is a disciple of legendary Cleveland Browns coach Paul Brown. Is it a dream come true?

I pinch myself to make sure I'm not dreaming. Then, sure that I'm awake, I say, "Dad, that *was* Coach Shula, and he just asked me to join the Miami Dolphins. *The* Miami Dolphins. What should I do? Should I actually do it?"

He pauses for a minute to think, then says without reservation: "Son, if you don't do it, you will regret it the rest of your life."

In a matter of days, *the* Sil Cornachioni, the legendary pro scout, is sitting at my kitchen table. I'm shocked to learn that Sil hails from Collinwood, of all places, born here in 1927, a 1945 graduate of Collinwood High School. (Sil lived a long life, passing in February 2015 at the age of 87. RIP, Sil, and thanks for signing me.)

With my dad's blessing, I sign the paperwork without even reading it and begin preparing for the biggest adventure of my life: playing quarterback for the world champion Miami Dolphins.

"When do you want Kenny in Miami?" Dad asks Sil.

Looking at me, Sil says: "Coach Shula wants you in camp sooner than the other players so he can work with you and have you get used to the heat and humidity."

"You got it," I reply. "But how will I get there?"

"Plane tickets will be sent to you by courier."

My talents are finally being recognized, I think to myself, and not just by any coach, but by one of the greatest of all-time. "Holy Cow, Batman!" I yell.

The weeks that follow are a blur. Before I know it, I'm on a plane to Miami International Airport, leaving from Cleveland Hopkins. With the ticket was the note that Coach Shula will pick me up at the airport himself. When my feet hit the hard carpet of the arrival gate, I scan the terminal looking for the legend, though I'm really doubting he will be the one picking me up.

That's when I spot Coach Shula marching down the terminal in my direction with a big smile on his face. Inside I almost do a somer-sault. The closer he gets, the bigger the smile, and then he starts to wave. Soon he's holding his arms out as if to give me a big bear-hug, though something seems off. Something's going on here, I think.

When he's about ten feet out, I smile back and hold my arms out awkwardly to bear-hug him in return. When he walks right past me without slowing, I turn around, wondering what he's doing. And there they are—his wife (Dorothy) and his kids are just feet behind me. They hail from Cleveland, no doubt returning to Miami after visiting family back in Cleveland.

No wonder Coach Shula was so happy to pick me up at the airport, I'm thinking to myself while sitting in the back of his station wagon loaded to the gills with what seem like 20 screaming kids. Welcome to the real NFL!

I get checked in that night and am so excited to get to the practice field that I have a hard time sleeping. The next day, I'm walk into the locker room of the team that won Super Bowl VII in 1973 after completing the only undefeated season in NFL history, and then repeated last year (1974) in Super Bowl VIII.

What an unbelievable leapfrog, I'm thinking, to go from the UD Flyers to the Miami Dolphins, the best team in all of football, with no draft in between. Jesus, there I am, in the same room with some of the best football players ever—quarterback Bob Griese, quarterback Earl Morrall (then second string to Griese), running back Larry Csonka, running back Mercury Morris, running back Jim Kiick and, of course, well, one more guy, to name only a few.

I put my things in the locker and then feel a tap on the shoulder. I turn around. It's the one more guy: Paul Warfield is standing there with a wide grin, having been picked up by the Dolphins a few years earlier. "I told you, Kenny, that you'd play in the NFL," he says with a big smile. "Are you ready?" Then he laughs. "Of course not. No one can be ready for the NFL."

I respond with a smile and reach out my hand. "You sure did. Thanks, Paul, for your confidence in me. I can't tell you what a difference it made playing with you and Frank."

"Well, welcome aboard. And get ready for the ride of your life."

He then turns and walks away, leaving me there to feel my first ever NFL out-of-body experience, and thinking: *I'm a God's honest Miami Dolphin. You've made it. You're not in Cleveland anymore, Poke Salad.*

~ ~ ~

I am instantly exposed to a radically different perspective on how this game should be played. I've always known that football is a violent sport played by violent men, but now my eyes are opened to the mental side of the game, the mental chess match, if you will. But this side is right up my alley. I feel confident, like Frank Ryan must have felt because I'm well-educated, having attended Catholic school all my life.

Building on the knowledge imparted to me by Ryan and Warfield back in high school, and, of course, my high school and college coaches, my learning curve is massive. Quickly, I learn to read defenses as the offensive coaches, led by Coach Shula, take me through my progressions from primary to secondary to tertiary receivers. Man-on-man coverage vs. zone coverage is no longer black-and-white, one or the other. I learn that professional defenses present a mixture of both in order to confuse the quarterback and keep him off balance.

But here's the big difference from college and high school, at least for me. I'm finally working with a coaching staff that I can learn something from, some of the best guys in the game, and my excitement transcends my focus to a whole new level. Grasping how to read defenses, in and of itself, giving me an edge like the house in Vegas.

As expected, training camp is brutal. A taskmaster, Coach Shula works us to the bone; but I enjoy approaching the game from a whole different perspective. As a consequence, I feel fully prepared for our first preseason game against the Cincinnati Bengals at Riverfront stadium. Yes, just a four-hour drive from the house where I grew up.

My dad arrives two hours early for the game. Mom could have accompanied Dad, of course, but she did not want to see me get mauled. Yes, that's right; she will never attend a single game in my entire football career, from high school to the pros.

Though Earl Morrall is the Dolphins' starter at QB, it's a preseason game so Coach Shula puts me in when we find ourselves down by 13 points. Also a rookie that year is a guy by the name of Nat Moore, converted to running back from wide receiver. (After an illustrious career with the Dolphins, Nat is now the Director of Player Personnel.) Let's just say, using Nat's own words, that he and I "lit it up that night under the night skies in Cincinnati."

Before the first half ends, we connect on two long bombs, pulling the game within reach as Coach Shula draws up the right plays, responding brilliantly to the mercurial Cincinnati defense.

Immediately after the game, the team begins boarding the buses to take us back to the airport to depart to Miami. I leave the locker room and go look for Dad. He's standing by himself, talking to anyone who will talk back to him. "Dad!" I yell.

He looks around until he sees me. A huge grin on his face, he walks over and shakes my hand, then we hug. "Great game, son. I am so proud of you. You and Nat looked great out there."

"Thanks, Dad. Follow me. Ready to meet Coach Shula and the team?"

"You bet I am, son," he replies, and we walk down the long corridor to the locker room, me leading and him following, a poignant reversal from when I was young.

Once inside, Dad is beside himself. This is the first time he has ever been inside a real professional team locker room. A few of the guys look over and say hello. One or two walk over, introduce themselves, and shake his hand before patting him on the back.

Then the moment comes. Coach Shula sees us and walks over. "Mr. Polke?" he says as he sticks out his hand. "Hi, I'm Don Shula."

My dad punches his hand out and gives Coach a vigorous handshake. Words cannot describe the pride beaming from his face.

"Kenny had a great game tonight, but, of course, there is still much to work on," Coach Shula tells my dad, who is speechless.

"Kenny has nothing but great things to say about you, Coach, and how happy he is to be learning from the best."

"Are you going back home to Cleveland with your dad tonight?" Coach Shula asks me.

"I thought we had to head back to Miami, Coach," I say.

"You have off till Tuesday morning. This isn't college anymore. Just be back in time for practice on Tuesday. See you then. You deserve it."

The following morning, my picture is plastered all over the Sports Section of the *Cleveland Plain Dealer*. Our phone rings non-stop all day, with family, friends and, yes, fans, calling to wish us the best. In the Polke household, those two days are unbelievable, not in the casual sense of the word, but in the actual meaning of *un-be-liev-able*.

I head back to Miami on Monday, in time for morning practice on Tuesday, with reporters mobbing me at Biscayne College—Dolphins' training headquarters at the time—when I arrive for practice. But again, the dance with fame expires quickly. Preseason continues, and because of that first exemplary game against Cincinnati, I receive more playing time, but that's not what it is about. I learn that Coach Shula had only brought me on board as a hedge against the NFL strike.

Now that the NFL strike is over (I didn't even know there was a strike when Coach Shula called me), it's all about the numbers. Only so many people can make the team, as there are only so many seats on the bench. And they already have two amazing quarterbacks, both Super Bowl winners for the Dolphins—Earl Morral and Bob Griese.

They don't need a third guy who didn't start until his junior year in college. I am released from the Dolphins the very summer I'm hired.

~ ~ ~

Thankfully, before the ink dries on my Dolphins release papers, I get a call from my hometown team, the Cleveland Browns. They want me, so I finish out the season on the taxi squad (reserve squad as it is known now) with the Browns. This means I sit in on all team meetings, but I don't dress for the games on Sunday. Which is not to say I'm of no value to them. The Browns coaches pick my brain for every detail they can get from me before we play the Dolphins, and we go on to defeat them because I had memorized their every move and strategy.

Apparently, Coach Shula is devastated by his loss to the Browns, later commenting it was "the toughest game of my career." To what degree I contributed to that, by sharing and discussing with my new team every detail I knew about the Dolphins' game strategy, no one will ever know. Then, after losing to us, the Dolphins are dealt another devastating blow after losing in the playoffs. Csonka, Warfield, and Kiick all leave the Dolphins and join the Memphis Southmen in the short-lived World Football League, ironically to play for my old UD college nemesis, none other than Coach John McVay.

EXERCISE:

You prepare for something all of your life. You achieve it. And it doesn't work out as you hoped. Has this ever happened to you?

_____

_____

_____

_____

_____

_____

_____

Life is a long road. When one dream does not work out, another takes shape on the horizon. Do you have a dream on the horizon? If so, what is it?

_____

_____

_____

_____

_____

_____

_____

What is your plan to achieve this dream?

_____

_____

_____

_____

_____

_____

_____

PART III
COMING HOME

"I am, he thought, a part of all that I have touched and that has touched me, which, having for me no existence save that which I gave to it, became other than itself by being mixed with what I then was, and is now still otherwise, having fused with what I now am, which is itself a cumulation of what I have been becoming. Why here? Why there? Why now? Why then?"

— Thomas Wolfe, *Look Homeward, Angel*

Chapter 31

COMING HOME, THE CLEVELAND BROWNS & "BOMB CITY, USA"

"You can learn a line from a win, and a book from a defeat."

— Paul Brown, Head Coach, Cleveland Browns

"I didn't dub Collinwood 'Bomb City, USA.' But what else would you call a neighborhood with 35 bombings over just a few years' time?"

— Dr. Kenneth J. Polke

Danny Greene, the Irish-American gangster who began his rise to prominence in Collinwood in the 1960s when I was a boy, is now a legend in our neighborhood. To some, he's a good family man who's become known as Collinwood's very own Robin Hood. But to many, he's a criminal and a thug. In reality, in my humble opinion he's all of those things rolled into one.

What I know about Danny Greene derives mostly from lore, from stories told by my mom and dad, by rumors filtering through the neighborhood, and by newspaper accounts. Sure, I would see him around, trolling the hood with his convertible top down, waving to people up and down the block. But that was mostly it. Occasionally, he would make an appearance at Collinwood events, e.g., little league games, fairs, and parades.

As the story goes, one of his early jobs is acting as the enforcer for Shondor Birns' numbers racket, and the muscle for mobster Frank "Little Frank" Brancato's garbage-hauling enterprise. Around 1968, when I was 14 and just starting high school, supposedly Birns directed Greene to handle a black numbers operator, and in the process, Greene almost blew himself up. That's apparently what inaugurated him into the bomb business.

In early 1971, when I was off to college at UD, it's reported that one of Greene's accomplices, Art Sneperger, blew himself up with a car bomb intended for Mike "Big Mike" Frato, who had formed a refuse-hauling organization that competed with the mob. Frato had previously complained about Greene bringing mob involvement to the garbage business in Cuyahoga County, where Collinwood is located. So the bombing was seen as Greene's reply to Frato's complaints.

It's not like Frato and Greene didn't know each other personally, either. At one point, they reportedly are partners and close friends, each naming their sons after the other. Then in November 1971, Frato is shot and killed in White City Beach, which is located in Euclid Beach Park only miles from our house. Greene is interrogated over the killing, but he is never arrested for it, credibly claiming that Frato had shot at him first while he was jogging and exercising his dogs.

Soon afterwards, Greene is again out jogging at White City Beach when a sniper takes aim at him and shoots several times, barely missing the mark (apparently a hit put out by Birns). This time,

Greene is so outraged that he whips out a revolver from his waist and starts charging in the direction of the sniper, reportedly firing full throttle. The sniper, rather than shoot back, flees from fright. That is the manner in which Greene sows his legendary reputation as fearless and invincible.

Plain Dealer and *Cleveland Magazine* journalist Ned Whelan, to whom Greene would send critiques in green ink, writes this of Greene, capturing the one side of his Dr. Jekyll and Mr. Hyde personae:

Imagining himself as a feudal baron, he supported a number of destitute Collinwood families, paid tuition to Catholic schools for various children and, like the gangsters of the Twenties, actually had fifty, twenty pound turkeys delivered to needy households on Thanksgiving.

On March 29, 1975, Birns is blown to shreds as he enters his car, which is parked behind Christy's Lounge. Christy's is a West Collinwood bar formerly known as the Jack and Jill West Lounge, located at 2516 Detroit Avenue NW, only miles from my house. The *Plain Dealer* reports that the explosive force of the bomb blew Birns through the roof of the 1975 Mark IV Lincoln Continental in which he was sitting. Apparently the police find fragments of Birns' body splattered on the front passenger door.

Police guess that the car's ignition was wired to sticks of dynamite. But their bigger concern is the potential for a mob war erupting in the wake of Birns' death. Revenge killings are anticipated, as is a bloody battle for control of his numbers racket since he died without leaving an heir apparent. When I arrive back in Cleveland to play for the Browns, I take up temporary residence at my parents' house, and so, the mob again casts a long, ugly shadow across my world.

Indeed, throughout the early '70s while I'm off at college, no fewer than 35 bombs explode in Collinwood. So, in the summer of 1975, bomb smoke is in the air when I report to Kent State University for training camp under the Browns' new head coach, Forrest Gregg, the team previously helmed for decades by legendary Head Coach Paul Brown...a team with a history of eight championships and a remarkable win-loss record at the time...a team that imbued me with pride as a little boy...a team that gave me some of my first heroes.

~ ~ ~

That summer, on Wednesday, July 23, 1975, the Browns hold their first scrimmage with me starting as quarterback. My biggest fan, my dad, sits in the stands rooting me on. I throw two touchdown passes and complete five of six passes for 79 yards. Nothing for the record books, but one completion is a 42-yard bomb to Billy Lefear, who had recently moved to wide receiver from his rookie slot as running back the previous year. Not bad for a start.

The veterans are present and in uniform, but most don't play, including starting quarterback Mike Phipps, and backup quarterback, Brian Sipe. These guys are my ultimate competition.

Dad rushes up to me after the game. "Son, you were fantastic."

"Thanks, Dad."

Excited as a kid in a candy shop, he crouches into a boxing pose and punches me on the shoulder, à la Uncle Eddie. "With that kind of performance," he says, "you might grab the starting position, don't you think?"

"I sure could, Dad. Crazier things have happened."

"Son, listen to me," he says. "You can do it. You can start. I know it."

But when exhibition season starts, the Browns are in a state of turmoil and morale is lower than a snake's belly. Under "horrendous leadership" from the new head coach (not my words), the team's roster is like a revolving door. Players never know from one minute to the next whether they will be on the team or gone. It's difficult to give your all under those circumstances, and it will show in one of the worst seasons in franchise history for the Browns, who will win only three games.

Predictably, players will be very upset and Coach Gregg's tenure will be short-lived. As an ex-player of the one and only one Vince Lombardi, legendary coach of the Green Bay Packers, when Coach Gregg tries to imitate the legend's coaching style, players see right through it as being phoney.

So, before the season even starts, I'm thinking it is time for me to re-assess my life's goals. Accordingly, in September 1975, after months of inner turmoil, I make the biggest decision of my life: I decide to leave football. After conquering so many adversities, and overcoming so many obstacles to get where I am, the decision is not an easy one. Quitting is just not in my genes. But I'm living at home and not even making enough money to survive on, with both Phipps and Sipe ahead of me, and more great quarterbacks entering the league every year.

With the weight of a lifetime on my shoulders, I walk into Coach Gregg's office and give him the news. He understands. "Thanks for your efforts, Kenny, and best of luck to you in your future endeavors."

"Send my check to the house, will you?"

"Of course. Got all your stuff?"

"Yeah, right over here." I point to an orange-and-brown mesh bag outside the door. It's bursting at the seams with my helmet, shoulder pads, home and away uniforms, and several keepsake footballs.

"Sorry, Kenny, but all the gear has to stay."

"No keepsakes for a lifetime of work?"

"'fraid not."

When I get home, it's about 7:00 p.m. (I usually grab a bite with one of the guys and don't get home until 9:00 p.m.), and the streetlights are just coming on. I grab the bag from the trunk by habit and lug what's left of my stuff to the front door.

Inside, Mom is cooking dinner in the kitchen, and Dad is studying the Cleveland Indians box scores in the living room while watching the news. Christine is playing dolls on the floor in front of the television while Dennis and Cheryl are off at college. The house seems empty and spacious as I stand awkwardly at the doorway for a few moments until Mom looks over and says, "Oh, Ken, what are you doing home so early? Is something wrong?"

"No, Mom, nothing's wrong."

Mom turns back to the sound of a loud sizzle on the stove.

I turn toward the living room. "Hey, Dad, wanna play some catch?"

Having taken him by surprise, especially since he is comfortable in his chair, he looks at me strangely before he says: "Ah, oh, okay, sure, Kenny. I'd love to."

I grab the old gloves and ball from the closet and we head out to the sidewalk in front of the house, taking our spots just like we used to do in the old days.

"What's going on, son?"

"Ah, nothing, Dad. Just thought I'd come home early for some of Mom's home cooking and a game of catch."

Dad squats and holds up the catcher's mitt, as I wind up and rip a fast ball down the sidewalk. Smack. "Ouch!" he yells. "Hey, you're not a kid anymore. Gotta take it easy on the old man."

About this time, Mom walks out and, after watching us for a moment, says with hesitation, "Men, dinner is ready."

"Hey, Mom, come on out for a minute, will you? I have something I want to tell you guys."

I tuck the glove under my arm and walk in between them in the grass of the front yard. They join me from both sides. A train whistle toots in the distance. Church bells chime from somewhere in the neighborhood—it's exactly 7:30 p.m.

"Everything all right, Kenny?" Mom asks, concern evident by the higher pitch of her voice. Both Mom and Dad look at me with long eyes, knowing something profound has happened.

"I won't beat around the bush," I say. "I've decided to quit football."

A long silence grips the air, except for the lone sound of a motorcycle engine ripping the quiet evening as it accelerates down the highway.

"I've decided to go to medical school."

Another long silence follows, until Mom breaks down and cries. She rarely cries, but now from the overwhelming force of the words, her crying transforms into deep sobs, except these are not sobs of sadness; these are sobs of joy. "I'm so glad," she says. "I was always so worried you'd get—"

"I know, Mom—hurt."

She shakes her head, then pulls up her apron to wipe the tears streaming down her cheeks.

"Let's go eat and celebrate, men," she says as she turns toward the house.

"Mom," I say. "Catch." I underhand the ball toward her, giving it a high loop. She turns and spreads her hands wide to catch the ball in her apron.

Dad reaches out his hand. "I'm proud of you, son, and you know, Mom and I support you in whatever you do."

No truer words could be spoken.

EXERCISE:

Have you ever made a life-altering decision that seems to go against the grain of everything you have worked for until that time? If so, describe it here.

_____

_____

_____

_____

_____

_____

As you sit here today, reading this book, do you have any unfulfilled passions and dreams? If so, what are they?

_____

_____

_____

_____

_____

_____

_____

What decision can you make right now to fulfill those passions and dreams while you still can?

_____

_____

_____

_____

_____

_____

_____

EPILOGUE

"Adversity introduces a man to himself."

— H.L. Mencken

"Those who live by the bomb, die by the bomb...."

— Lt. Andrew Vanyo, head of Cleveland's Criminal Intelligence Unit

Upon hearing of my retirement from the NFL, my mother's old friend, Mike Polensek, a fellow Catholic serving as our city councilman, asks me if I would like to give back to the community. I say, "Sure, Mike, what do you have in mind?"

"Ken, we've received federal funding to open up two Youth Centers in the community. This is a new project and we can't think of anyone better suited for the directorship position than you. We know these kids will look up to you, especially coming from the neighborhood itself."

"Sounds interesting, Mike," I say.

"Our mission will be to lend emotional and spiritual assistance to young men and women in need. You know, victims of some hard knocks. Some just need a place to feel wanted and pass time. Others need a major lift to get back on their feet. I'd love for you to take the lead on this."

Like me, Mike grew up in Collinwood, but unlike me, he attended the public schools—first Nottingham Grade School and then Collinwood High School, from which he graduated in 1969. I reply, "Let me think about it for a night, but sure, it sounds like something I'd like to do."

After mulling it over, the next day I call Mike and say, "I'll do it," and for the next two years, I work for the Youth Centers 24/7, living, breathing, and sleeping there every day and night, as I ready myself for my next big journey in life.

Sadly, while devoting myself to the Youth Centers from 1975 to 1977, 37 bombs explode in Collinwood, East Cleveland, and Cuyahoga County, giving us the reputation, "Bomb City, USA." It is hard to imagine this apocalyptic nightmare if you don't live here yourself, but it's the reality. Indeed, in April 1977, journalist Whelan writes: "Greene...leads a life that only a Hollywood scriptwriter could conjure up for an underworld character."

In the fall of 1977, I start Dental School at Case Western Reserve University. At that time, our dental class at CWRU ranks number two compared to all the other dental schools in the nation.

While attending school, I work the graveyard shift on the weekends at the Cleveland Clinic Blood Bank for beer money. People from all over the world come here to have open heart surgery. The clinic to this day pioneers many innovative techniques for open-heart surgery. One Middle Eastern king, along with his reported 75 wives, takes up an entire floor during his visit. He is so impressed with his care that he leaves an endowment of millions to the hospital.

A funny story comes to mind about an elderly Southern couple from Alabama. I am assigned to draw blood from the husband, who is undergoing open-heart surgery the following morning. Each open-heart surgery patient requires six pints of compatible blood for transfusion during surgery, and it is our job to have the appropriate blood matched and screened prior to surgery.

Upon entering the room, the patient's wife is very inquisitive about where her husband's blood for the transfusion will be coming from.

"Donors from the neighborhood," I reply.

This answer does not satisfy her curiosity, so she continues her line of questioning. As I finish obtaining blood samples, her *real* concern dawns on me: the clinic is located in an all-black community, and she is afraid her husband might be getting blood from a black man.

I assure both her and her husband that they are in great hands, and that the doctors and staff are the best in the world, but I can't help but add: "If, after the surgery, Mrs. Smith, you see your husband has developed a propensity for watermelon, barbecued chicken, and wanting to tap dance, please notify the doctors immediately." These are my exact words.

As I look over to her husband, I can see him looking at his wife, rolling his eyes in disgust, followed by a smile sent in my direction that says, "Thank you for tolerating her." A wink back from me conveys an understanding, "You're welcome." With few words spoken, a young Northerner and an elderly Southerner have bonded. He knows my prayers are with him because we share a common bond… his well-being.

The month after I start dental school, Danny Greene's nine lives run out when the Mayfield Road Mob gets its revenge. Like Birns before him, he is blown to shreds by a bomb, except in his case, it's a Trojan Horse Bomb placed in the car adjacent to his in the Brainard Place parking lot of his dentist, as I mentioned earlier.

Lt. Andrew Vanyo, head of Cleveland's Criminal Intelligence Unit, comments on his misfortune: "He knew the code: Those who live by the bomb, die by the bomb...."

In the trials of Greene's accused killers (some found guilty, some cleared), prosecutors and witnesses cast light on the dark, bizarre underbelly of Cleveland's criminal underground. But after weeks of testimony from dozens of witnesses, all seem to agree: other than for the mob being involved, there is no rhyme or reason for the bombings and the murders. No one knows the entire story, and no one ever will.

One lucky twist of fate resulting from Greene's murder, and the subsequent prosecutions, is the domino effect it causes. The FBI will crack down hard like never before, pressuring the new generation of gangsters to jettison their allegiance to *omerta*. Countless thugs, who would have laid down their lives before squealing in an earlier era, spill their guts to save their own skins, turning state's evidence against each other, leaping for deals and plea bargains like rats on a sinking ship.

When the ship sinks below the surface, the prosecutors achieve no less than 22 convictions, all of which are plastered across the headlines of the *Plain Dealer* and other newspapers and magazines. Before all is said and done, they will have cut the heart out of the mob from Cleveland to Chicago and as far away as New York, Los Angeles, and Las Vegas.

Married twice, Greene leaves five children. His oldest son, Danny Kelly, once described his father as "truly intrepid.... He probably could have been governor or senator if he hadn't gone the other way." Which is what I did. I went the other way, graduating from Case Western Dental School in 1981—a graduation that both my dad *and* my mom attended—a family first except for my high school graduation. My playing in the NFL made my dad proud, and now, graduating from Case Western Reserve Dental School, makes my mom even prouder.

The merger in 1990 of St. Joseph and Villa Angela High School enables both schools to get on their feet in a time of shrinking piety. Thankfully, the school that provided the best of private education, sports programs, and values to young minds for 140 years has since emerged as one of the fastest growing private schools in all of Ohio.

Credit must be given to Principal Richard Osborn, Class of '69. His efforts to rally the alumni have been invaluable. Of course, it has been said—behind Richard's back—that countless alumni made financial donations just to get Richard to stop talking. We love you, Richard, and appreciate you for all your hard work; but you can stop talking once the alumnus has signed the check!

In 1991, I propose to my wife Valerie on a mainland flight to Hawaii, where we are heading for a well-deserved vacation. Valerie is a country girl from Ashtabula, Ohio. I was introduced to her by Jeremy "Moe" Bratt. Jeremy was one of my dog walkers in the neighbourhood for my two Golden Retrievers, Nicklaus and Trevino. Jeremy was ten years old at the time. Out of all the blind dates I've been fixed up with, it took a ten-year old to introduce me to the girl of my dreams. Jeremy will later become the best man at our wedding.

You romantics will appreciate the next story. My plan is to propose to Valerie after we arrive in Hawaii. But Mom, still being old school in her thinking, compounded by being Catholic, warns me that I need to propose before leaving Cleveland. Not one to comply literally with my mom's wishes, I come up with an alternative plan. Upon boarding the plane, I ask the flight attendants whether they have champagne on board, because if they do, my plan is to slip the engagement ring into Val's glass.

"Sure," they say, and they join me in the conspiracy.

Like nothing unusual is up, they serve us champagne and then deliberately hover nearby in the aisle. Wanting to see Val's expression, they look busy serving others but get anxious because Val is buried in her paperback and not paying any attention to her glass of champagne. Finally, having to move down the aisle, they stop dead in their tracks when Val releases a huge scream. The pilot immediately announces over the P.A. that all is good. "It's just Dr. Polke asking Valerie to marry him. After all, what's a girl to do at 35,000 feet over the Pacific Ocean?"

The plane erupts into a thunderous applause, which leads to one heck of a party. Who says jocks don't have a sensitive side? Among the passengers are my parents. *It is their very first vacation ever, and they are here to witness my grand engagement—a very small payback for their life of sacrifice for our family.*

Our wedding takes place in Cleveland in June the following year. All the guys from our third floor "Animal House" make an appearance—both Radzik twins, Glenn and Gary, as well as Steve Jaye and Gerry McFadden. It's the last time we will ever come together in one place, and I smile ear-to-ear every time I look at them, sensing this is a very special moment. Sadly, cancer will take Gary's life and diabetes Gerry's in the years to follow. RIP, guys. I miss and love you both—words I write with tears in my eyes.

~ ~ ~

On November 17, 2015, almost 40 years to the day I left the NFL, I drive past the old crik and arrive for the event at my alma mater, now Villa Angela—St. Joseph High School. This night, I see many old friends and tell them about my upcoming book. They all ask for a copy.

EPILOGUE

When the entire 1969-1970 football team is called to the stage to be inducted into the Hall of Champions, I'm right there with them, beaming from ear to ear and patting the backs of the guys who crushed me in the brutal scrimmages of yesteryear. When the spotlight shines on me for a moment, I hold up a jar of peanut butter and jelly swirl…. Just kidding.

A few months later, to our total shock and surprise, Val suffers acute heart damage and requires a pacemaker to be installed to monitor her heart's rhythm. Because of this, we make a huge decision: We decide to move back home near Cleveland to be near her family. I sell my dental practice, my sights now set on coaching, consulting…and, of course, writing and publishing this book and starting my speaking tour entitled: "Values Matter."

For years, writing, speaking, coaching, and consulting has been my dream—what I really wanted to do with the rest of my life. Of my dental practice, frankly, I had become tired. Digging into patients' mouths every day no longer did it for me, if it ever did. But that doesn't make the decision or transition any easier. Nothing in life is a gift. It always comes with hard work, even when it seems to fall into your lap.

But finally, I am proud to say that I have achieved my dream. The book is finished. Poke Salad, baby, you've come home to your angels.

And that, ladies and gentlemen, is the rest of the story.

A Final Note

CONQUERING YOUR ADVERSITIES

"Consult not your fears but your hopes and your dreams. Think not about your frustrations, but about your unfulfilled potential. Concern yourself not with what you tried and failed in, but with what is still possible for you to do."

— Pope John XXIII

You have finished this book. What next? What are you going to do now to conquer your adversities and realize your dreams, or to help your family, friends, and/or team do so?

No matter how bold, ideas without action are academic. Success, an old doctor friend once said, is biased to action. Action means taking this book's lessons, your answers to the questions posed, applying them to your own life, crafting a game plan for you and/or your family/team, and taking the field of life with winning strategies that enable you to dismantle and conquer your adversities.

Can you do it? You bet you can. The insights, life lessons, and solutions provided by this book—and your own answers to the questions posed at the end of each chapter—can immediately become part of your life plan. And you know what? You have already come up with many of the solutions inspired by your own life, from family to kids you grew up with, to teachers and coaches, to people you know and your own heroes.

Grab a pen and write out on the blank lines below ten adversities that currently stand in the way of your goals, passions, and dreams. Then, when you are done, identify ten actions that will transform your life or the lives of those around you by conquering and overcoming those adversities.

The actions can be as simple as: Adversity: I never find time to read. Action: I will read one inspiring book per week that will help me accomplish my goals and dreams. Adversity: I'm afraid to sell my dental practice and pursue my dream of writing, coaching, consulting, and speaking. Action: I will write a book, sell my dental practice, and launch a career coaching, consulting, and speaking.

EXERCISE:

List ten adversities that currently stand in the way of your goals and dreams:

1. _____

2. _____

3. _____

4. _____

5. _____

6. _____

CONQUERING YOUR ADVERSITIES

7. _____

8. _____

9. _____

10._____

List ten actions that you promise yourself to accomplish in the next three months that will overcome, or start to overcome, these adversities:

1. _____

2. _____

3. _____

4. _____

5. _____

6. _____

7. _____

8. _____

9. _____

10._____

There you go. Now you have your action plan. Next, take action! I'm rooting for your success. Feel free to call me for a complimentary consultation to help launch your future success or call me just if you need someone to talk to: 440-990-4700. May God bless you on your life's journey.

ABOUT THE AUTHOR

Dr. Kenneth Polke was born in 1952 and was raised in Collinwood, a neighborhood within Cleveland, Ohio. He grew up attending Catholic school amid the mafia-ridden streets of Collinwood. A Hollywood movie, *Kill the Irishman*, starring Val Kilmer, Christopher Walken, Paul Sorivino, and Dan Ofinino would later be made of these Mafia-controlled streets depicting the life and times of Danny Greene, a notorious mob boss. Dr. Polke could have chosen a life of crime—the easy way out—but he chose sports and an education instead.

Ken played high school football at St. Joseph High School, the private Catholic school within the Collinwood neighbourhood and, co-incidentally, one of the top schools for football in Ohio. His throwing arm and other skills on the field led him to having numerous college recruiters interested in him. Eventually, he would be discovered by the pro scouts and signed by the Miami Dolphins and the Cleveland Browns before he decided to leave football and become a dentist. While football was the vehicle chosen, Christian values was the road taken to escape Collinwood.

After decades of dentistry in the Denver area, Ken has now returned to his native Cleveland, where he lives with his wife Valerie. Today, he is a writer, author, public speaker, life coach, and consultant. His goal is to inspire others to overcome the adversities in their own lives.

BOOK DR. KENNETH POLKE TO SPEAK AT YOUR NEXT EVENT

Finding just the right person to speak to a group of people can be a tall order, but if you want someone engaging with humorous knock-your-socks-off stories, look no further! When Ken Polke speaks to your group, not only will your audience and colleagues enjoy amazing stories and down-to-earth wisdom, but they will come away with a greater sense of empowerment and excitement for their futures.

Ken has a ton of inspiring stories that range from growing up in the streets of a Mafia-ridden Cleveland neighborhood to his glory days on the football field, including being recruited by the Miami Dolphins and the Cleveland Browns. He knows what it's like to fail and to try and try again until you succeed. After a lifetime of hard work and dedication, he now wants to bring his message to people of all ages and backgrounds, teaching them how to overcome their adversities so they can follow their dreams.

No matter whether you are in Ohio or anywhere else in North America, and whether your audience is 10 or 10,000, Ken can tailor a speech for your group or meeting that will inspire your audience. He knows your audience doesn't want to be bored but motivated through humor and wit and a unique story they can apply to their own situations so they can create effective change in their lives. He delivers on what he promises and will leave your audience wanting more.

To contact Ken for a complimentary pre-speech phone interview and find out whether he is available to speak to your group, contact him at:

DrKennethJPolke@gmail.com
440-990-4700
www.DrKennethPolke.com

HOW ELSE CAN DR. POLKE HELP YOU?
ABOUT DR. KENNETH POLKE'S BUSINESS BROKERAGE

Looking to retire soon? Want to cash-in on the sale of your business to invest the proceeds? Want to sell your business and still remain on to generate more income? Afraid that if you do sell, you will overpay in brokerage commissions? Then look and fear no more as Dr. Kenneth Polke is here to the rescue. We can assist you in these life-altering events.

Life comes with many experiences, most good, but some, called adversities, are unfortunately very bad. All aspects of life, whether it be in football, academics, practicing dentistry, practicing medicine, or even raising children, present adversities. I wrote this book to share how you might face these challenges and "CONQUER YOUR ADVERSITIES." Indeed, even most recently, I personally faced more "adversities" during the sale of my dental practice. Every phase of the sale presented roadblocks ranging from lazy and incompetent brokers and poorly written sales contracts to horrendous legal advice and dishonest and corrupt buyers. This was the absolutely worst experience in my life, and even the time I was attacked by someone yielding a machete pales in comparison. Don't let this happen to you.

I knew this book could be a bridge to helping other doctors avoid these landmines during the buying or selling of their dental or medical practices. Just like wisdom can be passed on both from an academic standpoint and from a coaching football standpoint, so too can it be passed on during the purchase and sale of a business. So this has become one of my major goals. In addition to consulting with coaches, players, parents, schools, and teams, I am now consulting with doctors. The practical experience and wisdom I gained from training with Pro Football Hall-of-Fame player Paul Warfield while still in high school has no substitute. The same can be said for the brutal eye-opening horrific experience I faced in selling my business. Wisdom comes from "CONQUERING YOUR AD-VERSITIES."

Call or text 440-990-4700 or email Dr. Kenneth Polke at DrKennethJPolke@gmail.com for a complimentary one-hour consultation regarding the buying or selling of your business.